Between Winnicott and Lacan

Between Winnicott and Lacan

A Clinical Engagement

Edited by Lewis A. Kirshner

Routledge
Taylor & Francis Group
New York London

Routledge
Taylor & Francis Group
270 Madison Avenue
New York, NY 10016

Routledge
Taylor & Francis Group
27 Church Road
Hove, East Sussex BN3 2FA

Routledge is an imprint of Taylor & Francis Group, an Informa business

Printed in the United States of America on acid-free paper
10 9 8 7 6 5 4 3 2 1

International Standard Book Number: 978-0-415-88373-3 (Hardback) 978-0-415-88374-0 (Paperback)

Library of Congress Cataloging-in-Publication Data

Between Winnicott and Lacan : a clinical engagement / edited by Lewis A. Kirshner.
p. cm.
Includes bibliographical references and index.
ISBN 978-0-415-88373-3 (hardback : acid-free paper) -- ISBN 978-0-415-88374-0 (pbk : acid-free paper) -- ISBN 978-0-203-84336-9 (e-bk)
1. Winnicott, D. W. (Donald Woods), 1896-1971. 2. Lacan, Jacques, 1901-1981. 3. Psychoanalysis. 4. Psychotherapy. I. Kirshner, Lewis A., 1940-

BF173.B48 2011
150.19'52--dc22 2010030213

Visit the Taylor & Francis Web site at
http://www.taylorandfrancis.com

and the Routledge Web site at
http://www.routledgementalhealth.com

Contents

Contributors

Jeanne Wolff Bernstein, PhD, is a psychoanalyst in Berkeley, California, and past president of the Psychoanalytic Institute of Northern California. She has written many articles on the work of Lacan, among them "Countertransference: The Royal Road to the Unconscious?" (*Psychoanalytic Dialogues*, 1999) and "Love, Desire and Jouissance: Two out of Three Ain't Bad" (*Psychoanalytic Dialogues*, 2007).

James E. Gorney, PhD, is a psychoanalyst in independent practice in Knoxville, Tennessee. He has served on the staff of the Austen Riggs Center in Stockbridge, Massachusetts, and is the author of articles exploring clinical applications of the work of Lacan.

André Green, MD, is a member of the Paris Psychoanalytic Society, of which he was president from 1986 to 1989. From 1975 to 1977 he was a vice president of the International Psychoanalytical Association and from 1979 to 1980 a professor at University College London. He is the author of numerous books and articles on psychoanalysis.

Mardy Ireland, PhD, is a practicing psychoanalyst in North Carolina. She is author of *The art of the subject: Between necessary illusion and speakable desire in the analytic encounter* (Other Press, 2003).

Lewis A. Kirshner, MD, is clinical professor of psychiatry at Harvard Medical School and training and supervising psychoanalyst at the Boston Psychoanalytic Institute. He is the author of *Having a life: Self pathology after Lacan* (The Analytic Press, 2003) and has led workshops at meetings of the American Psychoanalytic and International Psychoanalytical Associations on "Working Between Winnicott and Lacan."

Deborah Anna Luepnitz, PhD, is on the clinical faculty of the Department of Psychiatry at the University of Pennsylvania School of Medicine. She is the author of *Schopenhauer's porcupines* (Basic Books, 2002) and maintains a private practice in Philadelphia.

Mari Ruti, PhD, is associate professor of comparative literature at the University of Toronto and is author of *Reinventing the soul: Posthumanist theory and psychic life* (Other Press, 2006). Her articles have appeared in the *Journal of the American Psychoanalytic Association.*

Alain Vanier, MD, PhD, is a member of Espace Analytique, an independent Lacanian group. He is professor and director of graduate studies at the Centre de Recherches Psychanalyse, Médecine et Société of the Université Paris Diderot. He is an author of books and articles dealing with the work of Jacques Lacan and coeditor of *Winnicott avec Lacan* (Hermann, 2010), the collected proceedings of a London conference.

François Villa, MD, is a psychoanalyst, member of the Association Psychanalytique de France, professor of psychopathology, and member of the Centre de Recherches Psychanalyse, Médecine et Société at the Université Paris Diderot. He is the author of books and articles on psychoanalysis.

Introduction

Lewis A. Kirshner

The theme of this volume is the possibility of a psychoanalytic treatment that can move between two seemingly incompatible theories of the origins and structure of the human psyche. Whereas D. W. Winnicott developed a model of *self*, born in the context of a pediatrician's notion of a "good enough" mothering relationship, Jacques Lacan constructed a theory of the *subject*, derived from phenomenology and linguistics. Their contrasting approaches can be viewed as representing a bifurcation in the evolution of psychoanalysis, not only from an institutional perspective but also in widely held attitudes toward clinical practice. For Winnicott, the essence of psychoanalytic process was the here-and-now, dyadic relationship of analyst and patient, with its recapitulation of early infant development, contained within the setting of a holding environment. By contrast, Lacan emphasized close attention to the language of the analysand and placed the analyst in a nonrelational position as the other. Perhaps for this reason analytic writers have only very recently begun to address the possibility of working between and with Winnicott and Lacan in a complementary or dialectic way.

Arguably the major psychoanalytic innovators since Sigmund Freud, Winnicott and Lacan questioned received theory in ways that even now have not been fully integrated into practice. Their conceptions of psychic life address many issues in contemporary psychotherapeutic work, particularly those dealing with treatment of children, borderline disorders, and psychotic patients for whom problems in the development of self and intersubjective relations are crucial. Our objective in this volume is to clarify their major concepts, to differentiate between them, and to identify points of intersection to contribute to a more effective psychoanalytic practice. Our authors take a variety of positions on how, what, and when the two sets of ideas can be used clinically. They address the history of the Lacan–Winnicott relationship, the evolution of their theories, possibilities and obstacles to working between them, and detailed clinical examples of how their ideas have been put to work with varying types of patients.

Apart from his conceptual innovations about the earliest stages of psychic development, Winnicott has been revered for breaking psychoanalysis out of a reductionist view of the ego and its mechanisms of defense, encapsulated inside the mind of a mostly unconscious patient. I am referring here to a style of impersonal psychoanalysis that was taught through the 1980s, one in which the analyst, hidden behind a blank screen and assuming a position anchored in reality, attempted to detect and interpret a patient's defenses and hidden impulses. This model, although certainly a caricature of analytic practice (associated with the school of ego psychology in the United States), did influence clinicians, who were taught to be wary of engaging patients directly and to see the treatment relationship mainly in terms of a unidirectional transference. The patient's behavior was described as the product of a closed mental apparatus rather than as part of a two-person or intersubjective relationship, and it was the clinician's task to decipher and interpret it.[1]

The development of object relations theory in Great Britain by Melanie Klein and her followers changed this picture by seeing the subject as implicated from the beginning of life in a self–other dialogue. Despite the metaphysical complexities of her concept of instincts and her Hobbesian view of infancy, a notion of intersubjectivity began to emerge with Klein as she insisted on the inseparability of the psyche from object relations. Winnicott's version of this process took this step much further without her theoretical baggage by placing the self and its development at the center of his model of mental life. In doing so, he anticipated yet more drastic changes in theory and practice subsequently initiated by self psychology and relational psychoanalysis.

The innovations of Winnicott and object relations theories in general were strenuously resisted in North America. A joke circulating at the Boston Psychoanalytic Institute in the 1980s suggested that a plaque would be erected over the entrance stating: "Klein Not Taught Here." Today, colleagues are surprised that Winnicott's ideas were so fiercely attacked, notably when he presented them to a mostly hostile New York Psychoanalytic Institute audience in November 1968 (see Baudry, 2009). According to his biographer, "After the verbal critiques ... Winnicott muttered that he now knew why the Americans had become embroiled in the fighting in Viet Nam. After the talk concluded he returned to his hotel and had a massive coronary" (Kahr, 1996, pp. 118–119).

Lacan is much less familiar to most English-speaking analysts—harder to read and harder to connect with everyday clinical concerns. Yet, he, too,

[1] The term two-person psychology has been used in diverse ways, for example, by Charles Rycroft, Emmanuel Ghent, Stephen Mitchell, and Arnold Modell, but generally implies a critique of the so-called drive-defense model of psychoanalysis that viewed the subject as motivated principally by internal forces. The importance of the other in mental life and even of the role of the "third" (an entity or structure apart from the two protagonists in the analytic relationship) has been highlighted by French psychoanalysis since Lacan's early work on the paternal metaphor, notably by Andre Green, and has recently become part of North American theory through the writings of Lewis Aron and Jessica Benjamin.

was reacting against what he saw as a sterile, ritualized form of psychoanalysis that ignored its central aspect, the human subject. His writings were much more openly critical of then-current practices than Winnicott's and in turn aroused even fiercer opposition from official psychoanalytic circles. Eventually, he was expelled for his heresies from the International Psychoanalytic Association (IPA) in 1963.

Perhaps influenced by his early exposure to the rich philosophic tradition of phenomenology, Lacan increasingly focused his analytic teaching on questions concerning the nature of subjectivity and the subject. His division of psychic experience into three registers of the Imaginary, the Symbolic, and the Real provided a new framework for conceptualizing a triadic basis for the human subject. The nature of "the subject" has been a perennial philosophical problem since the Greeks, all the more so with the fading of religious belief in the existence of an inner essence or soul.[2] Lacan argued that Freud's discovery of the unconscious had radically changed the terms of this inquiry. Addressing subjectivity from the perspective of psychoanalysis not only had philosophical import for Lacan but also provided an alternative to the biophysical analogies of instinctual energy and discharge that underpinned Freud's model of the psyche.

The term *self*, often associated today with the work of Heinz Kohut, first came to psychoanalytic prominence through the writings of Winnicott. As a substantive entity, it was basically absent in Freud and has no equivalent intellectual history to the concept of subject. Apart from a few scattered uses, it entered psychoanalysis via the concept of self-representation advanced by Heinz Hartmann in ego psychology. He argued that a notion of *self* as a correlate to *object* was necessitated by Freud's exploration of narcissism, in which libido could flow outward to be invested in the object or return to be invested in the self. Similarly, the other could be loved either narcissistically as oneself via a process of identification or as a separate object, with all the real-life consequences of these oppositions. Hartmann proposed self-representation as an ego function to clarify this model (Kirshner, 1991). A phenomenological conception of the self as a vehicle of agency, however, even the Cartesian sense of subjectivity as an "I," was absent from Hartmann's use of the term. Later analysts influenced by Kohut's self psychology came to see the self as the cohesive essence of the person, a superordinate structure in the mind, and made it the focus of their analytic work.

The vocabularies of self and subject, as Deborah Luepnitz shows in her chapter, reflect important cultural and theoretical differences between

[2] The philosophical roots of this problem and their manifestations in Freud have been explored in depth by the French psychoanalyst Laurence Kahn in her book, *La Petite Maison de l'Ame*, in which she analyzes the problems of locating agency and intention in the structure of a mental apparatus.

schools of psychoanalysis and have an impact on the implicit goals of treatment. Her chapter uses what she calls the two organizing tropes of selfhood versus subjectivity in Winnicott and Lacan to build a "double description" of the nature of clinical work and proposes this dual perspective as a way to resolve the humanist and posthumanist impasse in contemporary analytic practice. At stake is a way of incorporating both an informed receptivity to unconscious processes as they unfold in psychoanalytic therapy and an engaged copresence. Conceptualizing the dual role of analyst as other and as intersubjective participant represents the basic challenge of a dialectical reading of the two theories. We can see this attempt to move across the two vocabularies at work in James Gorney and Mardy Ireland's chapters as well, where the two authors find a corrective to a naive "self-to-self" conception of transference and countertransference in Lacan's attention to words and language. It is rare to read a complete case report that explicates Lacanian concepts in a jargon-free manner, as these authors have done.

The contrast between the two vocabularies is present in everyday speech, when we say that one has or lacks a "self," while everyone *is* a subject. "Self" carries an atomistic ring, suggesting a discrete and autonomous entity that may evoke both a religious reference and an economic relationship of ownership and individual responsibility in a neoliberal world. Even Kohut's use of the term *selfobject* to convey the self's need to use others to sustain its major functions of self-esteem and cohesion suggests a solipsistic project of self-maintenance. To be a subject, on the other hand, carries the ambiguity of being "subjected to," as in being a subject of the king—a political entity, as Luepnitz observes. The notion of subject (and perhaps this is the result of its intellectual history) seems caught up in a quasi-juridical framework of definition. Moreover, in English, the word carries an impersonal quality, as in the subject of an experiment.

Nonetheless, it is possible to conceive of an overlap between the two concepts, especially in the way that Winnicott used the term "the true self." His famous distinction between the true and the false self bears some similarity to Lacan's differentiation of ego and subject. The false self represents a compliant, defensive shield of conformity with the expectations of others, whereas the true self seems to touch on natural impulses—"the spontaneous gesture," in Winnicott's terminology—of the preverbal child. Lacan's conception of the ego (*le moi* in French) as an alienating identification with the other seems close to this depiction, perhaps in the sense that every "self" is to some extent false, a mask of adaption. Likewise, his portrayal of a divided subject, while considerably more complex, can be analogized to the discrepancy between a forever hidden, private self evoked by Winnicott and the ego's adaptation to the mother. It is less well known that Lacan grappled with the Winnicottian notion of the self in his later work, as Jeanne Bernstein describes in her chapter.

Although they were contemporaries who had a history of interaction (with Lacan clearly the more eager to pursue their relationship), in the end Lacan and Winnicott failed to understand each other very well, a missed connection recounted by Alain Vanier. Lacan recognized the importance of Winnicott's transitional object and attempted to link it to his important concept of the *objet petit a*, as Vanier and Bernstein both report in detail. Bernstein sees Lacan's conception of the role of the *objet a* both in the origin of the subject and its power to animate the transference to be a major advance in our theoretical understanding of these processes. Despite similarities in their turn toward psychic origins for advancing theory and practice, however, Winnicott and Lacan were moving in different directions, and the promising first beginnings of dialogue were cut short. André Green reviews the major steps in this evolution, critiquing some of the more speculative ideas in Lacan's later seminars as leading away from useful applications to treatment. He sees the bifurcation in psychoanalysis to which I alluded earlier as a definitive one, with Lacan's increasingly mathematized theory moving far away from the clinical questions with which Winnicott struggled.

Of course, French psychoanalysis, in particular, was significantly influenced by Lacan, who is now read routinely in France by students in training, and many of his important ideas (especially around his attention to speech, the subject, the exploration of the imaginary mode, and the *après coup*) have become integrated into the mainstream in a way that is not true in North America. Green, in his comprehensive summation, continues to find the writings of the earlier Lacan on intersubjectivity and the use of language valuable in ways his later ideas are not, whereas Winnicott remains closer to his clinical practice. Green's own enormous contributions to the field—notably his work on the negative, the symbol, and the importance of the analytic third—owe some of their inspiration to his exposure to both (see Green, 2005a, 2005b). The notion of "self," as derived from Winnicott, however, has never been well accepted in the French tradition.

Among many places in which Winnicott spoke about the birth of the self are two principal texts: "Transitional Objects and Transitional Phenomena" (1953) and "Mirror-Role of Mother and Family in Child Development" (1967), both included in the volume *Playing and reality* (1971). I discuss these articles in my chapter on psychosis, and, of course, they remain seminal contributions to psychoanalytic theory and practice. The insight that a third area of transitional experience was necessary to supplement the conventional distinction between subjective and objective has become essential to the contemporary understanding of transference and holds obvious relevance to treatment of psychotic patients. Lacan (1949) wrote about analogous phenomena in his first major paper on the Mirror Stage, the basic elements of which were included in his presentation, "Some Reflections on the Ego," presented on May 2, 1951, in London at the British Psychoanalytical Society, subsequently published in 1953.[3] He also, as Vanier documents, spoke several times about the transitional object in his Paris seminars and arranged for the translation and publication of Winnicott's paper in the journal he directed, *La Psychanalyse*, in 1959.

As described already, Lacan attempted, without success, to equate his original idea of the *objet petit a*, the virtual object that is the cause of desire (and not, as some suppose, the object of desire) to the transitional object. Vanier's scholarly chapter explores this misunderstanding in depth and shows how the two concepts can be thought of together as attempts to grasp the same early processes of infant development. Both terms grapple with the beginnings of subjectivation and the birth of a separate self. Through clinical vignettes, Vanier demonstrates how they can enhance our understanding of clinical problems of early childhood. Read with Bernstein's discussion of Lacan's concept of the *object petit a*, his chapter suggests a revised formulation of the role of loss in early development that is specifically psychoanalytic. Bernstein emphasizes that the Lacanian process of becoming a subject carries with it an inevitable sense of loss of a part of the body, of the mother's body that the infant has experienced as belonging to him. She argues that acceptance of loss is central to a Lacanian approach rather than the attempt to repair it.

The notion of a transitional space in which, as Winnicott wrote, questions of subjectivity or objectivity do not pertain may, in fact, illuminate some of the difficulties in conceiving of the *objet petit a*, which was proposed by Lacan as a virtual leftover, a residue of psychic birth as a speaking subject. Like the transitional object, the object *a* is not real (both being fantasies, although the transitional object has material reality) but does have effects that play out in reality (the symbolic reality of social existence), especially as the subject has no alternative but to attempt to name it. The project of seeking symbolization (representation) of the *objet petit a* implies a creative process, a potential creative transformation of the subject, similar to the invention by the child of transitional objects. Mari Ruti argues this possibility in her chapter, in which she opposes both Winnicott and Lacan to a dehumanized and wholly contingent view of the subject that she finds in much postmodern writing. Her writings enlarge a dialogue with feminist, postmodern authors like Judith Butler, who has emphasized the imposition of a subjective position via social norms and the Althusserian process of *appellation*, a kind of labeling that sticks to the self but offers no support for an autonomous creative subject. To the contrary, Ruti places the potential for creative transformation at the center of psychoanalytic praxis. Through play and language, she suggests, the subject can grow beyond its determinations by social and economic structures, perhaps evolving a self that is not merely subjected (and subjugated) to these external forces.

[3] Lacan wrote a paper on the Mirror Stage for presentation at the IPA Congress in Zurich in 1935 and apparently sent a copy to Freud.

At the same time, the corresponding naiveté of a contemporary practice that conceives of the self as a cohesive entity, an interiorized superordinate agency, failing to acknowledge its dependency on language, shifting identifications, and social structures, as Butler (1990) argued, does not simply represent a shallow basis for psychotherapists on which to base their work but lends itself to ideologies about normality and appropriate behavior and feeling. Models of self associated with particular eras and entrenched ideologies that define normative gender, class, and economic relationships can then dictate goals and expectations for the subject in psychotherapy. When psychotherapists orient their practices around the goals of a normative healthy life in this way, they risk becoming agents of what Michel Foucault called a biopolitics that governs behavior within a given socioeconomic system. Our postmodern awareness of the hidden normative ideology within psychotherapeutic practice makes it important on many levels to think carefully about what assumptions may underpin the languages of self and subject that we employ and what they imply. What subject are we talking about, and what does it reflect about our work?

Subjectivity for Winnicott and Lacan had the paradoxical property of being both a product of external determinants and a unique sort of creative freedom. The infant–mother relationship, for example, facilitates ego identifications and construction of a false self but also the possibility of an emergent transitional space—the space of a "third"—in which the child can create its own meanings. French psychoanalysis, Green in particular, has elaborated this conception of *tiercity* (thirdness). By sustaining her position as a third (as opposed to a purely dyadic relation), the psychoanalyst holds a crucial role both in deconstructing the effects of unconscious forces that have shaped the self and in enabling construction of new figurations of subjectivity. This dual function may be most important in the treatment of severe mental disorders, which exemplify par excellence the difficulty of sustaining a separate self, with which Winnicott and Lacan were significantly concerned. My own essay examines their respective contributions to understanding and treating psychosis, reviews the concepts they introduced, and applies them critically to case material with a paranoid patient. It calls for analysts to devote more attention to major mental illnesses, which they have by and large abandoned to more biological psychiatric approaches.

It is challenging for the analyst to sustain an active role in uncovering and interpreting unconscious wishes and beliefs that in many respects determine the thoughts and behavior of the subject and also to maintain a receptive openness to the novelty that may emerge in the treatment process. The analysand's creative expressions are inevitably shaped by the analyst's participation, implicating her as a subject with convictions and desires of her own, and make the old notion of neutrality important in new ways. The analyst's first obligation is to be wary of imposing a personal or professional ideology, as the American psychoanalyst Arnold Modell

(1991) rightly emphasized. "Whose Reality Is It?" was the title of one of his important papers, which stressed intersubjectivity in the clinical encounter. From this perspective, the analyst has the double task of occupying the position of authority implicit in the transference (the Other) while maintaining a subjective place apart. This goes to the issue of the doctrinaire style of interpretation allegedly characteristic of classic technique and criticized by Winnicott and Lacan. As Lacan repeatedly insisted, the analyst is not a subject of knowledge (one who knows the truth) but rather is a facilitator of the analysand's quest for meaning. Winnicott's view of the analytic relationship, especially in his work with more damaged patients, may have erred in viewing the dyadic relationship too literally, as a regression to actual dependency on a primary object rather than as a shared construction. In this respect, he may have imposed his own reality at times, seeking to become the good object his patients lacked, as Green (2005a) suggested. On the other hand, Lacan's advocacy of a position of abstinence and nongratification of demands may have failed to recognize the symbolic needs of many patients for more personal involvement by the analyst in the analytic process.

The contrast between Lacan's avoidance of shared relatedness and Winnicott's assumption of a maternal role suggests that the clinician's greatest challenge in attempting to work between their models, moving back and forth across their overlapping and at times opposed conceptions of subjectivity, is to sustain presence and connection while not imposing an interpretation of reality that merely compounds an earlier developmental alienation. A dialectical way of listening to the analysand involves attunement to transference and desire while remaining receptive to acknowledgment of the analyst's part in the design of the new fabric being woven "transitionally" in the space between them. In their respective contributions, Gorney, Ireland, and Luepnitz illustrate possible ways of working between Winnicott and Lacan and provide examples of how they apply this approach to practice. They show how close attention to language and its effects can take us beyond the simple dyad of analyst and patient, which can often lead to an endless intrication of two subjects immersed in the here and now of immediate experience. Attention to the signifier, to the words being spoken, rather than interventions at the level of a reparative relationship and nurturing responses to conscious feelings, can sustain a third position that, in turn, opens a transitional zone for creative growth. Ireland's attention to the significance of the actual letters as they appear in her patients' discourses is a rare illustration of use of this aspect of Lacanian theory.[4] In her interpretation, the letters themselves hearken back to the earliest stages of emergence of the subject. For his part, Gorney recounts the crucial emergence of a signifier as

[4] Freud used a similar method in his analysis of the Wolf Man's word *wespe*.

linking early experience and transference in the unconscious fantasy of his patient. Both authors stress their commitment to a Winnicottian holding function as the basis of the analytic relationship yet make it clear how their readings of Lacan sensitized their listening to their patients, leading to emergence of crucial unconscious connections previously absent from the treatments.

Underlying the writings of Winnicott and Lacan is a complex struggle to conceive of subjectivity as a natural expression of the living person who is and is not part of the natural world and who overflows any unitary constructions of identity. They were interested not in adaptation or successful functioning as an ideal (if incomplete and illusory) therapeutic goal but in catalyzing a more authentic form of existence (that, itself, may be at once utopian and reflect an intrinsic dynamic of human beings). This "philosophical," truth-seeking aspect of psychoanalysis comes to the fore in Winnicott's posthumous book *Human nature* that is interpreted for us in the chapter by François Villa. Villa unpacks the propositions advanced in Winnicott's frequently somber reflections in the light of other theories and shows how they are to variable degrees implicit in clinical practice. He joins other contributors in reminding us that psychoanalysis goes beyond its functional role as a method of treatment or techniques. Rather, it aims at understanding the basic human situation, a desire that continues to attract students to the field. Villa shows that Winnicott's thinking was surprisingly close to the preoccupations of philosophically minded psychoanalysts like Wilfred Bion and Lacan by returning us to the fundamental question of what makes a meaningful life possible.

The perennial human problem addressed by these powerful thinkers was how to sustain personal life and identity against the pressures of biological needs and limitations while living among others in an intersubjective world. Patients seek the help of psychoanalysis not so much to deal with discrete symptoms as to find meaning in their personal histories and relationships without unbearable pain. Winnicott and Lacan were pioneers in exploring these pathways. It would be a great loss if their works were left as isolated historical relics in the stream of fragmented therapeutic methods and diverse approaches that characterizes the current psychoanalytic scene. We have argued that many of the dilemmas and contradictions of contemporary psychoanalysis are embedded in the distinction between self and subject, between the interpersonal and the intersubjective dimensions of experience. As the following chapters argue, issues of personal desire, identity, self, and subjectivity are the heart blood of psychoanalytic therapy, often obscured by the diverse vocabularies and ideologies of psychoanalytic schools. Our authors' suggestions of how to use their ideas in a complementary manner advance the critical dialogue that the field of psychoanalysis badly needs. We hope it will inspire others to attempt the path of working between Winnicott and Lacan.

REFERENCES

Baudry, F. (2009). Winnicott's visit to the New York Psychoanalytic Society and Institute: A contextual view. *Psychoanalytic Quarterly*, *78*, 1059–1090.
Butler, J. (1990). *Gender trouble: Feminism and the subversion of identity*. New York: Routledge.
Green, A. (2005a). *Jouer avec Winnicott*. Paris: Presses Universitaires de France.
Green, A. (2005b). *Key ideas for a contemporary psychoanalysis*. London: Routledge.
Kahr, B. (1996). *D. W. Winnicott: A biographical portrait*. London: Karnac Books.
Kirshner, L. A. (1991). The concept of the self in psychoanalytic theory and its philosophical foundations. *Journal of the American Psychoanalytic Association*, *39*, 157–183.
Lacan, J. (1953). Some reflections on the ego. *International Journal of Psychoanalysis*, 34, 11–17.
Modell, A. H. (1991). A confusion of tongues, or whose reality is it? *Psychoanalytic Quarterly*, *60*, 227–244.
Winnicott, D. W. (1953). Transitional objects and transitional phenomena. In *Through paediatrics to psycho-analysis* (pp. 229–242). New York: Basic Books, 1975.
Winnicott, D. W. (1967). Mirror-role of mother and family in child development. In *Playing and reality* (pp. 137–138). London: Tavistock, 1971.
Winnicott, D. W. (1971). *Playing and reality*. London: Tavistock.

Chapter 1

Thinking in the space between Winnicott and Lacan[1]

Deborah Anna Luepnitz

> In the same river, we both step and do not step, we are and we are not.
>
> Heraclitus (Fragment 49a)
>
> ... What we saw and grasped, that we leave behind; but what we did not see and did not grasp, that we bring.
>
> Heraclitus (Fragment 56)

Following an interview in 1990, British Middle Group analyst Marion Milner showed me her paintings from the 1930s and 1940s. Pointing to a canvas with two hens tearing each other apart—blood and feathers flying—Mrs. Milner said, "I like to say it's Anna Freud and Melanie Klein fighting over psychoanalysis."[2]

She was referring, of course, to the 1940s battle that derailed careers, ended friendships, and nearly destroyed the British Psychoanalytic Society. It culminated with the group's bifurcation into the A and B groups, each member bound to choose allegiance. The person whom both Klein and Anna Freud trusted, and who refused to choose sides, was Donald Woods Winnicott. While he did not set out to create a third, nonaligned faction, Winnicott became identified with the Independents, or "Middle Group," which was to have a lasting impact on psychoanalytic thinking the world over. Few contemporary analysts, whether their primary identification be Freudian, Kleinian, Jungian, Kohutian, or relational, have not been influenced by constructs such as the good-enough mother, the transitional object, potential space, borderline states, the squiggle game and—perhaps most importantly—the clinical use of countertransference as a source of information about the analytic process.[3]

Another schism in the psychoanalytic world occurred some 20 years later—this one ending with no comparable *entente*. I am referring to the

[1] This chapter is a revised and expanded version of the original article from *International Journal of Psychoanalysis, 90*(5), 2009, pp. 957–981. Reprinted with permission.

[2] Author's unpublished interview with Marion Milner, November 23, 1990, London.

[3] Winnicott reportedly said to Guntrip (1975), "We differ from Freud. He was for curing symptoms. We are concerned with living persons, whole, living and loving" (p. 462). Whether this statement is fair to Freud, it does seem to anticipate the work of the American relational school (e.g., Aron, 1996; Greenberg & Mitchell, 1983; Mitchell, 1988, 1993).

events that began with the International Psychoanalytical Association's (IPA's) investigation of Lacan's experimentation with analytic time and ended with what he called his "excommunication" from that body (Lacan, 1981, p. 3). Lacan established his own school, the *École Française de Psychanalyse*, which was renamed the *École Freudienne de Paris*.[4] Despite this schism, Jacques Lacan maintained a cordial relationship with Donald Winnicott. Lacan arranged for the French translation of Winnicott's paper on the transitional object—certainly a sign of respect—but he also gently mocked his British colleague for years as a "nurse analyst" susceptible to reducing Freud's radical project to a practice of "Samaritan aid" (Lacan, 1977, p. 36).

Winnicott (1971) wrote, "Jacques Lacan's paper *Le Stade du Miroir* [The mirror stage] (1949) has certainly influenced me..." (p. 111). However, he neither described that influence nor appeared to comprehend Lacan's widely cited piece. Winnicott, who acknowledged in a letter to Ernest Jones "a neurotic inhibition to reading Freud" (Rodman, 1987, p. 33), not surprisingly found Lacan's re-reading of Freud incomprehensible. Many followers of Lacan and of Winnicott perpetuated the nonreading or aggressive misreading of the other man. For example, Middle Group analyst Charles Rycroft wrote, "... I found his [Lacan's] writings a real load of rubbish" (1985, p. 5).

Many Anglophone clinicians persist in dismissing Lacanian psychoanalysis as a fringe movement. By some estimates, however, half the world's practicing analysts identify as Lacanian (Fink, 2007, p. xii; Hill, 1997, p. 3). Consider also the perspective offered by Joyce McDougall, despite never being a member of Lacan's circle: "In France, we are all Lacanians, just as we are all Freudians" (Forrester, 1990, p. 112). Jacques-Alain Miller (1981), while noting that Lacan was generally "pro-Winnicott," made it clear that he himself was not. Miller argued that the preoccupation of Winnicott and the Middle Group with the role of the mother—all but ignoring a paternal element—constituted as normative a kind of phallic woman. Miller went so far as to claim that this fixation on an all-powerful mother would lead to a perverse system of thinking ("*une propédeutique pérverse*") (Miller, 1981, p. 43). The same position was taken by Laurent (1981).

Following the 1977 translation of the *Écrits* into English, Lacan developed a following among Anglophone academics, and the relationship between Lacan and Winnicott attracted critical interest. A number of authors contrasted the two psychoanalysts' theoretical positions, in most cases tendentiously. Some inveighed against the familiar humanism of Winnicott and the Middle Group in favor of the iconoclastic Frenchman, whom one author described as "the most important thinker in France since René Descartes" (Ragland-Sullivan, 1986, p. ix; see also Elliot, 1991; Finlay, 1989; Lonie, 1990; Mitchell, 1974; Moi, 1985.)

[4] For an exhaustive history of those events, see Roudinesco (1990).

Others campaigned for the delightfully imaginative, guileless, environment-sensitive Winnicott over Lacan, the "narcissist" who rejected the mothering role of the analyst, overvalued the paternal/phallic function, and whose "opaque" style seemed designed to frustrate the reader (Flax, 1990; Rudnytsky, 1991; Rustin, 1991).[5]

Have no clinicians set themselves to studying both Middle Group and Lacanian psychoanalysis? Even as early as the 1960s, there were a few. For example, Maud Mannoni, a member of Lacan's circle, traveled regularly to London for supervision with Winnicott (Boukobza, 1999). And in 1984, Anne Clancier and Jeanne Kalmonovitch published a book of interviews with eight French analysts about Winnicott, revealing keen interest both in his theoretical and clinical contributions (Clancier & Kalmanovitch, 1987).

Conversely, interest in Lacan by Anglophone analysts has continued to grow as Lacanian training and study groups have arisen in the United Kingdom, Canada, Australia, and the United States. Further evidence is found in volumes such as *Lacan in America* (Rabaté, 2000) and *Lacan and the New Wave in American Psychoanalysis* (Gurewich, Tort, & Fairfield, 1999). (See also Fink, 1997; 2007.) For many years, a number of relational analysts have at least cited Lacan, and his impact on their thinking, while indirect, may be more profound than those passing citations would suggest (Benjamin, 1988; Mitchell, 1993).[6]

Until very recently, the only psychoanalyst on either side of the Winnicott–Lacan divide whose original work reveals a deep understanding of both traditions was André Green (1986; 2000). Green, a onetime colleague of Lacan, chose at a crucial point to break ranks:

> I had followed Lacan in the name of freedom of thought, and now he was upbraiding me for thinking for myself. It was the end of our collaboration.... The more familiar I became with their [Middle Group] frame of mind, the more I had the feeling that this was where I could

[5] Rudnytsky (1991), unlike Flax, finds Lacan's tragic worldview "compelling and coherent" and suggests that "... it may be possible to synthesize Lacan's view with object relations psychoanalysis" (pp. 83–84).

[6] As Jessica Benjamin (1997) correctly observed, "Psychoanalytic theory here [in the U.S.] (apart from the academically based Lacanians...) only very recently has taken up the postmodern challenge to identity" (p. 707). I would amplify her implication to argue that American analysts were introduced to "the postmodern" to some degree through their encounter with those academically based Lacanians (e.g., Brennan, 1989; Felman, 1987; Gallop, 1982; Mitchell, 1974, 1982; Rose, 1982). In the United States, Lacan is often linked with the word *postmodern*, a term used somewhat idiosyncratically. For example, Rudnytsky prefers "postmodern" Lacan to "humanist" Winnicott, whereas Flax (1990), who reviles Lacan, sees Winnicott as postmodern.

find what was missing in Lacan's approach, which seemed to me unsatisfactory, even misguided, in its abstraction. (1986, p. 9)

In contrast to the view of Winnicott as a "nurse analyst" without intellectual rigor, Green (1986) asserted: "I consider *Playing and Reality* to be one of the fundamental works of contemporary psychoanalysis" (p. 10). Although Green clearly admired Bion, Klein, and many others, his esteem for Donald Winnicott and Jacques Lacan appeared overarching:

> After Freud, I see two authors who have pushed their research and coherence very far on the basis of two quite different points of view, and which up to a certain point converge. These two authors are Lacan and Winnicott.[7]

For Green, constructs such as the pre-oedipal period, the borderline diagnosis, and the use of countertransference—all anathema in Lacan's school—became *sine qua non*. Green qualified his enthusiasm by adding, "I am not an unconditional Winnicottian.... [A]n analyst who really wants to think about practice cannot dispense with a reflection on language, a reflection that is absent in Winnicott" (p. 124).[8]

A number of analysts in the past few decades, working independently of one another, have continued to build a conceptual bridge between Middle Group and Lacanian theory (Bernstein, 1999, 2006; Eigen, 1981; Gorney, 2003; Ireland, 2003; Kirshner, 2004; Lonie, 1990; Luepnitz, 2002; Mathelin, 1999; Rogers, 2006; Satorsky, 1993). These practitioners have placed themselves in a position that, in one sense, is analogous to that of London's original Middle Group. Engaged by both Lacan and Winnicott, and disinclined to discipleship, they work in the area between two schools of allegedly incompatible thought. It might be useful to describe this area with Winnicott's term "potential space," which, by definition, both separates and joins two people or entities. The goal of these bridge-building authors, I believe, is not to forge a synthesis amounting to one master discourse, but rather to bring two radically different psychoanalytic paradigms into provocative contact. In an early draft of this chapter, I suggested that the abovenamed authors were moving toward something that could be called a new Independent tradition, or even a "New Middle Group." Responses to this notion were univocal: The last thing psychoanalysis needs is another sect, a new "ism." There is, indeed, no reason to refer to the contributors to this volume as anything other than analysts interested in both Winnicott and Lacan.

[7] Interview of André Green by Anne Clancier (Clancier & Kalmanovitch, 1987, p. 121).

[8] Ibid., p. 124. In a later interview, Green renounced Lacanian theory and practice, describing himself as a "foe" of Lacan (Benvenuto, 1995). The present author is not an unconditional Greenian.

But why these two? Why not Lacan and Fairbairn or Winnicott and Bion? While pairing any two psychoanalytic authors can be heuristically useful, I argue for Winnicott and Lacan because, in addition to their exceptional impact on audiences both popular and professional—an impact few analysts since Freud could claim—they represent equally important ends of the analytic spectrum. Winnicott, it has been said, introduced the "comic tradition" into psychoanalysis, in contrast to Freud's tragic vision (Phillips, 1988; Rudnytsky, 1991; Schafer, 1976).

Winnicott achieved this through both an emphasis on spontaneity and play, and through his meliorism. He sounded an occasional melancholic note (e.g., "… social health is mildly depressive—except for holidays," Winnicott, 1989, p. 175), but his theoretical work, like his immensely popular BBC broadcasts about child development, was persistently upbeat. He believed that happy families are possible and that mankind is changing for the better. His position is 180 degrees out of phase with that of Lacan, who resonated with Freud's pessimism, adding a gravitas that was all his own. One of Lacan's most famous teachings is: "*Il n'y a pas de rapport sexuel*" (There is no such thing as a sexual relationship). More sweeping still are his assertions: "There is something originally, inaugurally, profoundly wounded in the human relation to the world" (Lacan, 1954–1955, p. 167), and "Life does not want to be healed" (ibid., p. 233). If his rhetoric is hyperbolic, it was precisely to distinguish his position from that of the Middle Group, which did not shrink from terms like "health," "wholeness," "maturity," and "mature intimacy."

Just as Winnicott became a household name in England of the 1940s, so did Lacan become widely known in France in the 1960s and 1970s. Neither in his engagement with the student demonstrators of 1968 nor in his later television interviews would he spare his audience either his somber view of the world and the prospects for social change, or his famously recondite style of speaking.

Lacan and Winnicott addressed themselves to many of the same theoretical problems from obverse points of view, which is most evident in their writings on the mirror stage. Winnicott's (1971) mirror stage is straightforward and full of promise. The True Self of every individual is called into being in the mirroring gaze of the good-enough mother. Absent such a mother, the individual has a second chance with a good-enough analyst who can foster the self's coherence and experience of wholeness. Winnicott (1971) uses the phrase "when the family is intact and a going concern" (p. 118), revealing his view of human households as potentially benign, humming along like successful businesses.

Lacan's mirror stage, in contrast, is the site of a necessary alienation. The infant who recognizes its image in the mirror—often while hearing the words: "Look—that's YOU!"—begins a lifelong course of searching outward instead of inward for identity. We spend our lives captivated by images of ourselves, struggling for reassurance that we are more intact than we feel. For Lacan, what emerges in the mirror stage is *le moi* (the ego), which he saw as the source of all neurotic suffering. The ego, far from being the hero of the story, is instead our shared symptom. Rather than help patients shore up their identity, Lacan aimed to point out the degree to which all identities are mistaken. We cannot learn who we "truly" are in the gaze of anyone else; even the mirror on the wall deceives by reversing right and left. The word "family" does not occur in Lacan's mirror stage paper, and the mother makes but a brief appearance. This does not mean he felt mothers and fathers were unimportant. Rather, it was his goal to resist what he saw as an increasing familialism in psychoanalytic theory, and to emphasize the structural over the developmental. Confronting our desire for the illusion of wholeness was something Lacan saw also as subversive to capitalism, since the wish to appear whole leads to greater and greater consumption (Declercq, 2006; Lacan, 1990; Stavrakakis, 1999; Žižek, 1989).

The two mirror stages constitute distinct creation myths about the origin of the individual, which inevitably shape clinical practice. What would it mean, then, for a practitioner to think in terms of both Lacan and Winnicott? One possibility is to regard Winnicott and Lacan as complementary or mutually limiting. One can turn to Winnicott and the Middle Group as a corrective to Lacanian abstraction, and can turn back to Lacan as a corrective to the absence of reflection on language. Winnicott (1971) was interested in the "symbolic," but his notions of it overlap with what Lacan placed in the register of the "imaginary."

Bernstein in *Countertransference: Our new royal road to the unconscious?* (1999), used Lacanian constructs to titrate what she views as the excessive concentration on countertransference by some analysts. Bernstein believes that Winnicott and the Middle Group made a vital contribution in turning our attention to the analyst's interiority, but cautions that its overuse can simply cover for the "analyst's narcissism." She trains her sights on the relational school:

> Although the American relational school has contributed much to humanize the analytic encounter ... an overly democratic use of 'working in the countertransference' risks trapping the analyst in the glass cabinets of what Lacan calls the Imaginary order (Bernstein, 1999, p. 291).

With biting wit, she offers the example of a leading contemporary analyst who had recently devoted three-fourths of a professional paper to his personal musings, and only one-fourth to a portrait of his patient. Bernstein asked if the castration fears of the patient in question

> could not have been attained without learning about [the analyst's] own competitive conflicts with his father and brothers, his recollection

of a suit in disconcordance, his grandparents' mezuzah ... his memory of a bleeding nose at age eight, and his attendance at a recent *bris* (1999, p. 281).

Bernstein devotes the rest of her article to an explication of Lacan's early teaching on the role of the signifier as a way of limiting what he perceived to be an overemphasis by Winnicott and other British analysts on the role of phantasy and the imaginary (see also Greenberg, 2001; Mills, 2005).

This brings us to the point of examining the most elemental difference between Lacan and Winnicott, which might be described by posing the question of who shows up for analysis—the *self* or the *subject*? The second essential difference concerns the goals or aims of treatment.

SELF VERSUS SUBJECT

Apart from whether a prototype of the self can be found in Freud, we know that his preferred trope was *die Seele*, which translates "soul" or "mind." Both Rank and Ferenczi had invoked the "self," but Winnicott, apparently confident in the transparency of the term, cites no previous usages.

According to the *Oxford English Dictionary*, the word *self* probably derives from the Latin stem *se*, used to connote sameness or identity. (Latin *per se*, "in itself," is used for emphasis.) But *self* used as a noun to refer to what is really and intrinsically a person does not appear until the Renaissance. By 1595, Spenser is referring to "myself, my inward selfe...." And five years later, Shakespeare's Polonius urges "to thine own self be true." This semiautonomous, perfectible entity, born of secular humanism, was not welcomed by everyone. In 1680, Charnock, a Puritan theologian, wrote, "Self is the great Anti-Christ and Anti-God of the world."

The British Romantic poets attempted an apotheosis of self as it struggled against tyrants and industrialization. The exaltation of self remains a motif of Anglo-American poetry of the modern period, best illustrated by Whitman's *Song of Myself*. Hopes for the self's wholeness or coherence were dimmed in the early work of T. S. Eliot (1963). Winnicott, who occasionally quoted Eliot, did not believe in a self necessarily split or alienated. For Winnicott, only in illness is the self divided.

While the Winnicottian self with its "incommunicado element" is neither as positivist nor as pastoral a concept as critics allege, Winnicott's metaphors are consistently organic, and his trust in nature everywhere apparent. The self that emerges through contact with a good-enough mother can *grow, develop, and mature to wholeness*. Eigen (1981) wrote of helping patients "to grow a self." That trope is interesting in light of the use of "self" as a transitive verb around 1900, meaning "to fertilize by means of pollen from the same plant." One could thus "self" a flower. And Middle Group analysts hope to foster the flowering of the self.

It was precisely this collection of gardening metaphors that Lacan rejected. In a harsh critique of developmental models in Anglo American analysis, Lacan demanded:

> Can you really, you analysts, in all honesty, bring me testimonies of these splendid typical developments of the ego of subjects? These are tall stories. We are told how this great tree, man, has such a sumptuous development.... A human life is something entirely different (Lacan, 1988, p. 155).

Lacan's "subject" is by definition not a natural but a political entity. The *Oxford English Dictionary*'s earliest definition of the word is "One who is under the dominion of a monarch." In the 18th century it became central to philosophical discourse (e.g., Kant's "thinking subject") and remained a key word for Hegel. Althusser (1971), who believed that Lacan's work had laid the groundwork for a meeting of psychoanalysis and Marxism, is well known for his aphorism: "*Être un sujet, c'est être un sujet*" (That is: To be a subject in the sense of having agency is to be a subject in the sense of being limited by the laws of a culture).

If one wished to map the Winnicottian self, one might look no further than his paper on the transitional object, where he drew a mother's breast pointing in the direction of an infant. In the space between them he placed arrows indicating their creation together, first of "illusion" and later of the "transitional object" (Winnicott, 1953). His aphorism—*there is no such thing as a baby*—means that where there is self, there is always already mother.

In contrast to this three-point structure, the Lacanian subject is mapped as a quadrature. The Lacanian diagram known as "Schema L" (Lacan, 1977) includes the following four points: S, o, o', and O. The S at the top left of the rectangular schema does not, as is often assumed, stand for "subject." S is a pun on the Freudian "*das Es*"—the It, which Lacan glosses as "our stupid ineffable existence" (1977, pp. 193–194). The small o (at top right) stands for one's objects. The o' (bottom left) stands for the ego, and the O (bottom right) for the big Other. Note that the ego is just one of the subject's objects, albeit a privileged one. The subject is stretched across these four points; it has no core or center. Subjectivity does include the feeling of immediacy and intimacy ("This is *me*") designated by o'. But it is marked equally by the opposite—a radical alterity labeled O in the diagram. This big Other refers not to a person but to a place; it is a locus of extreme alterity some associate with God, fate, or death itself. A key term for Lacan is *desire*—a word that scarcely appears in Winnicott's *oeuvre*. Lacan's insisting famously that "man's desire is the desire of the Other" means that there is no desire that is unmediated (by language, culture, the unconscious), a fact that speaks to the trouble we normal/neurotics face in struggling to know what we want. Lacan (1977) asks poignantly, "Who then is this Other to whom I am more attached than to myself?" (p. 172). It is this second degree of otherness that most clearly marks the difference between Lacanian and non-Lacanian theory. Consider, for example, the oft-quoted maxim of interpersonalist Harry Stack Sullivan: "We are all more human than otherwise." Lacan, pointing to our ineluctable relation to the Other, might say: "We are all more Otherwise . . . ."

Ragland-Sullivan (1987) made the point that the contemporary Western subject is "a mixture of the medieval 'I' believe; the Cartesian 'I' think; the Romantic 'I' feel; as well as the existential 'I' choose; the Freudian 'I' dream, and so forth" (p. 10). To these we might add the Winnicottian "I" relate and the Lacanian "I"/it speak(s).

The distinction between *self* and *subject* generates many other differences between the two traditions. For Lacan, the analyst starts out in the position of O, not o—the place of the Winnicottian analyst. For Lacan, an interpretation should be "halfway between a quotation and an enigma"—not a "good feed." For Winnicott, the central drama will turn around the infant's loss or feared loss of maternal connection. For Lacan, while loss is obviously important, something even more profound is at stake—the *lack* built into subjectivity by the mere existence of the unconscious.

More difficult than describing the theoretical difference between *self* and *subject* is conveying how this difference affects practice. The most helpful heuristic I have found thus far is a remark made by novelist Salman Rushdie during a lecture in 2000. Rushdie mentioned in passing that the first line of his novel *Midnight's Children* originally ran as follows: "Most of what matters in your life happens in your absence."[9] If that seems to be terribly obvious, consider that it runs counter to everything Winnicott taught. For Winnicott, and for the countless analysts influenced by him, what matters—what forms us psychically—is how we were held, fed, loved and, above all, recognized as infants. Those early gestures involving touch, listening, seeing, call the inchoate self into being. It is a psychoanalysis of *presence*.

In contrast, Lacan insists that before we are touched and fed by mothers and others—before we speak—we have been spoken about. We are given a name already stuffed with hope, fear, expectation. Our birth was anxiously awaited or dreaded. We come into a world not of our making—into war or peacetime—into a caste or class that will inform everything we do and say. It is a psychoanalysis organized around the knowledge of limits and death and always in the key of the signifier.

[9] Lecture by Salman Rushdie at the University of Pennsylvania, Philadelphia, PA, April, 2000.

THE AIMS OF PSYCHOANALYSIS: LACAN VERSUS WINNICOTT

To contextualize the question of the aims of psychoanalytic treatment, it is wise to begin with Freud's memorable *lieben und arbeiten*—to love and to work. Those simple words were to take a strange turn in the hands of some English-speaking analysts of the 1930s and 1940s. For example, in an interview about Freud's work, Karl Menninger (1930) replied, "There are two fundamentals in life. One is the business of making love, the other is the business of making a living."[10]

Less businesslike, but nonetheless problematic is Melanie Klein's view of the goals of analysis. In "On the criteria for the termination of a psychoanalysis" she included "an established potency and heterosexuality" (1975, p. 45). These are sentiments that Freud would not have endorsed and that Lacan spent a career renouncing.

"Psychotherapy has to do with two people playing together," Winnicott wrote (1971, p. 38). His notion of the goals of analytic treatment is often understood as love, work, and play. In his posthumously published volume *Home Is Where We Start From* (1986) Winnicott wrote, "Health ... includes the idea of tingling life and the magic of intimacy" (p. 31). Harry Guntrip, analyzed by Winnicott, said he was helped by "... Winnicott entering into the emptiness left by my non-relating mother so that I could experience the security of being myself" (1975, p. 465). Guntrip here is referring to the True Self, defined by Winnicott as "the source of what is authentic in a person."

In contrast to what Buccino (1993) condemns as the "commodification of the object in object relations theory," Winnicottian mothering—whether in the home from which we start or in the analytic home to which we repair—is as much serendipity as commodity. That is, Winnicott insisted that the breast the mother offers is not the one the baby finds. And the breast the infant demands is not the one the mother presents. This paradox reveals itself clinically all the time. It accounts for Guntrip's (1975) claim that he had his Fairbairnian analysis with Winnicott and his Winnicottian analysis with Fairbairn. The illusion of harmony arises in the "potential space"—the area where meaning is created—between baby and mother or patient and analyst. The matrix of the Winnicottian self, as pointed out already, is not a simple dyad but a three-point structure: mother, baby, area of illusion. Furthermore, as is well known, Winnicott taught that a mother remains "good enough" only through failing her infant.

This is one area where one might speak of a correspondence between Winnicott and Lacan, given Lacan's notion, variously stated, that to love is to give what one does *not* have (Lacan, 1977). Such convergences, however,

[10] Karl Menninger, quoted in *The Baltimore Sun*, 30 March 1930, p. 8.

should not blind us to the differences in their views of practice. Winnicott felt that the analytic atmosphere should be a "holding environment"—a place of safety and trust. Just as Winnicott closes many of his articles with a "summary of major points," so did he, when asked, generously summarize for a patient the themes of the previous session (e.g., Winnicott, 1972, p. 25). Winnicott, like Lacan, experimented with analytic time, but he did so by extending the hour to maximize the patient's experience of safety. His idea was that a person deprived of maternal provision could use the "good breast" of the analyst; offering more access thus could be reparative. In some cases, only a "regression to dependence" would be sufficient to break through the False Self system so that the patient could begin to exist as a person. Such was the case with Margaret Little (1990), who describes regressing to an infantile state—a terrifying experience made bearable by Winnicott's holding of her face and head in his hands in sessions that sometimes went on for hours. Little mentions that these sessions always ended "with tea and biscuits," and that she was charged each time only for the first hour. She credits her life to his devotion and willingness to work with people whom others would find too mad for analysis.

Lacan, like Freud, believed that the analytic atmosphere should be mildly frustrating. Lacan wrote, "Everybody agrees that I frustrate the speaker, him first, but me, too. Why? If I frustrate him it is because he asks me for something. To answer him, in fact" (1977, p. 254).

Unlike Freud, Lacan applied to the analytic session a technique currently known as "scansion." That is, in order to underscore the fact that the ego cannot control the analytic process, and to keep the unconscious open, the analyst cuts the session off at a propitious moment. That moment might come just after the patient has made a connection the analyst deems worthy of further reflection. Stopping the session unpredictably tends to keep the analysand working actively in between sessions. Clearly, the point here is neither to soothe the individual nor to compensate for early losses, and anyone who has experienced the cut can testify that it reinforces the nonmutuality of the analytic relationship. The cut is by design nonnegotiable, nondemocratic. While the present author knows from experience that the variable length session can be used responsibly and effectively, it is certainly true that many contemporary analysts would feel uncomfortable with the amount of authority implied in this notion of the analyst's role.

For Jacques Lacan, home is not "where we start from." Because we are spoken about long before we speak, the subject's origins can be said to lie at a time anterior to the birth of the individual—and not just months but decades before birth. Furthermore, whereas Winnicott emphasized the patient's capacity to relate more fully to others, to experience the "magic of intimacy," and to communicate better with the living, Lacan placed equal emphasis on the subject's improved relationships with the dead. Lacan's goal of supporting the truth of the subject, as we will see, is not the same as Winnicott's goal of fostering the emergence of the True Self.

In discussing the aims of Lacanian analysis, it is customary to speak of several phases of his work. In the first, Lacan was intent on returning language and the Symbolic to their rightful place in psychoanalysis. Thus, he spoke of the goals of treatment in terms of *pleine parole*—full speech. The purpose of treatment was to turn the subject of suffering into the subject of speech, to lift the requirement—most evident in hysteria—that the body speak for us. This idea is also referred to in terms of *le bien dire*—the capacity "to say it well" (Lacan, 1990). There may be no Middle Group equivalent of this idea.

In the second period, Lacan emphasized the mortifying effect of the Symbolic on the subject. That is, as much as we experience the empowering effects of language, it is nonetheless the case that we are born into a network of signifiers in which we, in many ways, will remain entangled. Lacan (1958) gave the example of the Rat Man, pointing out that his predicament, like that of Oedipus, was in effect present before his birth.

As a result of the signifier's power over us, we are marked not simply by the loss of objects and by trauma but also by an irremediable *lack* that not even ideal mothering and fathering could prevent. There is no hope for the subject without recognition of this constraint. The alternatives lie either in the foreclosure of lack, known as psychosis, or in its disavowal, known as perversion.

In the third phase, Lacan became most concerned with the register of the *Real*. (It is crucial to keep in mind that this has nothing to do with the English word *reality* but describes an area excluded by the Imaginary and the Symbolic.) At this time, Lacan (1978) was most likely to describe the goals of analysis in terms of "crossing the fantasy" or "crossing the plane of identification" (p. 273). He passionately opposed the idea of the patient's identifying with the ego of the analyst. Throughout, he maintained that the analysand must experience the destitution of the analyst as "subject supposed to know" and see him or her finally as no more nor less than the *objet a*—the cause of desire.[11]

In the spirit of the later Lacan, Jacques-Alain Miller (2007) goes so far as to say, "The age of interpretation is behind us" (p. 3). The analytic act in a "post-interpretative world," according to Miller, "takes its bearings on the cut" (p. 8). Interpretation risks creating coherence instead of letting "it" (the unconscious) speak.

Some Lacanians, in insisting on the later seminars in which Lacan introduced *lalangue* and the *sinthome* in his push toward the Real, discount the early seminars. I disagree with the all too familiar notion that the only valid

11 Doron Almagor has made the intriguing suggestion that, just as Lacan of the 1950s urged a return to Freud, Lacan of the 1970s—with his emphasis on the Real, the body, and *lalangue*—points to a "return to Winnicott."

reading of Lacan (or Freud) is a developmental one, in which what comes later is understood to improve on—or even to render obsolete—what came before. In clinical practice, it is clear that Lacan never gave up his theory of the signifier, any more than Freud forgot the importance of trauma.

In the clinical vignette that follows, I will be drawing mainly from what is known as early and middle Lacan. The focus here will be on the patient's coming to grips with her desire as evidenced in *le bien dire*—the capacity to say it well. *Le bien dire* refers not so much to a performance as to an ethic that becomes clearer when refracted through Lacan's retranslation of Freud's "*Wo Es war soll Ich werden.*" The Strachey translation of this line is, "*Where id was, there ego shall be.*" Most analysts today, thanks to Bettelheim (1983), understand the violence done to the work by the introduction of the Latinate terms id, ego, and superego. French, like German, uses the literal equivalents of "it," "I," "over–I." Lacan (1977) argued that Freud did not mean "*Le moi doit déloger le ça*" (The ego should displace the id), pointing out that Freud did not say, "*Wo* das *Es war, soll* das *Ich werden*" (p. 128). He retranslated the line several ways, such as "*Là où fut ça, il me faut advenir*" (There where it was, I must go) (Lacan, 1966, p. 284). And stronger still: "*Là où c'était...c'est mon devoir que je vienne à être*" (There where it was...it is my duty to come into being) (Lacan, 1966, p. 227).

Thus does a statement that the ego psychologists took on as their motto become, in Lacanian teaching, an ethical imperative. The "*ça*" here refers not only to the drives but also to the "roll of the dice" at the time of the subject's origins, including everything we place in the register of the Symbolic: for example, culture, social class or caste, race. Instead of an ego determined to master the drives, the re-translations connote a search and a return to a place (*Là*). To this starting point, the analysand must commit—in the first person singular—to return.

The re-translations are cited often precisely because they evoke so much—from the journey of Oedipus from Corinth to Thebes, to our own impulses to learn or turn away from the truths of our history and prehistory. Lacan (1992) employed the Greek "ἄτη" ("*até*"), used slightly idiosyncratically to refer to the subject's family or lineal "curse." Those who remain ignorant of it are bound to relive it, unto generations. The first-century Stoic, Seneca, observed that there are two choices in life: one can be led by fate, or one can be dragged by fate. What Lacan's work does is to insist on a place for the aspect of our lives that preceded us, the aspect that was always already beyond our control. Winnicott and the Middle Group seem to make no place for it.[12] Six years into an analysis with one patient, Winnicott (1972) asked, "Do you know of mother's early history? Had she childhood difficulties?" (p. 146). It is as though he was so focused on mother and child that a psychology infinitely more complex than dyadic–triadic became inarticulable.

[12] Bollas's (1989) use of "fate" and "destiny" does not insist on the multigenerational *até*.

Another way to say this is that Winnicott assumed that whatever had occurred to a mother historically could be passed on to a child only through their relationship—through holding, handling, seeing, impinging. Family history might be nothing more than a backdrop until enacted through the physicality of the nursing couple.

Lacan took the opposite view. That is, long before the adult Oedipus made his ruinous choices, he had carried the name that means "swollen foot," a name that he, while clever enough to solve the Sphinx's riddle, had never thought to question. Furthermore, as Lacan saw it, simply being born into the House of Labdacus was as determinative for Oedipus as any subsequent act of holding, nursing, abandoning, or rescuing might be.

Lacan took up this matter in his seminar on the transference, in which he uses a trilogy of plays by Paul Claudel to show a connection between the bringing to light of the multigenerational story or curse and any question of realizing desire (Lacan, 1991). In her commentary on Lacan's use of Claudel, Marie-Magdeleine Chatel (1992) remarked, "In order to decipher a symptom, one must explore not one but two generations preceding the subject."[13] The preliminary sessions can be used to begin this process.

No mere description of technique will allow the reader to imagine what an analysis with Lacan himself was like. Memoirs written by his analysands (Godin, 1990; Haddad, 2002; Rey, 1989; Schoonejans, 2008), none of which has been translated into English, reveal a clinical practice that was *sui generis* and certainly as different from Winnicott's as chalk and cheese.[14] Gérard Haddad, a Tunisian-born engineer who spent 11 years on Lacan's couch, describes beautifully his personal metamorphosis, as he discovers his desire in the last place he might have expected. Haddad describes Lacan's famous waiting room (there were three, in fact), where patients might wait hours before being called for a session that might last an hour, 5 minutes, or mere seconds. Lacan's provocations and enigmatic interventions have led detractors, but also supporters like Haddad, to evoke a comparison to the Zen student and master. For countless analysands whom Lacan saw during 40 years of full-time practice, the results justified the frustration. According to Haddad, when a patient was in crisis, Lacan saw him or her every day. It was Lacan's "radical engagement" at key moments that allowed Haddad to survive what he himself called the "bitter pill" of the short sessions (p. 148). The usual transferences developed. Haddad mourns Lacan, who was "both father and mother to me in the transference" (Haddad, 2002, p. 318).

The present author is probably not the first to wonder whether Lacan's devoted assistant, Gloria Gonzalez, who presided actively over that

13 Lecture by Marie-Magdeleine Chatel related to Lacan's seminar VIII, Après-Coup, New York, 1 February 1992.

14 For a memoir in English of a Lacanian analysis conducted by someone other than Lacan, see Gunn (2002).

crowded waiting room, did not provide his patients with a Winnicottian holding environment that allowed them to tolerate his severity (Godin, 1990; Haddad, 2002; Rey, 1989. See also Luepnitz, 2010).

CLINICAL FRAGMENT

During the initial phase of treatment with a patient in acute distress (described subsequently), my goal was to provide a holding space, all the while listening carefully for her key signifiers. We scheduled two regular meetings per week, and—as Winnicott might do—I allowed her additional sessions "on demand." Just as the infant needs to believe it has created the breast, and can control it, so can a patient functioning at a regressed level benefit from being offered more time. (With a patient in crisis, I prefer to offer more sessions of fixed length rather than sessions of variable length—whether long or short.) When she moved to the couch and appeared ready to make use of an analytic atmosphere less supportive of the *self*, my position more closely approximated the Lacanian Other. The first phase of treatment evokes Winnicott, not without Lacan, while the later phase evokes Lacan, not without Winnicott. Another patient might call forth a different kind of borrowing from the two traditions. Note that this clinical fragment turns on the patient's name, which has been changed to protect confidentiality. Every effort has been made to replicate the multiple resonances in her name, relying—much as dream disguises do—on metonymy and metaphor.

Alvareth Stein was a 35-year-old artist, referred for depression. Despite her brilliance, she had lost two jobs due to erratic performance and stopped paying her rent. The referring doctor, sensing that she was on the brink of homelessness, asked if I would see her for a low fee.

Alvareth arrived late for her first appointment. She was expressionless, short and obese with waist-length matted hair. My visceral response was not difficult to locate; I experienced a mix of sympathy, helplessness, and disgust, but this led to no particular idea of how to begin. Her first name was one I had never heard before, and I found myself posing a question that, based on my Lacanian training, I eventually ask every patient during one of the preliminary sessions: "What can you tell me about your names?".

Alvareth paused, looking a bit flummoxed. (Many patients, even those with long prior analyses, mention that they have never been asked this question.) Her answer happened to be particularly poignant, since she had been named for a great grandmother who died of starvation in a concentration camp and about whom she claimed to know "nothing." Talking about her name thus meant speaking about the Holocaust—a topic on which her late parents had been exceptionally reticent. Alvareth had already had 6 years of psychoanalytic psychotherapy, which she described as "lifesaving." The focus had been on her relationship with her critical mother and favored brothers, and not on other family history. The Holocaust had not been mentioned. My goal is not primarily to contrast her first and second treatments: different material is almost certain to emerge with different analysts (and even in two experiences with the same analyst). Alvareth conveyed the impression that her first treatment had provided a good-enough facilitating environment that allowed her fragmented self to cohere enough to "go on being." In my work with her, moreover, Winnicott's ideas remained crucial. For example, during bouts of depression, her hygiene suffered, and her clothes reeked of urine. My disgust, my fear that other patients would encounter a bad smell in my office would have been less tolerable and more distracting if not for Winnicott's (1949) permission "objectively to hate" the patient. That particular oxymoron absorbed my aggression toward her and freed me to speculate on the meanings of feeling "peed on." My goal was to continue to provide a holding environment, surviving her dirt and destructiveness—but also to move the treatment further along the lines of the (Lacanian) Symbolic in order to help her grapple with the question of desire.

One month into treatment she said, "My last name, Stein, means 'stone.' I like having a simple, pronounceable name. But as a fat girl, it was trouble because kids called me 'beer stein' and 'Steinway piano.'"

This was the first time her size had come up, and I asked if she wanted to say more. She replied, "I have a big problem with food: I don't eat."

For years she would subsist on coffee by day, and at night she would "shovel" carbohydrates, especially sweets left over at her workplace. She had never considered a connection between her own "not eating" and the starvation that killed her great grandmother.

Two weeks later she said, in mid-session, "By the way, my parents never called me 'Alvareth.'" They had used her middle name, which begins with the letter *D*. She liked this name because her father's name also began with *D*, giving them the same initials. She would later connect this with the first letter of my name.

In college, her professors had assumed she went by Alvareth, and she began introducing herself as such. I asked what it was like to change names, and she replied she felt she was hearing it then for the first time. The first two syllables reminded her of *aleph*, the first letter of the Hebrew alphabet, and she liked the idea of being first—first born, first in her class, the first to earn an advanced degree. But at 35, her high hopes had turned to bitter irony.

"Now I'm a number one failure. No job, no relationship, no nothing. Just a bag of anxiety, phobias, and fears."

A fear of flying preoccupied her. Ever since mentioning the Holocaust, she reported a sense of duty to visit the site where her great grandmother had been interned. "A part of me needs to go there, but how can I? I would never be able to be on a plane for that long."

After much exploration of this overwhelming fear, my (Winnicott-influenced) intervention was, "You may feel differently one day, of course. Maybe you need me to hold the hope!" In the silence that followed, she seemed to take in what I had offered—a statement of belief in her still-fragile self's ability to grow. She followed with a joke about taking tranquilizers on the plane. After a pause, I shifted from the voice of good-enough mother to that of the more cryptic Other, saying, "Not every journey calls for flight." My words might have pointed to the analytic journey (at that point, three times per week) and could be taken also as cautionary. That is, coming to know one's desire takes time: Beware of the "flight into health." In Lacanian terms, the value of the intervention lies in its very ambiguity. Working against closure, it keeps the analysand analyzing.

Alvareth brought in the following dream: *I am in high school. My mother is alive and reading my report card, all upset. "This is covered with Bs!" she says.*

The day residue had to do with awaiting an evaluation that she hoped would save her new job. She laughed about the dream because she was always an A student; she never got Bs. When I repeated the line verbatim—"This is covered with Bs"—she said it sounded like something one would say at a picnic: "The cake is covered with ants or bees." Her very next association, prompted perhaps by the sound of "ant," was the only story she remembered hearing about her great grandmother's wartime experience. It was her *great aunt* who had told my patient, "Your great grandmother was walking hungry in the street when a woman dropped a jar of honey and kicked it to the curb. There were bees all over it. She bent over and shoveled honey into her mouth with her fingers."

Alvareth was intrigued to hear the word "shoveled"—so closely linked to her own symptom—emerge from what she felt was a clear memory of her great aunt's account.

Metabolizing these findings took time. My sense was that the family's partial repression of the memory of the elder Alvareth had resulted in what Lacan would call "a return in the Real" of another starving Alvareth. To vindicate the family's loss, the younger woman had vowed to make a name for herself at college, to be number one—*aleph*. In the unconscious, a number one loser is not so different from a number one winner. As another patient of mine once said, "The unconscious seems to put an absolute value sign on things. Winning big and losing big are the same distance from zero." Being number one drove Alvareth; it became her *jouissance*, written as it was directly into her name. The great grandmother's pushing away bees to shovel in some honey was replicated in the great granddaughter's furtive eating and pleasureless existence. She allowed herself to dig deeper with the help of an analyst willing to hold the hope and with whom she could associate her nonimpinging father.

Alvareth came to a session months later announcing she had made the decision to "*do it*"—to travel to a Holocaust museum that is 2 hours, by car, from my office. Although I never mentioned the museum, Alvareth believed that this was what I had meant to convey with, "Not every journey calls for flight."

This pilgrimage profoundly affected my patient. On return, she appeared less depressed and much sadder, crying openly for the first time. Only after that visit could she bring herself to contact relatives who told her, for example, that her great grandmother was the only family member who had refused to leave Germany, insisting that, because she had sent three sons to the Front during the Great War, the Reich would protect her.

As we approached the end of 1 year of treatment she said: "I was named for a woman who couldn't face reality. I've built my own prison out of Alvareth Stein/stone. I can't really imagine life outside. But I think we've loosened the bars a bit!"

This might be considered an example of *le bien dire*—something she would elaborate throughout the course of our work. Her journey to the memorial—a journey that was not on my mind, although it was present in my words—argues for the significance of Lacan's re-rendering of "*Wo Es war, soll Ich werden.*" Where it was, it is my duty to come into being.

While it could be argued that something as simple as vigorous history taking could have led to these discoveries, my experience is that insights gained through exploration of one's name and what has always been hidden there in plain view are, like the recovery of Poe's "purloined letter," particularly valuable for the subject.

It was not until the second year of treatment that Alvareth chose to use the couch. Shortly afterward, she confessed to "snooping" into my first name and learned that, in addition to being the name of a biblical judge, "Deborah" in Hebrew means "bee." She recalled the dream phrase "bees all over it" and shielded her eyes, adding: "You know I can't talk about the birds and the bees." The most important intervention during that session probably was simply repeating the word "snooping" at several junctures. This had the effect of keeping her associations going. "A 'snoop,'" she said, "is someone who means no harm, but who likes—you know—to look." She recalled snooping in her parents' closet as a child. She compared her mother's "dark beauty" to her analyst's "sweet face," which she missed seeing while lying on the couch. "Snooping!" She had stared at a pretty woman on the bus that morning and imagined the woman's long fingernails scratching her back. "Snooping" allowed her to reveal the first stirrings of erotic transference as she both desired and feared closeness with another woman. (It would be years before I discovered that "snoop" has its origin in the Dutch "*snoepen,*" meaning "to eat on the sly," uncannily linking her problems with seeing/being seen and eating/being consumed.)

It is widely understood that patients tend to bring the kind of material they sense is valued by the analyst. Even a simple intervention like repeating a signifier can "lead the witness," of course, but probably less than interventions that are more narratively complete. What emerged in this session involved what Lacan called the "scopic" drive, plus a curiosity about the analyst's name in a way that leaned on negative oedipal remnants and pointed in the direction of a particular kind of desire that took the patient by surprise. Alvareth was to find the couch at turns liberating and deeply frustrating. She was surprised at first that I would not answer some questions or, more precisely, that I would answer them with silence. In these gaps, not only her grief but also her sexual longings found a voice for the first time in her life, feelings she had somehow assumed were never meant to be hers. No longer a victim, no longer not eating/shoveling for two, she was to lose the sense of being mocked by fate. Having grasped something of the family *até*, she was able to forge a different relationship to it.

Commentary on the case

Despite the genius of Winnicott and despite the obvious influence of his work on my treatment of this patient, there are two features that never could have been learned from his example. The first has to do with the multigenerational account that supports the symptom. Simply, there is no mention of this in any of his clinical writings (Winnicott, 1971, 1972, 1975, 1977) nor in the memoirs written by his analysands (Guntrip, 1975; Little, 1990).[15]

Over the past two decades, intense interest in what is now called "the intergenerational transmission of trauma" has emerged in the work of various analysts—some, but not all of whom—were influenced by Lacan (e.g., Davoine, 2007; Faimberg, 2005; Harris, 2007; Volkan, 2002). (Some family therapists, in fact, have made this exploration central to their work for years; cf. Bowen, 1978; Stierlin, 1977.) My point here is thus mainly historical, i.e., that Lacan, by insisting on the role of the family *até* in his seminar of 1959–1960 on the ethics of psychoanalysis, showed this matter to be part of the pursuit of desire for every suffering subject.

The second feature is the attention to a split subjectivity, divided by language, which seems rarely to be given its due outside of Lacan's "return to Freud."[16] Of course, one occasionally sees a reference to the meaning of a patient's name in Anglo-American case reports. For Lacanians, however,

[15] In the 1990s, the author interviewed Marion Milner, Enid Balint, Charles Rycroft, and others about their personal experiences of analysis with Winnicott. The author asked specifically if Winnicott had explored family history beyond parents and siblings. Each analysand said "No," and only one—Balint—said that exploring three generations was important to her own work as an analyst.

[16] Some relational analysts today refer to "multiple selves" or "multiple subjectivies." Fairfield (2001), however, points out how different such constructions—which emphasize the manifold possibilities of the individual—are from subjectivity as explored in contemporary European discourses, such as Lacan's.

attention to signifiers is not optional or occasional; it is as elemental as attention to countertransference is to the Middle Group. Thinking back to Schema L—Lacan's map of subjectivity—recalls that there is no subject without its arising in the speech of the Other.

The word *analysis* comes from the Greek verb αναλυειν (*analyein*), meaning to loosen or untie. Lacan (1949) writes, "Psychoanalysis alone recognizes this knot of imaginary servitude that love must always undo again or sever" (p. 7). For Winnicott, analysis may untie or free the True Self from its moorings in compliance. For Alvareth Stein, psychoanalysis began to "loosen the bars" in a way that speaks both to the development of the self and to the transformation of subjectivity.

To juxtapose more clearly the potential contributions of both Lacan and Winnicott to this vignette, we might ask if my impulse to begin the analysis with the question of names was driven by my countertransference. That is, could it be that my feelings of "sympathy, helplessness, and disgust" were actually the responses her family had *to her name*—stored in me through projective identification? As she was to mention only later, her parents, for reasons of their own, had chosen to call her by another name—one that did not belong to a Holocaust victim. They had dutifully given her the name of "Alvareth" ... but couldn't say it.

A passage from T. S. Eliot's *Four Quartets* (1963) glosses this clinical fragment:

> We are born with the dead:
> See, they return, and bring us with them.
> ...A people without history
> Is not redeemed from time... (p. 208)

TEACHING IN THE SPACE BETWEEN WINNICOTT AND LACAN

When I am supervising a student trained only in the Middle Group tradition, while listening to reports of object relations and countertransference, I find myself asking, Who is speaking? Who is the subject of this suffering? And when sitting with a student trained exclusively by Lacanians, while listening to a great deal about the production of signifiers, I find myself asking: Who are you to this patient? What's it like in the room?

In one of Winnicott's rare etymological observations, he noted correctly that "... 'cure' at its roots means care" (1986, p. 112). Middle Group students, whose formation often includes many hours of infant observation, tend to be alert to attachment issues and not embarrassed by their caring for the patient. Lacanian students, whose training encourages reading widely (from Freud and post-Freudians, Plato, Sade, Claudel, Joyce, and others), are less intimidated by the language of dreams.

The question of how to train analysts, with its corollary issue of breadth versus depth, is an old one not resolvable here. This author has found that teaching students even a single course on Winnicott and Lacan offers clarifying endpoints on the comic/humanist versus tragic/posthumanist continuum. Teaching Lacan to Anglophone students has become more feasible than it was 20 years ago when so many key texts were untranslated. Many then turned to secondary sources by academics, which did not address clinical practice. Recent texts by Lacanian analysts such as Paul Verhaeghe (2004) can be used in conjunction with primary sources.

A fine pedagogical example is offered by Mardy Ireland (2003), who describes her project as "a squiggle game between the analytic figures of Winnicott and Lacan" (p. 211). Ireland suggests teaching that every patient can be understood both as self and as subject by use of the analogy of the wave–particle theory of light. That is, it is now a commonplace of Western science that light is both a particle and wave. If we are able to hold in our minds so astounding a paradox when it comes to light, might we not also be able to imagine human beings in terms of both a substantive *self* and a structural *subject*? In Ireland's (2003) elaboration, Winnicott's thinking:

> ... can be depicted more by the metaphor of psyche as ... dispersed particles, and treatment as what enables their organization .... The Lacanian field is better presented by the metaphor of psyche as embedded within preexisting wave patterns (setting degrees of freedom concerning love, desire, thought, etc.) within which each individual must find/create a place. (p. 6)

In Ireland's clinical practice—in which she used artwork to "cut into the Real"—one sees an oscillation between the two points of view. Ireland resonates with Kristeva (1986), who, in a different context, urged

> a constant alternation between time and its 'truth,' identity and its loss, history and that which produces it: An impossible dialectic of two terms, a permanent alternation: never one without the other. (p. 156)[17]

The risk of teaching psychoanalysis from two radically different perspectives is the dilution of both streams of thought. Lacan worked throughout his life to undo the damage done by the popularization of Freud. Any attempt to make psychoanalysis easier to understand was for him extremely dangerous. In purely practical terms, it does no good for an analyst with

17 Jay Greenberg (2001) makes a point not unlike Kristeva's: "To my mind, the best prepared analyst is one who is strongly committed to a particular psychoanalytic point of view, but who is (more or less) constantly nagged by voices from outside..." (p. 421). To think with both Winnicott and Lacan is one way—but by no means the only way—of building-in the nagging voice.

little linguistic aptitude to begin asking patients about their names. One always ends up simplifying concepts when translating them from one tradition into another. For this reason, there will always be analysts from both camps who encourage students to commit to one school of thought and work creatively within it.

On the other hand, one risks something also in choosing not to titrate Lacan with Winnicott, Winnicott with Lacan. For example, critics have decried the dangers of Lacanian practice for years, insisting that it lacks the necessary environmental provision. Correctly or not, many suicides were attributed to Lacan (Roudinesco, 1990).[18] Just as Anglophone supervisees need help attending to language, so Lacanian students need help attending to what arises in them while sitting with a patient. Lacanians speak of examining what they call "the desire of the analyst," but students trained in Middle Group and relational theories seem to be the ones more adept in this area.

Analysts inspired in large measure by Winnicott and the Middle Group risk a *reductio ad matrem*—reduction of everything to the mother. While Winnicott made a great contribution by reminding us of our dependency on mothers, he paid too little attention to fathers, grandparents, and, it must be said, to our dependency on words.

Teaching in the space between Winnicott and Lacan could result in a fuller reading of Freud. Many contemporary clinicians read only Freud the humanist, the Freud whose thoughts about alleviating suffering grew out of Enlightenment ideals. This is the Freud who advocated public clinics where the poor were analyzed free of charge (Danto, 2005). This humanist Freud (1933), eager to communicate with a large audience, delivered and published his highly accessible *Introductory Lectures*.

Lacan (1992), in contrast, wrote, "As for us, we consider ourselves to be at the end of the vein of humanist thought" (pp. 273–274). Lacanians read Freud the antihumanist, or posthumanist. This is the Freud who, from his earliest writings, described a linguistic unconscious (Freud, 1895), insisted on the importance of the drives, and believed psychoanalysis could only turn neurotic suffering into "everyday unhappiness."

Finally, working in the potential space between Winnicott and Lacan not only fosters appreciation of both traditions, but also points out where both fail, clearing a place for new ideas. Leanh Nguyen, who runs psychoanalytic therapy groups for victims of torture, while relying heavily on Middle Group and relational theory, has criticized what she sees as its "sunny optimism," a quality she associates with American culture. As a corrective,

[18] There have been several accounts of Lacan's outrageous, even physically violent behavior with patients. The most recent is Schoonejans' 2008 memoir in which she describes fist-fighting with Lacan in her session. Winnicott's life, in contrast, is often viewed as scandal-free. But see Hopkins' (2006) biography of Masud Khan, which shows another side of Winnicott. As Brecht says, "Unhappy the land that needs heroes."

Nguyen (2004) welcomed Lacan's insistence on language, the symbolic, and death but was put off, as many have been, by the cultish allegiance of his followers. She has argued also that both Anglophone and French traditions have more work to do in theorizing race. (See the excellent contributions on race by Altman, 2000; Gherovici, 2003.)

Similarly, critics have pointed out that both Winnicott and Lacan occupy "patriarchal positions" (e.g., Sprengnether, 1990) and that the project of writing a nonnormative psychoanalysis must be ongoing (Corbett, 2001; Dean & Lane, 2001; Dimen & Goldner, 2002; Gherovici, 2010; Irigaray, 1977; Luepnitz, 2007; Magee & Miller, 1997; Mitchell, 1974; Verhaeghe, 2004). While Lacan never wrote anything as explicitly antifeminist as Winnicott's (1964) article "This Feminism," his refusal to engage certain texts and interlocutors cost his theory of feminine sexuality complexity and resonance (Luepnitz, 2003).

Another area ripe for improvement in both traditions is discursive style. Better psychoanalytic writing would require some analysts to forgo the *jouissance* of mimicking the master and others to forgo the reckless pleasure of using words as if they had no histories.

IN CONCLUSION

Adam Limentani (1977) once remarked that psychoanalysis is not only an impossible profession, it is also very difficult. Practicing or teaching in the manner described above does not make our work easier. Nor can it eliminate the rivalry depicted in Mrs. Milner's painting of the two hens. Somewhere between the healing illusion of devotion and the disciplined listening for desire, the "cure through love" must be reinvented for each patient.

ACKNOWLEDGMENTS

The author is grateful to Drs. Patricia Gherovici, Ellie Ragland, and Murray M. Schwartz for their comments on an early draft, and to Bernard F. Stehle for editorial help.

This chapter is a slightly revised version on an article published in the International Journal of Psychoanalysis in October 2009 (Volume 90, Number 5), reprinted here with kind permission of the editors.

REFERENCES

Almagor, D. (2010). Winnicott and Lacan. Discussion at the American Psychoanalytic Association meeting, January 13, New York.

Althusser, L. (1971). *Lenin and philosophy, and other essays*. New York: Monthly Review Press.

Altman, N. (2000). Black and white thinking: A psychoanalyst reconsiders race. *Psychoanalytic Dialogues, 10*, 589–606.
Aron, L. (1996). *A meeting of minds: Mutuality in psychoanalysis*. Hillsdale, NJ: The Analytic Press.
Benjamin, J. (1988). *The bonds of love: Psychoanalysis, feminism, and the problem of domination*. New York: Pantheon.
Benjamin, J. (1997). Psychoanalysis as a vocation. *Psychoanalytic Dialogues*, 7, 781–802.
Benvenuto, S. (1995). Against Lacanism: A conversation of [sic] André Green with Sergio Benvenuto. *Journal of European Psychoanalysis*, 2, 1–17.
Bernstein, J. W. (1999). Countertransference: Our new royal road to the unconscious? *Psychoanalytic Dialogues*, 9, 275–299.
Bernstein, J. W. (2006). Love, desire, jouissance: Two out of three ain't bad. *Psychoanalytic Dialogues*, 16, 711–724.
Bettelheim, B. (1983). *Freud and man's soul*. New York: Knopf.
Bollas, C. (1989). *Forces of destiny*. London: Free Association Books.
Boukobza, C. (1999). Maud Manoni and the retarded child. In J. de GroefJ & E. Heinemann (Eds.), *Psychoanalysis and mental handicap* (pp. 7–22). London: Free Association Books.
Brennan, T. (Ed.). (1989). *Between feminism and psychoanalysis*. New York: Routledge.
Bowen, M. (1978). *Family therapy in clinical practice*. New York: Aronson.
Buccino, D. L. (1993). The commodification of the object in object relations theory. *Psychoanalytic Review, 80,* 123–134.
Chatel, M. (1992). Presentation on Lacan's seminar VIII, Après-Coup, New York, 1 February 1992. Unpublished.
Clancier, A., & Kalmanovitch, J. (1984). *Winnicott and paradox: From birth to creation* (A. Sheridan, Trans.). London: Tavistock.
Corbett, K. (2001). Non-traditional family romance. *Psychoanalytic Quarterly, 70,* 599–624.
Danto, E. A. (2005). *Freud's free clinics: Psychoanalysis and social justice, 1918–1938*. New York: Columbia University Press.
Davoine, F. (2007). The characters of madness in the talking cure. *Psychoanalytic Dialogues*, 17, 627–638.
Dean, T., & Lane, C. (2001). *Homosexuality and psychoanalysis*. Chicago: University of Chicago Press.
Declercq, F. (2006). Lacan on the capitalist discourse: Its consequences for libidinal enjoyment and social bonds. *Psychoanalysis, Culture and Society*, 11, 74–83.
Dimen, M., & Goldner, V. (Eds.) (2002). *Gender in psychoanalytic space: Between clinic and culture*. New York: Other Press.
Eigen, M. (1981). The area of faith in Winnicott, Lacan and Bion. *International Journal of Psychoanalysis*, 62, 413–433.
Eliot, T. S. (1963). *Collected poems, 1909–1962*. New York: Harcourt, Brace & World.
Elliot, P. (1991). *From mastery to analysis: Theories of gender in psychoanalytic feminism*. Ithaca, NY: Cornell University Press.
Faimberg, H. (2005). *The telescoping of generations*. London: Routledge.

Fairfield, S. (2001). Analyzing multiplicity: A postmodern perspective on some current psychoanalytic theories of subjectivity. *Psychoanalytic Dialogues, 11*, 221–251.

Felman, S. (1987). *Jacques Lacan and the adventure of insight*. Cambridge, MA: Harvard University Press.

Fink, B. (1997). *A clinical introduction to Lacanian psychoanalysis: Theory and technique*. Cambridge, MA: Harvard University Press.

Fink, B. (2007). *Fundamentals of psychoanalytic technique: A Lacanian approach for practitioners*. New York: Norton.

Finlay, M. (1989). Post-modernizing psychoanalysis/psychoanalysing post-modernity. *Free Associations, 16*, 43–80.

Flax, J. (1990). *Thinking fragments: Psychoanalysis, feminism, and postmodernism in the contemporary west*. Berkeley: University of California Press.

Forrester, J. (1990). *The seductions of psychoanalysis: Freud, Lacan, and Derrida*. Cambridge, UK: Cambridge University Press.

Freud, S. (1895). Project for a scientific psychology. In J. Strachey (Ed. & Trans.), *The standard edition of the complete psychological works of Sigmund Freud* (Vol. 1, pp. 160–172). London: Hogarth Press, 1949.

Freud, S. (1933). New introductory lectures on psycho-analysis. In J. Strachey (Ed. & Trans.), *The standard edition of the complete psychological works of Sigmund Freud* (Vol. 22, pp. 1–182). London: Hogarth Press, 1949.

Gallop, J. (1982). *The daughter's seduction: Feminism and psychoanalysis*. Ithaca, NY: Cornell University Press.

Gherovici, P. (2003). *The Puerto Rican syndrome*. New York: Other Press.

Gherovici, P. (2010). *Please select your gender: From the invention of hysteria to the democratizing of transgenderism*. New York: Routledge.

Godin, J. G. (1990). *Jacques Lacan, 5 rue de Lille*. Paris: Seuil.

Gorney, J. (2003). Winnicott and Lacan: A transformational clinical conversation. Paper presented at the International Federation for Psychoanalytic Education, November 7, Pasadena, CA.

Green, A. (1986). *On private madness*. Madison, CT: International Universities Press.

Green, A. (2000). *André Green at the Squiggle Foundation* (J. Abram, Ed.). London: Karnac.

Greenberg, J. (2001a). The analyst's participation: A new look. *Journal of the American Psychoanalytic Association, 49*, 359–381.

Greenberg, J. (2001b). Response to commentators (The analyst's participation: A new look). *Journal of the American Psychoanalytic Association, 49*, 417–426.

Greenberg, J., & Mitchell, S. (1983). *Object relations in psychoanalytic theory*. Cambridge, MA: Harvard University Press.

Gunn, D. (2002). *Wool-gathering, or how I ended analysis*. London: Routledge.

Guntrip, H. (1975). My experience of analysis with Fairbairn and Winnicott: How complete a result does psycho-analytic therapy achieve? *International Revue of Psychoanalysis, 2*, 145–156.

Gurewich, J. F., Tort, M., & Fairfield, S. (1999). *Lacan and the new wave in American psychoanalysis: The subject and the self*. New York: Other Press.

Haddad, G. (2002). *Le jour où Lacan m'a adopté: Mon analyse avec Lacan*. Paris: B. Grasset.

Harris, A. (2007). Analytic work in the bridge world: Commentary on paper by Françoise Davoine. *Psychoanalytic Dialogues*, *17*, 659–670.
Hill, P. (1997). *Lacan for beginners*. New York: Writers and Readers Publishing.
Hopkins, L. (2006). *False self: The life of Masud Khan*. New York: Other Press.
Ireland, M. S. (2003). *The art of the subject: Between necessary illusion and speakable desire in the analytic encounter*. New York: Other Press.
Irigaray, L. (1977). *Ce sexe qui n'en est pas un*. Paris: Minuit.
Kirshner, L. A. (2004). *Having a life: Self pathology after Lacan*. Hillsdale, NJ: The Analytic Press.
Klein, M. (1975). *Envy and gratitude, and other works, 1946–1963*. London: Hogarth Press and the Institute of Psycho-Analysis.
Kristeva, J. (1986). *About Chinese women*. In T. Moi (Ed.), *The Kristeva reader* (pp. 139–159). New York: Columbia University Press.
Lacan, J. (1949). The mirror stage as formative of the function of the I as revealed in psychoanalytic experience. In *Écrits: A selection* (A. Sheridan, Trans.) (pp. 1–7). New York: Norton, 1977.
Lacan, J. (1954–1955). *The seminar of Jacques Lacan, Book II: The ego in Freud's theory and in the technique of psychoanalysis* (S. Tomaselli & J. Forrester, Trans.). New York: Norton, 1988.
Lacan, J. (1958). The direction of the treatment and the principles of its power. In *Écrits: A selection* (A. Sheridan, Trans.) (pp. 226–280). New York: Norton, 1977.
Lacan, J. (1959–1960). *The Seminar of Jacques Lacan: Book VII. The ethics of psychoanalysis* (J.-A. Miller, Ed., D. Porter, Trans.). New York: Norton, 1992.
Lacan, J. (1960–61). *Le séminaire, Livre VIII, Le transfert 1960–61*. Paris: Seuil, 1991.
Lacan, J. (1964). *Seminar XI. The four fundamental concepts of psychoanalysis* (J.-A. Miller, Ed., A. Sheridan, Trans.). New York: W. W. Norton & Company, 1978.
Lacan, J. (1966). *Écrits I*. Paris: Seuil.
Lacan, J. (1977). *Écrits: A selection* (A. Sheridan, Trans.). New York: Norton.
Lacan, J. (1990). *Television*. New York: Norton.
Laurent, E. (1981). Lire Gabrielle et Richard à partir du petit Hans. *Quarto*, *1*, 3–20.
Limentani, A. (1977). Affects and the psychoanalytic situation. *International Journal of Psychoanalysis*, *58*, 171–182.
Little, M. (1990). *Psychotic anxieties and containment: A personal record of an analysis with Winnicott*. Northvale, NJ: Aronson.
Lonie, I. (1990). The concept of impingement in Winnicott and Lacan. *Analysis*, 2, 30–42.
Luepnitz, D. A. (2002). *Schopenhauer's porcupines: Intimacy and its dilemmas: Five stories of psychotherapy*. New York: Basic Books.
Luepnitz, D. A. (2003). Beyond the phallus. In J. Rabaté (Ed.), *The Cambridge companion to Lacan* (pp. 221–237). Cambridge, UK: Cambridge University Press.
Luepnitz, D. A. (2007). Accentuate the negative: Two contributions to a non-normative oedipal theory. *Psychoanalysis, Culture and Society*, *12*, 44–49.
Luepnitz, D. A. (2010). Lacan *Furioso*. Paper presented at the annual conference of Division 39 of APA, April 24, Chicago.

Magee, M., & Miller, D. (1997). *Lesbian lives: Psychoanalytic narratives old and new*. Hillsdale, NJ: The Analytic Press.
Mathelin, C. (1999). *Lacanian psychotherapy with children: The broken piano*. New York: Other Press.
Menninger, K. (1930, 30 March). *The Baltimore Sun*, p. 8.
Miller, J. A. (1981). Problèmes cliniques pour la psychanalyse. *Quarto*, *1*, 31–43.
Miller, J. A. (2007). Interpretation in reverse. In V. Voruz & B. Wolf (Eds.), *The later Lacan* (pp. 3–9). New York: SUNY Press.
Mills, J. (2005). A critique of relational psychoanalysis. *Psychoanalytic Psychology*, *22*, 155–188.
Mitchell, J. (1974). *Psychoanalysis and feminism*. New York: Vintage.
Mitchell, J. (1982). Introduction I. In J. Lacan (Ed.), *Feminine sexuality: Jacques Lacan and the École Freudienne* (pp. 1–26). New York: Norton.
Mitchell, S. (1988). *Relational concepts in psychoanalysis: An integration*. Cambridge, MA: Harvard University Press.
Mitchell, S. (1993). *Hope and dread in psychoanalysis*. New York: Basic Books.
Moi, T. (1985). *Sexual/textual politics: Feminist literary theory*. New York: Methuen.
Nguyen, L. (2004). Recognizing the other, narrating the self. Paper presented at the Spring Meeting of Division 39 of the American Psychological Association.
Phillips, A. (1988). *Winnicott*. Cambridge, MA: Harvard University Press.
Rabaté, J., (2000). *Lacan in America*. New York: Other Press.
Ragland-Sullivan, E. (1986). *Jacques Lacan and the philosophy of psychoanalysis*. Urbana: University of Illinois Press.
Rey, P. (1989). *Une saison chez Lacan*. Paris: R Laffont.
Rodman, F. R. (1987). *The spontaneous gesture: Selected letters of D.W. Winnicott*. Cambridge, MA: Harvard University Press.
Rogers, A. G. (2006). *The unsayable: The hidden language of trauma*. New York: Random House.
Rose, J. (1982). Introduction II. In J. Lacan (Ed.), *Feminine sexuality: Jacques Lacan and the École Freudienne* (pp. 27–57). New York: Norton.
Roudinesco, E. (1990). *Jacques Lacan & Co.: A history of psychoanalysis in France, 1925–1985*. Chicago: University of Chicago Press.
Rudnytsky, P. (1991). *The psychoanalytic vocation: Rank, Winnicott, and the legacy of Freud*. New Haven, CT: Yale University Press.
Rudnytsky, P. (1993). *Transitional objects and potential spaces: Literary uses of D. W. Winnicott*. New York: Columbia University Press.
Rushdie, S. (2000). Lecture at the University of Pennsylvania, Philadelphia, PA, April.
Rustin, M. (1991). *The good society and the inner world: Psychoanalysis, politics, and culture*. London: Verso.
Rycroft, C. (1985). *Psychoanalysis and beyond*. London: Chatto & Windus.
Satorsky, D. (1993). Implications and use of the symbolic area of experience in Winnicott and Lacan. Smith College of Social Work. Unpublished paper.
Schafer, R. (1976). *A new language for psychoanalysis*. New Haven, CT: Yale University Press.
Schoonejans, S. (2008). *Le geste de Lacan*. Brussels: Luc Pire.
Sprengnether, M. (1990). *The spectral mother: Freud, feminism, and psychoanalysis*. Ithaca, NY: Cornell University Press.

Stavrakakis, Y. (1999). *Lacan and the political*. London: Routledge.
Stierlin, H. (1977). *Psychoanalysis and family therapy*. New York: Aronson.
Vanier, C. (2008). A baby that does not exist. *Analysis, 14*, 233–241.
Verhaeghe, P. (2004). *On being normal and other disorders: A manual for clinical psychodiagnostics* (S. Jottkandt, Trans.). New York: Other Press.
Volkan, V. (2002). *The Third Reich in the unconscious: Transgenerational transmission and its consequences*. New York: Brunner-Routledge.
Voruz, V., & Wolf, B. (Eds.) (2007). *The later Lacan*. Albany: State University New York Press.
Winnicott, D. W. (1949). Hate in the countertransference. In *Through paediatrics to psycho-analysis* (pp. 194–203). New York: Basic Books, 1975.
Winnicott, D. W. (1953). Transitional objects and transitional phenomena. In *Playing and reality* (pp. 1–25). London: Tavistock, 1971.
Winnicott, D. W. (1964). This feminism. In *Home is where we start from: Essays by a psychoanalyst* (pp. 183–194). New York: Norton, 1986.
Winnicott, D. W. (1971). Mirror-role of mother and family in child development (pp. 111–118). In *Playing and reality*. London: Tavistock.
Winnicott, D. W. (1972). *Holding and interpretation: Fragment of an analysis*. New York: Grove Press.
Winnicott, D. W. (1975). *Through paediatrics to psycho-analysis*. New York: Basic Books.
Winnicott, D. W. (1977). *The Piggle: An account of the psychoanalytic treatment of a little girl*. London: Hogarth Press.
Winnicott, D. W. (1989). *Psychoanalytic explorations*. Cambridge, MA: Harvard University Press.
Žižek, S. (1989). *The sublime object of ideology*. London: Verso.

Chapter 2

The bifurcation of contemporary psychoanalysis

Lacan and Winnicott

André Green

After having opposed the names of Lacan and Winnicott, today it is frequent to bring them together. Having witnessed the ascension of each myself, I had the opportunity to observe these two authors evolving, each in his own way. Occasionally, one could even bring them together on a given theme. For my part, I regularly followed the teaching of Jacques Lacan, especially in his seminars, from 1960 to 1967. Otherwise, I had what I could call amicable relations with him until 1967 when I felt the need to take my distance from him. If I frequented him assiduously between 1960 and 1967, I had many other occasions to retrace his path. I will begin with this, following with an analysis of the work of Donald Winnicott, the specificity of which is differentiated sharply from the thinking of Lacan and founds his own originality.

To bring together these two eminent figures of European psychoanalysis is to proceed to a curious marriage. If they both began to make themselves known around 1930, everything else, in fact, opposed them. The difference between their original training is well known. Lacan was the product of a generation of psychiatrists, part of the phalanx of Professor Henri Claude's assistants who founded modern psychiatry. All did not become psychoanalysts. Some of them, attentive to the renewal of psychiatry, oriented themselves toward other domains in psychiatry whose existence was just beginning to hatch. Very early, Lacan showed his interest in psychoanalysis. Having frequented surrealist milieux, he had entered into modernity and was on the lookout for all that pursued novelty. Psychoanalysis seems to have inscribed itself in this context, but it would be fair to say that Lacan perceived very early the originality of Freudian thought.

As for Winnicott, his pathway was different; he had a training that was essentially pediatric. Yet it must be underlined that from the onset he had knowledge of Sigmund Freud's work and had subscribed very early to his principles. Although allied to the theories of psychoanalysis, he quickly founded his own system of thought, different from Freud's on quite a few points.

Each of these two authors, therefore, was exposed to very different influences. Lacan very soon gained entry into the reigning cultural milieux of the time, well beyond medicine, and established new contacts with cultural and philosophical circles. One must add, however, that those belonging to psychiatric milieux were inclined in general to seek out and frequent intellectual circles—especially those in the entourage of Henri Ey. Kept more or less at a distance from medicine, they sought other allies. The English psychoanalysts, to the contrary, were scarcely interested in solidifying contacts with academics or intellectuals. One could say that in Great Britain psychoanalysis remains confined to psychoanalytic practice, with an exclusive concern for treatment. Probably from the same inspiration, the psychoanalysis of children saw an early expansion, always oriented toward prevention and treatment. We could affirm that psychoanalysis has remained in Great Britain a therapeutic activity without reverberations on the debate of ideas, as was the case in France. One can see that British psychoanalysis was primarily concerned with matters related to its objective of providing care to patients, whereas the French took a more intellectual turn by seeking to contribute to contemporary debates over theory.

JACQUES LACAN

At the time of publishing *Écrits* (1966), Lacan wrote his Chapter 2 titled "À nos antecedents" ("To our predecessors"). He recalled diverse steps: his thesis on paranoia about the case of Aimée, his article on the Papin sisters, the teaching of de Clérambault, "our only master in psychiatry," a reference going against the contemporary current during a period when Henry Ey combated the "mechanistic" thought of the man who had also been his master. Finally, the mirror stage[1] marked the arrival of Lacan in psychoanalysis. In this inaugural work to which Lacan and his commentators have never ceased to return, he referred to the imaginary relationship with the mother. This piece of writing studied the recognition of the child and the mother in front of the mirror, reflecting his own image of the fragmented body (primordial discord) in contrast to the totalized image of the mother. To this primordial incompletion was opposed the first "orthopedic" image of the mother, which resurges in dreams. As many steps from the formation of the specular "I" to the social "game" (from "*je*" to "*jeu*" in the French), a process that, at the mirror stage, permits identification with the imago of the counterpart: "I" as a stranger to "me." One must again recall the article in the *Encyclopédie Française, tome VIII*, on "The Family" (1938). From this moment, the conception of the ego pretending to a relationship with reality is attacked.

Today, we have available a new documentation that is not suspect of partiality. Dana Birksted-Breen and Sara Flanders (2010) are the authors of an

[1] First reference to Lévi-Strauss (1958), for his article on l'efficacité symbolique (symbolic effectiveness). On page 95 appear the first allusions to language.

excellent introduction to French psychoanalysis and particularly to the role of Lacan at the heart of it. They recognize the revolutionary influence of Lacan (p. 2). They recall his impact on its conception of unconscious processes, the importance that he accorded to language, the specificity he underlined of the *après-coup*, the distinction he put forward between instinct and drive, separating the biological from the psychic, the role of the other in the formation of the ego, the centrality of the Oedipus complex where the paternal role is recognized as having priority, and the conceptual importance of the castration complex. It is to him moreover that we owe the capital role of reading Freud. On the other hand, many of his disciples turned away from him afterward on account of the deviations that he defended against classical views of technique. We were equally opposed to his ideas concerning the body, the neglect of affect, the minimizing of pregenital drives, the preverbal, and so on. All these observations are highlighted under the pen of the two authors from the British Society (Birksted-Breen & Flanders) who comment on the positions of those who have held to placing themselves outside his influence. Nonetheless, this English view did not have difficulty in recognizing his real importance beyond institutional polemics.

I should like to define my own position vis-à-vis Lacan's contributions. I divide these into two categories. On one hand, there is an indisputable series of works having as their purpose to recall the force and pertinence of Freudian concepts. There is scarcely any doubt in what concerns those works about the importance of Lacan's rectifications and reminders of the axes of Freudian psychoanalysis. I myself have abundantly drawn from these sources. But there is also a second series of works underlining the contributions proper to Lacan, such as his own conceptions of structural linguistics without much concern for their compatibility with the original ideas of, for example, Ferdinand de Saussure. Concerning this second series of contributions, my opinion has evolved considerably over time, and my adherence to their content has become much more reserved. It is thus suitable to distinguish between the first and second group. Time has worn thin the ideas born of Lacanian hypotheses—on the fecundity of structural linguistics for psychoanalysis, for example.

All through the pages that mark his course, Lacan's thought closes up and does not suffer any improvisation. Lacan entered the psychoanalytic literature on equal footing with his intervention on the transference *à propos* Freud's case of Dora, one of the most striking texts in the collection.[2] However, it is in the fourth part of the Rapport de Rome that Lacanian theory was introduced (1966, p. 234). "The Function and Field of Speech in Psychoanalysis" (pp. 237–322) was the fundamental step. Did it have to have waited 21 years before Lacan found his way? What happened then for this choice on the relations between unconscious and language to be taken?

[2] Congrès des Psychanalystes de Langue Française de 1951 (pp. 215–224).

When one reads through the entire period before the Rapport de Rome of 1953, one can confirm the presence of master ideas considerably removed from those that would be developed after this date. Could one conclude that it was clinical experience that produced this change of direction? Nothing to my sense proves it. On the other hand, taking into consideration some of the ideas that imposed themselves at this time permits the recognition of themes born outside of psychoanalysis. In 1947 the monumental work of Claude Lévi-Strauss, *Les Structures élémentaires de la parenté* (1949), appeared. It was an event that saw the birth of what would be called structuralism. This movement was born of the encounter in the United States during the Second World War (in 1941) of Lévi-Strauss and Roman Jakobson, linguist of the celebrated Vienna school. This fact did not escape the attention of Lacan, who cited Lévi-Strauss. The reference to language intervened only halfway into the Rapport (Lacan, 1966, p. 285).

One could not say that the new alliance between Lacan's thinking and structuralism was predictable, yet, in sum, Lacan's ideas in 1953 seem to have been imported from anthropology and linguistics under the influence of Lévi-Strauss and Jakobson. Subsequently, the interest that Hegel held for Lacan would be transferred to Saussure, of whom Maurice Merleau-Ponty had already recognized the importance. Lacan (1966) engaged the problem closely in "The Freudian Thing" ("*La chose freudienne*") and "Psychoanalysis and Its Consequences" ("*La psychanalyse et ses conse-quences*"). It was thus after the middle of the 1950s that Lacan found the distinctive features with which his thought can be identified. "The Instance of the Letter in the Unconscious" ("*L'instance de la lettre dans l'inconscient*") stands out in particular. Here, Saussure was used to serve Lacan. During these years Lacan was the most brilliant in constructing his oeuvre, which advocated a conception of psychoanalysis that founded his practice. He referred to this in the "Direction of the Treatment and the Principles of Its Power" ("*La Direction de la cure et les principes de son pouvoir*"). We can note the following: Winnicott was cited in the bibliography of his paper à propos his article on transitional objects and phenomena, first presented in 1951, but Lacan was more involved in juggling with the signifier and its algorithms. He postulated, against the linguists, the separation of signifier and signified, the sliding of the signified under the signifier, and the development of an algebraic notation (p. 325).

Some of his other writings were notable. I cite especially "The Subversion of the Subject and the Dialectic of Desire in the Freudian Unconscious" ("*Subversion du sujet et dialectique du désir dans l'inconscient freudien*"). This period coincided with the move of Lacan's seminar to the École Normale Supérieure, where he began his lessons with "Science and Truth" ("*La Science et la vérité*"). The subject in question in his discourse could be only the subject of science. Lacan sought here without success, I fear, to convince Lévi-Strauss of this: "*Moi, la vérité, je parle*" ("Myself, the truth,

I speak"). By this complicated statement he informed us that the truth could be sought only out on the side of speech, of which it is the function to reveal the truth for whomever knows how to listen for it.

It would be to know Lacan very poorly to imagine that the publication of the *Écrits* in 1966 would have sufficed to complete a body of doctrine arrived at its culmination. In fact, the expansion of the theory of the signifier was far from indicating the closure of his work. So decisive was this step in his thought that many identify it as the essence of Lacanian theory, but it would be a mistake to rest there. In fact, Lacan next distanced himself from theories of language after having placed Saussure and then Noam Chomsky in position as doctrinal references. Nonetheless, by the reception by the linguists of his hypotheses, he distanced himself from them and struck out for new horizons. Henceforth, topology is what pushed him toward a growing mathematization. His listeners would have to acquaint themselves with the torus, the cross-cap, and other models intended to clarify psychoanalytic theory. Some mathematicians were attracted by these Lacanian conceptions. The theory of borromean knots took over the task, with the real, the symbolic, and the imaginary, the new triad, outlining complicated pathways, one of these terms passing under, the other over, the third tracing some mostly mysterious criss-crossings, lacking which the unconscious would remain opaque to those claiming to be concerned with it.

At the time, Lacan experienced the agonies of a second split. His colleagues who had previously separated from la Société psychanalytique de Paris (SPP) could put into question those lagging spirits who had not taken the time to be formed by Lacanism. But how to explain, unless by reasons of interest, that those who had all their time to acquaint themselves with the finest subtleties and the finesse of Lacan's thinking took the decision to reaffirm their disagreement with him? Some prestigious names—Jean Laplanche, Jean-Bertrand Pontalis, Didier Anzieu, Piera Aulagnier, François Perrier, Jean-Paul Valabrega, and Guy Rosolato—all became dissidents in turn. They were to form the future advancing wing of former disciples of Lacan. In any case, they remained with the theory of the signifier, declining to follow the master in his explorations on the side of topology or the borromean knots. By a paradoxical phenomenon, the more difficult it became to follow Lacan in these elaborations, the more recruitment to his cause, inspired by demographic or political motives, was extended with little difficulty.

In the meantime, a new tendency came to light. After the split of 1963, Lacan and his followers formed the new École Freudienne de Paris. Those who had separated from Lacan either regrouped in the ranks of the young and ephemeral Société Française de Psychanalyse or founded the new Association Française de Psychanalyse around Daniel Lagache, which was admitted at the International Psychoanalytical Association (IPA); some others then came to join Lagache: Jean Laplanche, Jean-Bertrand Pontalis, Didier Anzieu, Vladimir Granoff. Some others formed the spearhead of the *Nouvelle Revue de Psychanalyse* around Pontalis. The Lacanians ceased having the monopoly of opposition to the IPA. All the same, the quantitative criterion remained the sign of success, the Lacanians having the advantage of numbers, which, happily, signified only the power of the media. Soon after, at the initiative of Aulagnier, Perrier, and Valabrega—the Quatrième Groupe—split off in turn. Henceforth, the Lacanian group, having lost a notable fraction of Lacan's students—who were among its best representatives—found itself greatly weakened. To remedy this important loss, l'École Freudienne de Paris, born after the split of 1963 under the impetus of Lacan, opened its doors to nonanalysts who flocked there.

We come to the essential. What to think of the work of Lacan? His success was assured by the number of adepts it attracted. I will not limit myself to this perspective but prefer to insist on my own judgment. Of Lacan himself, I will begin by recognizing that he was a great stimulator, a mind of great erudition, animated by a remarkable dynamism, possessing indisputable gifts that made him leader of a school. On the other hand, one regrets his aggressive attitude, his sarcasm, the need he found to make his interlocutors believe that they comprehended nothing of what they were speaking about and that he alone understood. From this angle, he used the means of paradox for polemic ends. His adversaries, however, were not always weak opponents to the controversies he animated. In France, we might cite Maurice Bouvet, to limit ourselves just to him. Outside France, in the ranks of Anglo Saxon psychoanalysis, opponents of stature were not lacking. Melanie Klein, D. W. Winnicott, and W. R. Bion cannot be considered negligible any more than Loewald, Lewin, and others still. The aforementioned attributes of Lacan are weaknesses that do not bring honor to the person. Still graver were the liberties he took with his practice: arbitrary shortening of sessions, put-downs and public humiliations, even sometimes violence practiced on analysands lying on his couch. The more one permitted him liberties, the more he abused them. It remains to be decided whether his attitude was on behalf of a technique inspired by the search for truth or whether it rather indicated the mark of total authority, a thirst for domination and of a power without limit, reserved to him alone.

Yet, beyond all that, what is Lacanian theory worth? On the scale of time, recognizing that it was able to seduce me when I was in search of novelty (and, I must acknowledge, when the official theory, sinning by insufficiency, often proved itself disappointing and threatened to follow the path of decline), I cannot deny its appeal. But once Lacan gave us to suppose that he was really at odds with the conception of a psychoanalysis that he purportedly defended, there was a lot to beware of. Said in another way, after the Rapport de Rome (1953), during what I call the opulent period of Lacanism, around the years 1953 to 1960, Lacan produced a series of articles that still today make his renown but that remained outside of clinical practice.

Having subsequently gone more deeply into the thought of Saussure, I was able to become aware of the degree to which he was a great mind, worthy of respect and admiration, and how much it seemed increasingly evident that his thinking had little to do with what psychoanalysis talked about, even according to Lacan (Green, 2003). While Saussure used the concept of the unconscious, the way he understood it did not leave the slightest chance of an encounter between him and Freud. In this regard, it is useful to recall that Raymond de Saussure, Ferdinand's son, became a renowned psychoanalyst who had an analysis with Freud. He found it suitable to transmit to Freud the work of his father. Freud thus had between his hands Saussure's writings but scarcely accorded them any interest. The "adaptations" that Lacan made the works of Saussure undergo, of which, said in passing, he knew only the approximate versions (since corrected, thanks to Rudolf Engler), have hardly convinced linguists. That "the unconscious [was] structured like a language" has not held the attention of Benveniste or of Culioli or Simon Bouquet, to speak only of those three. The position of Lacan, who sought to separate the signifier from the signified, is today considered unacceptable by many. Akhmatova judged that Lacanian theory in a more general fashion was not acceptable to linguists. But above all, Rastier and Bouquet (Green, 2003, pp. 273–274) recognized that the field of linguistic studies has to be divided into two parts. On one hand, there is the work attaching itself to the *logico-grammatical pole*, of which grammar is the representative, and, on the other, is the *rhétorico-herméneutique pole*, represented by semantics. The thought of Lacan, however, was connected to the *logico-grammatical*.

That Lacan did not fail to refer to Lévi-Strauss was without a doubt remarkable. Unhappily, the anthropologist declined this honor, awaiting the death of Lacan, with whom he had a friendly relationship, to admit his total disagreement with, first, Freud's thought, and, even more, with Lacan (in *Le Regard Éloigné*; Lévi-Strauss, 1983). Let us recognize, nonetheless, the value of Lacan's ideas on the relationship between certain theories of language and the poetic function. I must add, though, that Jakobson (1963), author of a theory which classifies in six functions the givens of language, put in the first position the emotional function that was ignored by Lacan. Because Lacan did not want to hear affect spoken of, as I have shown clearly in *Le Discours Vivant* (Green, 1973a), Lacan could not deprive himself of reaching back to mathematics, to the algebra of Boole and Frege, concerned to remind us that the only subject of value to his eyes was that of science. He oscillated between a conception of the symbolic and references to science, and his attempt to anchor psychoanalysis in these choices stimulated many efforts. Lacan (1966) wished to arrive at a primal language, *un langage premier*, which obliged him to forge a new concept, *lalangue* (one word), to designate the primitive forms of language, anterior to its secondary formalization.

Certain felicitous formulas made their appearance here: "Language thus constitutes a communication in which the sender receives from the receptor his own message in an inverted form" (Lacan, 1966, p. 298), and, again, what is scarcely disputable for an analyst, "The function of language is not to inform, but to evoke" (p. 299). Above all, for Lacan, the analyst remained a "master of the truth" (p. 313). I imagine that Winnicott and Bion would not approve of that. Let me conclude with "the murder of the thing .... In this way, the symbol manifests itself first as murder of the thing, and this death constitutes in the subject the perpetuation of his desire" (p. 319). I comment in passing that the text closes with many references to the negative and to negativity.

It is important to understand that, for Lacan, the source of every manifestation of the unconscious is "the place of the other." This other, which is not accessible to the subject, manifests itself only by its desire—the desire of the other that carries the mark of the unconscious. The sole consideration to take note of is this reference to the place of the other, "the treasure of the truth." Every manifestation issuing from the conscious then can be only a ruse or the product of a rationalization.

Who speaks? "*It* speaks there where it is suffering" (the "It," *le Ça*, the unconscious). "Myself the truth, I speak." Myself who? Then appears the other. *It speaks*, "a subject in the subject, transcendent to the subject." We confront here another aspect of Lacan's talent. As much as his linguistic prowess appears dated today, his words on the intersubjective relation of analytic speech continue to make us reflect and make for captivating reading. Said another way, when Lacan sticks with metaphor, you have to read him. One rediscovers him in areas far indeed from the sources where he began, for example, in the psychoses. On the other hand, when Lacan pronounces himself on the direction of treatment (*la cure*), he scarcely convinces me. He is broadly surpassed in this regard by Winnicott or Bion. How indeed could he have spoken about it, he who had so battered its frame. It is hardly astonishing that he lost the fundamental markers of analytic technique (Lacan, 1966, p. 793); he deliberately ignored them.

I will leave to the side other of his contributions, whatever might have been their importance, but will conclude the period of the *Écrits* in drawing attention to the significance of the article "Subversion of the Subject and the Dialectic of Desire in the Freudian Unconscious" ("*Subversion du sujet et dialectique du désir dans l'inconscient freudien*") (1966). It concerns a veritable theoretic summation around one of those Lacanian schemas, called "*l'ouvre-bouteille*" (the bottle opener), which could not be summarized. Lacan is here at the antipodes of Anglo Saxon psychoanalysis and especially of the British Society. If we plunge into a reading of the works of Winnicott and of Bion, we are in the psychoanalytic literature most opposed to Lacan. When I reread from a distance the Lacan of this period, I find myself before constructions that are seductive but are far away from any clinical reality, which is to say everything that concerns my practice.

And this is why I leave deliberately to one side the torus, the cross-caps, and the borromean knots, which are of no help to me. To the contrary, when I read and reread Winnicott and Bion, I am directly at the heart of my practice. I am open to what they say to me. While I am sometimes seduced by the elegance and the correctness of his formulations, I have no need to follow the acrobatics of authors who bring me into their experiences; I must admit to disappointment in the writings of Lacan that are not a reference as for my practice as a psychoanalyst. I can recognize the poetic beauty of some of his fulgurations, but I cannot be convinced that it has to do with psychoanalysis, as Freud is always able to make one feel.

One remark to terminate: whereas Winnicott discovered, through a properly psychoanalytic research, the importance of the frame as a theoretical concept that had to impose itself on the future of psychoanalytic thought, Lacan from his side took no account of this advance. How could he have done otherwise, he whose practice had so ill treated the rules that his colleagues recognized as fundamental? But there is more. Lacan preferred to pass beyond the basic principles of treatment, reducing them to formal rules denuded of interest. He contested that technique could be compared with the grandeur of ideas of which he made himself the herald. In fact, the method was replaced to serve the same function, or an equivalent one, by a reflection on language; the deepening of language played an equivalent function in Lacanian theory to that of the frame. Language served as the frame for theoretical observation—except that Lacan would ultimately have to rebaptize his linguistic conception of the unconscious as "*linguisterie*," to punish the linguists for not having wished to hear him. And since analysis limited itself to an exchange of words, how could one not find its justification in a speculative deepening of language? Henceforth, to elucidate the mysteries of psychic life amounted to elucidation of the mysteries of language. Few linguists let themselves be convinced by this disappearing trick, and still fewer psychoanalysts belonging to other schools of thought. Today one can hardly let oneself be fooled.

In sum, the revaluation of the Lacanian influence on French psychoanalysis can be only nuanced. Without any contest, the Lacanian charisma touched many psychoanalysts, even among those who declared themselves in opposition to him. One cannot challenge that he also had a healthy influence during a period when the ensemble of work by non-Lacanian analysts—with the exception of Bouvet—was scarcely enlightening and often threatened psychoanalytic thought with its impasses. One had to await the following generation for a healthy rebound. On the other hand, today, the innovations of Lacanism appear disputable indeed. One cannot say that structural linguistics has permitted any notable advances and still less topology or the theory of the borromean knots. The psychoanalysis of the future has drawn more of its resources from the side of the British Society. Once again, Winnicott and Bion have been recognized in French psychoanalysis as authors of the first rank and of an incontestable utility. At the opposite end, Winnicott's writings were new according to their reference to psychoanalytic practice.

D. W. WINNICOTT

Although I know the work of Winnicott fairly well, I cannot pretend to speak with the same competency as I can about Lacan, who was part of my psychoanalytic landscape. His work, without a doubt polemic, contested, and revolutionary, was the object of incessant commentary, as much on the part of his admirers as his adversaries. But in a certain way, the youth of the period, taken with his novelty, had no choice. Before the poverty of contemporary psychoanalytic productions (with a few exceptions), which could not escape us, the works of Lacan imposed themselves. The scent of scandal that surrounded them gave us hope of a renewal of which we had great need. The discovery of Winnicott, which was a bit belated, placed itself under other auspices. Gallimard, which had promoted the translation of a number of his works, founded the *Nouvelle Revue de Psychanalyse* under the urge of Pontalis, which helped us to know him better. This publication aimed to leave the ghetto in which French psychoanalysis was enclosed. Having included Masud Khan on its editorial team, Pontalis benefited from his advice and direction and did a lot to familiarize us with Winnicott. Khan introduced us to his writings that were for us an authentic source of novelty. Already from 1961, I began to know better the work of authors of the British Psycho-Analytical Society. The Kleinians were a novel source for those of us (the great majority of the French) unfamiliar with the *oeuvre* of Klein. Our elders had grave reserves about adopting her views. But there was not only Melanie Klein; it was an entire school that aroused our admiration—Segal, Rosenfeld, and Joseph, among others. By the same circumstance, we also got to know Klauber and, Stewart, and James, non-Kleinians authors, as well as other talented clinicians from whom we learned a lot. Winnicott, after the turbulence of Lacanism, permitted us to think in other ways again by helping us discover other horizons than those of French thought and, as well, remaining far from the systematic theory of Melanie Klein. He offered a valid new way of thinking, fundamentally clinical, free of prejudices, and, before all else, creative. The thought of Winnicott was perhaps better accepted and welcomed in France than it sometimes succeeded in making itself heard in the United Kingdom, where the Kleinian hegemony and the orthodoxy of Anna Freud strongly resisted its penetration.

When I became interested in the origins of Winnicottian thought, I learned how, inspired by psychoanalysis, this pediatrician had tried to write about it. His analyst at the time broke with his customary neutrality by telling him, "If you are applying psychoanalytic theory to children you should meet Melanie Klein" (Rodman, 2003, p. 106). This he did, even though he was ignorant of almost all of Kleinism. He was profoundly impressed by Klein and was undoubtedly appreciated by her. For her part, she thought that she could do no better than open the doors of her group to make him one more disciple. Winnicott, however, was in horror of endangering his independence of mind and for nothing in the world would have accepted the proposition to become even the most talented of her "students." Throughout his life, he never ceased to reproach the disciples of Klein for rendering a very bad service to her thought by blindly repeating all that she had discovered. Nothing was worthy of criticism. It took the powerful originality of Bion to defend a Kleinism renewed by his own ideas. Shortly, the thought of Bion did not delay its secession, but without rupture or dissidence. He remained Kleinian, although one cannot deny that his thought carried an originality that allowed it to be distinguished in the heart of Kleinism. It was not by chance that Winnicott should later express to Bion his admiration for an *œuvre* to which, despite everything, he felt himself close. His letters are witness to this (see notably his letter of October 7, 1955; Rodman, 1987, p. 89). But this encounter was late, and Winnicott for his part had a long road to travel before being considered a major author, after having succeeded in tracing his path outside the ways marked by Klein. He went so far as to affirm his (partial) disagreement with her ideas and did not agree with those of her disciples who referred to them without departing one iota from what she had written.

I will limit my discussion to several of Winnicott's significant works, as it is not possible to cite the totality. Several excellent studies of Winnicott exist: those of Masud Khan (1975), Madeleine Davies and David Wallbridge, Adam Philips, and especially one by Jan Abram, who has studied in detail the monumental corpus of his completed works. I permit myself to append to this list some of my own publications. Finally, I mention the study by Michel Gribinski (2000, pp. 17–29).

The first collection of articles by Winnicott appeared in 1958, and included earlier articles. In "Primitive Emotional Development" (1945), Winnicott defended the idea that the patient's fantasies about his insides are important in themselves, more important at first than the child's relationships to differentiated others:

> The main object of this paper is to present the thesis that the early emotional development of the infant, before the infant knows himself (and therefore others) as the whole person that he is (and that they are) is vitally important: indeed that here are the clues to the psychopathology of psychoses. (p. 149)

Winnicott described what he called dissociation. Over time, mother and baby have a shared life (p. 112), but fantasy is more primary than reality.

Winnicott also postulated a state of precocious cruelty ("primitive ruthlessness," p. 154) as well as the fear of disintegration (p. 155). Finally, he described primitive vengeance ("primitive retaliation," p. 155). The object was said to be born of desire because it was created from this origin. We can note a point of convergence here between Winnicott and Lacan, without them having ever communicated their conceptions. It is evident that the basic suppositions of Winnicott differed profoundly from the fundamental Kleinian theorems, which he never accepted.

Other important articles accompanied these beginnings, such as, "Hate in the Countertransference" (1949, p. 194). This was the first time that hate was not interpreted as arising from feelings attributed to the analysand but was recognized in the analyst. This was another difference from the Kleinian perspective that presumed most often a state of clarity and innocence with which the analyst cloaked himself. Then followed Winnicott's descriptions concerning illusion and the birth of the transitional object, accompanied by schemas (p. 223). Shortly after, the first version of "Transitional Objects and Transitional Phenomena" was published under the title of "A Study of the First Not-Me-Possession" (1953), an article that would be the object of constant revisions, the last of which dates to his collection *Playing and Reality* (1971b). The preoccupation of Winnicott with the problem of "mind and its relation to the psyche soma" (1988) had already appeared. This problem haunted Winnicott, who made diverse contributions to the subject. But it was in 1954 that a very important article appeared, a veritable point of departure for what one might call the Winnicottian clinical method, "Metapsychological and Clinical Aspects of Regression Within the Psycho-Analytical Set Up" (1954). This innovative article proposed a new interpretation of regression in analytic treatment and showed how treatment could fail, in spite of a very advanced technique. Winnicott draws attention to patients for whom analysis must address the earliest stages of emotional development preceding the establishment of the personality, an entity prior to the acquisition of the concepts of space and time. One could end up in these cases with a "freezing of the failure situation" (1954, p. 281). Winnicott conceived the idea of regression in the setting of a very organized defense of the ego that implied the existence of a false self (1954, p. 281). The failure did not relate to an individual reaction but to a failed environment. One can see here the notion that regression can be a part of healing. Winnicott laid out the succession of phases that punctuate the events in treatment. The dominant concept was that of the setting as a support for a regression of the patient to a state of dependence. The self that has been hidden until this point submits to the whole ego, succeeds in freezing its environment, and follows by a complete thaw as an expression of freedom. Regression to dependence can end under this circumstance with progress toward independence, with drives and desires becoming realizable.

In this latter case, the analyst *is* the mother: she does not represent the mother; she is her incarnation. It is not her representation but her incarnation in the transference that is in question. The existence of a true self is still lacking. To terminate this collection of papers, I cite the work on primary maternal preoccupation (Winnicott, 1956a) and the antisocial tendency (Winnicott, 1956b). The novelty of the ensemble is impressive, especially the independence of thought, the originality, and the refusal of any dogmatism that rests on blind adhesion to the ideas of master thinkers.

The second volume of Winnicott's work, extending from 1958 to 1963, appeared under the title *The Maturational Processes and the Facilitating Environment* (1965). From this period, we can recognize a few contributions that have become famous, such as "The Capacity to Be Alone" (1958), in which he dealt with the capacity to be alone *in the presence of the mother.* He proposed the concept of a relationship of the self between two persons, one of whom is alone. "I am alone" could be interpreted in different manners. In this context, the relation with the Id is reinforced when it unfolds in a setting of *ego-relatedness*, a conception that implied a distinction according to Winnicott. By its excess, the threat of an orgastic excitation can destroy the satisfaction of the play.

Another important article, presented at the Congress of the International Psychoanalytical Association (IPA) in Edinborough in 1961, in this volume is "The Theory of the Parent–Infant Relationship," a topic widely debated at the time and to which Winnicott brought a new vision. In it, he limited the scope of projection but specified that for a child who develops in the frame of the relationship setting the outcome will appear to him as a projection. Winnicott underlined the incidental note of Freud, in his 1911 article on the "Two Principles of Mental Functioning," according to which an organism that was a slave to the pleasure principle and inclined to ignore the reality principle would be unable to survive except under the condition of including the role of maternal care (p. 36). "Provided one includes with it in the care it receives from the mother," Freud underlined with clairvoyance. Winnicott commented there on the necessary role of separation from the parents. In sum, the primitive drive was destined to fade and give place to independence. He gave his own interpretation of the primitive phases of development, presenting his conception of the progression from the subjective object to the object objectively perceived (p. 45) as well as the steps that mark the journey from absolute dependence to independence. With precision, he described the role of the maternal provision and the modifications of this role confirmed on the mother's part. This important article did not escape the attention of the international public. All the ideas of Winnicott were not adopted, however, and it took them a long time to be recognized for their true value.

In 1963, Winnicott wrote "The Development of the Capacity for Concern," a text where he described the important step of acquisitions from the depressive phase. This feature was of fundamental importance for him. To be more precise, it must be recognized that Winnicott was never convinced by Klein's descriptions of the paranoid-schizoid phase, whereas to the contrary he shared many of her ideas about the depressive phase. The "capacity for concern" did not exist for him from the beginning but resulted from an evolution that was completed at the same time as the unification of the object (Klein). At this moment, the subject discovers concern for the object that is important to handle carefully and to avoid attacks that are too openly destructive.

In a general manner, Winnicott, instead of referring to a linear temporal evolution, preferred the idea of a voyage—a voyage from the original state of absolute dependence to one of relative independence, a voyage from the condition of the subjective object to the object objectively perceived. In other terms, it concerned arriving at the idea of an object originally created by subjective omnipotence, thus given over to internal conditions, evolving to one at a later state perceived in external reality and existing out of that reality, not as the effect of a subjectivity that gave it birth.

Winnicott opened the question of direct observation in "On the Contribution of Direct Child Observation to Psychoanalysis" (1957), in which he differentiated "profound" from "primitive" (p. 109): "Deep is not synonymous with early because an infant needs a degree of maturity, before becoming gradually able to be deep" (p. 111). Another important idea was presented here: "Now the direct observer of infants must be prepared to allow the analyst to formulate ideas about very early infancy which may be psychically true and yet which cannot be demonstrated" (p. 112). To conclude: "In two words a human infant must travel some distance from early in order to have the maturity to be deep" (p. 114). Winnicott was not one of those who, under the pretext of adopting a dynamic version, neglects problems like those of psychiatric classification (1959–1964). His reflections took up well-known basics but gave them a new importance. For example, he introduced the idea of the *false self*, which he invented (1960a). In psychosis, one can find a primitive organization of defenses that form the fundamental basis for it.

We can also admire the talent for observation of the author in "String: A Technique of Communication" (1960b). The reader who seeks a well-argued study of Winnicott's criticisms of the theory of Melanie Klein can benefit from reading the chapter "A Personal View of the Kleinian Contribution" (1962). There he recounted his first meetings with Klein, with whom he soon found himself in disagreement.

Winnicott next took up the problem of communication. He highlighted the necessity of a favorable environment for it to succeed and further developed his ideas on the two states of the object—subjectively created and objectively perceived. He considered the problem of consent given by the patient when he feels found by the analyst and its contrary, the absence of communication.

I will rest here for what concerns the important contributions between 1958 and 1965 and will not speak either about *Therapeutic Consultations in Child Psychiatry* (1971a), a marvelous book in which one can admire the skill of the great clinician Winnicott was, or about *The Piggle* (1978), a passionate account of the treatment of a little girl where one can see Winnicott attempting to place himself in their play at the level of the identification the patient required.

Now I come to the essential contribution, *Playing and Reality* (1971b), which is the final book by Winnicott. It was published after his death. In my eyes, it is the most important psychoanalytic work since Freud's death. For me, its interest surpasses *Envy and Gratitude* and even the most prestigious contributions of Lacan. Almost all of it deserves to be cited, but a few chapters merit passing on to posterity. For lack of space, I will mention only certain of them. The book opens with a new version of "Transitional Objects and Transitional Phenomena," in which Winnicott recalls the principle theses dating from the first version of this famous article (1953). The author considered *Playing and Reality* to be a further development of this article, which formed its first chapter. Let us recall its essential ideas. Winnicott wrote, "There is a wide variation to be found in a sequence of events that starts with the newborn infants fist-in-mouth activities, and leads eventually on to an attachment to a teddy, a doll or soft toy, or a hard toy" (p. 1). Winnicott specified that alongside the objects born from either internal or external reality there exists a third category that we cannot ignore, an intermediate area of experience. We could locate this intermediary category as belonging to *tiercéité* (thirdness) (Green, 1990). Winnicott pleaded for recognition of this area as one of *illusion*, which can become pathological in situations outside the familiar forms of art and religion. Winnicott described its different aspects, the end of a blanket, a soft object, and other items of the same genre. These objects are destined to be caressed and are the support of an autoeroticism. They constitute "*the first 'not-me' possession*" and are in relation to manifestations of the symbolic. Treated with affection, these objects must never be changed or washed, and they resist being invested with erotic or hateful drives. They come neither from inside nor from outside.

The Kleinians have never agreed to recognize the discovery of transitional phenomena, which precede reality testing. These pass from a stage of magic, omnipotent control to one of manipulation. They undergo evaluative transformations (fetishism, anal eroticism). In this respect, Winnicott made his conception more explicit, opposing it to that of Melanie Klein; the transitional object *is not* an internal object. As a consequence of his discovery, he affirmed the category of *illusion*: "The intermediate area to which I am referring is the area that is allowed to the infant between primary creativity and objective perception based on reality-testing" (Winnicott, 1971b, p. 11).

To these basics presented first in 1951, Winnicott added a second part written in 1969 on the baby's limited tolerance of maternal absence, at the end of which her representation is lost. He presented clinical material relative to "*fantasizing*" and also dealt with patients interested only in "*the negative side of relationships*." For them, two figures take on considerable importance, "*the gap*" (the effect of absence as death) and *blankness*. The negative of certain objects (lost) can become more important for them than the positive of those that were supposed to replace them: "The real thing is the thing that is not there" (1971b, p. 23). It is the reality of objects that are symbolized that raises doubt about the effectiveness of their symbolization and questions the reality to which they belong: "All I have got is what I have not got" (p. 24). In my practice, I have been able to confirm the authenticity of these remarks.

I cite Chapters 3 and 4, "Playing: Theoretical Statement" and "Playing: The Search for the Self," without a doubt the most profound contributions on play. The chapter "Creativity and Its Origins" presented a complement to the Freudian theory of bisexuality. Winnicott postulated a *pure feminine element*, source of the creativity and vitality of the child, who receives these gifts from the mother. The well-known patient whom Winnicott hears as a girl, when he knows that he is a boy, is among his most inventive interpretations (1971b, pp. 72–75). It is a remarkable illustration of the way Winnicottian theory was doubled by an appropriate technique (Green, 2010). Finally, we conclude with a concept to which Winnicott gave its full importance, "The Use of an Object and Relating Through Identifications." He dealt here with the attempt to place the analyst "outside the area of subjective phenomena" (p. 87). This goal is attained through multiple efforts aimed at destruction of the object, which survives all attempts to destroy it. It is the very survival of the object that ends by giving it a reality able to resist all attempts at subjective omnipotence. Winnicott wrote, "Without the experience of maximum destructiveness (object not protected) the subject never places the analyst outside and therefore can never do more than experience a kind of self-analysis, using the analyst as a projection of a part of the self" (p. 91).

I will finish with a work essential to my purpose, permitting Winnicott to dialogue explicitly with Lacan. Reading Lacan's article "*Le Stade du Miroir*" (1949) suggested a new idea to Winnicott. Different from Lacan, Winnicott imagined that the *original mirror* was represented by the mother's face. This occurred before the separation of the infant from the mother. Separation is accomplished when the face of the mother becomes an object objectively perceived, sometimes precociously. Winnicott maintained that when babies regard their mother's face at the beginning what they see is themselves (p. 112) and that "what she looks like is related to what she sees there" (p. 113). It is important that babies not perceive the moods of the mother on which they depend too precociously. Their inner sense of who they are ought not to rely excessively on her moods, such as what her mind might be preoccupied with outside the baby. This condition will permit children to acquire the feeling of their own reality by making their internal state coincide with what they perceive of the mother's face.

As I have stated, Winnicott died before he was able to participate in the conclusion of his work, and many unpublished articles remained, too numerous to list. One of them in particular deserves mention, "Fear of Breakdown" (1974), prepared shortly before his death and published posthumously. In it, Winnicott attempted to show that a present fear of mental collapse could cover a past event that had not yet been integrated. Said in another way, the initial experience of a fear of breakdown had not been identified, recognized, felt, assimilated, or recorded. By this fact of having been lived *without being integrated*, the event became the object of an ignorance, as if it had never existed. From this state of nonknowledge, it could return as something feared, an event to come; it belonged to the past, but to an unrecognized past. For Winnicott, this situation concerned the collapse of the institution of a unified self. *It is therefore the fear of a breakdown that has already taken place*, part of a defense against a primitive disorganizing anxiety. The condition for overcoming this anxiety requires that the fear return, so that at a later time it can be integrated and recognized. This work of Winnicott dealt with his original conception of anxiety as anxiety of death, which to his eyes had nothing to do with a death instinct. The outcomes of this early experience were identified by Winnicott as states of void and nonexistence.

Now we arrive at the conclusion of our journey. It remains to speak about his posthumous book, never published during his lifetime, an uncompleted work that I personally find remarkable, *Human Nature* (1988). The synopsis of the book has two parts, the first dating to August 1954 and the second to around 1967. In it, Winnicott retraced his path from pediatrics to psychoanalysis. As he said, his knowledge of very regressed adults permitted him to understand better the psychology or early childhood, "much of which could not be learned by direct observation of infants, nor from analysis even of children of 2½ years" (p. 2). It is of course impossible to summarize the contents of a work that is of largely speculative character and explores such a vast range of psychic life, taking up many of the author's conceptions.

Winnicott sought to establish distinctions between the *psyche-soma* and *the mind*: "The psyche begins as an imaginative elaboration of physical functioning" (1988, p. 19). He did not place the drive at the origin of psychic life. The absolute dependence of mental life on the body preceded this evolution. "Instinct-freedom promotes body health and from this it follows that in normal development with increasing instinct control the body has to be sacrificed at many points, instinct-freedom being normally curtailed in the child socialisation process" (1988, p. 24). Assessing the contribution of Freud, he criticized theories that ignore his discoveries: "Any theory that denies or bypasses these matters is unhelpful" (p. 36). "The clue to healthy early childhood ... is INSTINCT" (p. 39). Erotic drives, just as destructive ones, play their roles. Next a game of illusion in the mental space between baby and mother makes possible the hallucination of the breast as the precedent for gratification. And here, to conclude, a capital idea:

> As we go back to the earlier stages we go towards the complete merging of the individual in the environment, that which is implied in the words primary narcissism. There is an intermediate between this and interpersonal relationships which has great importance of which it could be said that between the mother who is physically holding the baby and the baby there is a layer which we have to acknowledge, which is an aspect of herself and at the same time an aspect of her baby. It is mad to hold this view and yet the view must be maintained. (p. 157)

We will stop with this.

The comparison between the work of Lacan and Winnicott is for me instructive. I was fascinated by Lacan, and I counted a lot on his attempt to renew the theory during an epoch when I had to face the poverty of the current theoretical approach. The "return to Freud" did not take long to reveal what it actually was: an invitation to move toward Lacan, that is, to language. Lacanian thought was born not from experience but from the introduction into psychoanalysis of theoretical conceptions arising elsewhere, in other fields of knowledge (anthropology, linguistics). Although many of Lacan's reflections showed a certain analytic sensibility and contributed to correction of errors committed by his contemporaries, the Lacanian breakthrough around the aphorism "the unconscious is structured like a language" revealed itself over time to be a disputable slogan, contested and rejected, moreover, by all the linguists and non-Lacanian analysts. As I have maintained, the years when Lacan pretended to reject "linguisterie" signaled a defeat. His theoretic expansion toward topology and the borromean knots has been ignored by many in his own movement. Today, I would say that if the reading of Lacan continues to be instructive, his theorizations have aged and serve only to turn analysts away from true psychoanalysis. For having mixed up the classic rules of technique, he ended up with an enormous confusion, put to work by a brilliant mind little interested in the practice of analysis or in basing itself on guide posts as sturdy as Freud.

I thank heaven for having allowed me to know Winnicott. I had the privilege not only of hearing him, approaching him, and being dazzled by his analytic creativity but also of following one of his patients after his death. I am thus able to attest to the absolute sincerity and authenticity of his ideas. Winnicott was an authentic creator. He did not hesitate to oppose the views of Melanie Klein, to propose a theory completely different from hers, not to accept any compromise, and to force himself to criticize his adversaries with modesty. His views on the roles of the environment, original dependence, the construction of first the subjective object and then the object objectively perceived, of illusion, the invention of and the construction of external reality as resistance to destruction, and so on, are of a great richness. They have the value of an acquired knowledge and permit me to use the theory as the fruit of his experience.

A final word: If I were asked today to pronounce on the value of certain psychoanalytic theories, I would no longer be satisfied to oppose the contribution of Lacan based on the experience of the neuroses to those of the contemporary clinic, built on the *borderline states*. I am not unaware that Lacan was quite interested in psychosis and more specifically in paranoia. Nonetheless, I remain persuaded that the main source of his most enlightening reflections was neurosis, following on the paths of Freud. Of psychosis, he was content to rely on Schreber, without making allusion to contemporary clinical experience as have other authors like Bion. In what concerned the borderline states, he was able to say nothing, affirming the inexistence of this clinical category. His pupils followed him after his death.

I would not content myself with affirming that the lively force of Winnicott's elaborations was drawn from his experience with borderlines and his familiarity with nonneurotic states revealing a psychotic organization. Winnicott, there is no doubt about it, was the one who allowed us to understand these conditions at the frontier of psychosis. Beyond these fecund hypotheses, Winnicott for me was the author of a developmental conception going further than Freud or Klein, both credible and sufficiently imaginative to gain general acceptance. To the duo Freud–Winnicott, I would add today the considerable work of W. R. Bion, a major author for understanding the psychoses. This triangulation seems to me a stronger and more complete representation of the psychoanalysis. Even more, Bion appears to me the author who for several years has had the most profound influence on psychoanalytic thought since Freud.

REFERENCES

Abram, J. (2007). *The language of Winnicott: A dictionary of Winnicott's use of words* (2nd ed.). London: Karnac Books.

Birksted-Breen, D., & Flanders, S. (Eds.) (2010). *Reading French psychoanalysis*. London: Routledge.

Davies, M., & Wallbridge, D. (1981). *Boundary and space: An introduction to the work of D. W. Winnicott*. London: Karnak Books.

Freud, S. (1911). Two principles of mental functioning. In J. Strachey (Ed. & Trans.), *The standard edition of the complete psychological works of Sigmund Freud* (Vol. 12). London: Hogarth Press.

Green, A. (1973a). *Le discours vivant*. Paris: PUF.
Green, A. (1973b). *The fabric of affect in the psychoanalytic discourse* (A. Sheridan, Trans.). London: Routledge, 1999.
Green, A. (1990). De la tiercéité. In *La Psychanalyse: Questions pour demain* (pp. 243–277). Paris: PUF.
Green, A. (2000). *André Green at the Squiggle Foundation* (J. Abram, Ed.). London: Karnac Books.
Green, A. (2003). Linguistique de la parole et psychisme non conscient. In *Ferdinand de Saussure* (pp. 272–284). Paris: Cahier de l'Herne dirigé par S. Bouquet Éditions de l'Herne.
Green, A. (2005). *Jouer avec Winnicott* (M. Lussier & C-M. François-Poncet, Trans.). Paris: Presses Universitaires de France.
Green, A. (2010). Sources and vicissitudes of being in D. W. Winnicott's work. *Psychoanalytic Quarterly*, *79*, 11–35.
Gribinski, M. (2000). En guise d'introduction: Sur D. W. W. par D. W. W. In M. Gribinski (Ed.) & J. Kalmanovitch (Trans.), *La crainte de l'effondrement et autres situations cliniques* (pp. 17–29). Paris: Gallimard.
Jakobson, R. (1963). Essais de linguistique générale (N. Ruwet, Trans.). In *Linguistique et poétique* (pp. 209–248). Paris: Seuil.
Khan, M. R. (1975). Introduction. In D. W. Winnicott, *Through paediatrics to psychoanalysis*. London: The Hogarth Press.
Lacan, J. (1938). La famille: Le complexe, facteur concret de la psychologie familiale. Les complexes familiaux en pathelogie. *Encyclopédie Française*, Tome 8. Paris: Larousse.
Lacan, J. (1966a). *Écrits*. Paris: Le Seuil.
Lacan, J. (1966b). Le stade du miroir. Théorie d'un moment structurant et génétique de la constitution de la réalité, conçu en relation avec l'expérience et la doctrine psychanalytique. In *Écrits*. Paris: Seuil.
Lévi-Strauss, C.-L. (1947). *Les Structures élémentaires de la parenté* (2nd ed.). Paris: Presses universitaires de France, 1967.
Lévi-Strauss, C. -L. (1958). L'efficacité symbolique. In *Anthropologie structurale* (pp. 225–226). Paris: Plon.
Lévi-Strauss, C.-L. (1983). *Le Regard Éloigné*. Paris: Plon.
Phillips, A. (1988). *Winnicott*. Cambridge, MA: Harvard University Press.
Rodman, F. R. (Ed.) (1987). *The spontaneous gesture. Selected letters of D. W. Winnicott*. Cambridge, MA: Harvard University Press.
Rodman, F. R. (2003). *Winnicott: Life and work*. London: Karnac Books.
Winnicott, D. W. (1945). Primitive emotional development. *International Journal of Psychoanalysis*, *26*, 137–143.
Winnicott, D.W. (1949). Hate in the counter-transference. In *Collected papers: Through paediatrics to psychoanalysis* (pp. 194–203). London: The Hogarth Press and the Institute of Psychoanalysis, 1975.
Winnicott, D. W. (1953). Transitional obejcts and transitional phenomena. A study of the first not-me-possession. *International Journal of Psychoanalysis, 34*, 89–97. In *Through paediatrics to psychoanalysis* (pp. 229–242). London: The Hogarth Press and the Institute of Psychoanalysis.

Winnicott, D. W. (1954). Metapsychological and clinical aspects of regression within the psycho-analytical set up. In *Through pediatrics to psychoanalysis* (pp. 278–294). London: Hogarth Press, 1975.

Winnicott, D. W. (1956a). Primary maternal preoccupation. In *Through paediatrics to psychoanalysis*. London: The Hogarth Press and the Institute of Psychoanalysis, 1975.

Winnicott, D. W. (1956b). The antisocial tendency. In *Through paediatrics to psychoanalysis* (pp. 306–315). London: The Hogarth Press and the Institute of Psychoanalysis, 1975.

Winnicott, D. W. (1957). On the contribution of direct child observation to psychoanalysis. In *The maturational processes and the facilitating environment*. London: Hogarth Press, 1965.

Winnicott, D. W. (1958). The capacity to be alone. In *The maturational processes and the facilitating environment*. London: Hogarth Press, 1965.

Winnicott, D. W. (1959–1960). Classification in relationship. In *The maturational processes and the facilitating environment*. London: Hogarth Press, 1965.

Winnicott, D. W. (1960a). String: A technique of communication. In *The maturational processes and the facilitating environment*. London, Hogarth Press, 1960.

Winnicott, D. W. (1960b). The false self relationship. In *The maturational processes and the facilitating environment*. London, Hogarth Press, 1965.

Winnicott, D. W. (1961). The theory of the parent-infant relationship. In *The maturational processes and the facilitating environment*. London: Hogarth Press.

Winnicott, D. W. (1962). A personal view of the Kleinian contribution. In *The maturational processes and the facilitating environment*. London, Hogarth Press, 1965.

Winnicott, D. W. (1963). The development of the capacity for concern. In *The maturational processes and the facilitating environment*. London: Hogarth Press, 1965.

Winnicott, D. W. (1965). *The maturational processes and the facilitating environment*. London: Hogarth Press.

Winnicott, D. W. (1971a). *Therapeutic consultations in child psychiatry*. London: Hogarth Press.

Winnicott, D. W. (1971b). *Playing and reality*. London: Tavistock Publications.

Winnicott, D. W. (1974). Fear of breakdown. *International Review of Psychoanalysis, 55*, 103–107.

Winnicott, D. W. (1975). *Collected papers: Through paediatrics to psychoanalysis*. London: The Hogarth Press and the Institute of Psychoanalysis.

Winnicott, D. W. (1978). *The Piggle*. London: Hogarth Press.

Winnicott, D. W. (1988). *Human nature*. London: Free Association Books.

Chapter 3

Winnicott and Lacan

A clinical dialogue

James E. Gorney

The richness of the clinical encounter is so complex that the organizing beam of any one psychoanalytic theorist never seems to provide full explanatory illumination. Insular explanations of clinical process from a single theoretical perspective often constrict vision just as they provide insight; they amplify some of the leading themes, while they simultaneously ignore and obscure many others. It has been my experience that transformational dialogue among different psychoanalytic paradigms stimulates a dialectical, hermeneutic synergy. This synergy may then provide a theoretical and technical perspective that is greater than the sum of its parts. To amplify this proposition, I shall engage a transformational dialogue between aspects of the work of Donald Winnicott and Jacques Lacan. The resulting dialectic will be then used to illuminate clinical material drawn from a psychoanalytic case in which a threatened impasse was avoided.

I begin with the proposition that some of Winnicott's fundamental contributions to theory and technique are congruent with and may even facilitate the overall goals of Lacanian praxis. During their respective lifetimes, Lacan and Winnicott were well aware of each other's writings. Lacan himself arranged for the first translation into French of Winnicott's seminal paper on transitional phenomena. In Winnicott's *Playing and Reality* (1967), he made reference to and respected the importance of Lacan's (1949) "Mirror Stage" paper. In addition to several admiring references to Winnicott's work in the texts of Lacan, an investigation that I undertook of their unpublished correspondence in the Winnicott archives of New York Hospital during the 1980s revealed a long-standing intellectual and personal relationship between these two masters of psychoanalysis. Despite significant differences in regard to theory and practice, the correspondence documents a demonstrable sphere of conversation and mutual influence. In particular, this can be observed in both theorists' writings related to the structure and function of symbolism. Of course, their approaches to symbolic processes were different. While their correspondence also reveals a discernable climate of personal respect, admiration, and affection (Rodman, 1987), there are also fundamental theoretical differences and divergent clinical implications in the work of Lacan and Winnicott, many of which have been outlined in a recent study by Luepnitz (2009).

To begin with the clinical perspective of Lacan (1953), a patient's litany of empty speech can often become the most formidable obstacle to treatment. The rigidified, ossified, and frozen discourse of the Mirror Stage ego tends to trigger in the analyst powerful countertransference reactions ranging from boredom to anger to contempt. The more primitive and deeply disturbed the patient, the more likely that the analytic discourse will become petrified in this manner into a two-way nondiscourse of empty words, fueled by a transference–countertransference impasse—at root, an ego-to-ego struggle on the field of the imaginary (Lacan, 1958). In this regard, key theoretical and technical contributions of Winnicott, particularly his conceptions of transitional phenomena (1953), play (1971), and the holding environment (1960), can be very useful in enabling the analyst to avoid swallowing the imaginary lure that the regressed patient casts out to tempt the analyst into an ego-to-ego struggle. I propose that application of a Winnicottian perspective to this clinical difficulty can enable the analyst to facilitate the emergence of a more vital and productive symbolic discourse. Here, I refer to the Lacanian conception of a process in which the repetitive litany of demand can be cut and, in the gap thus formed, the articulation of signifiers of desire become possible. Along these lines of integration between the two theories, Kirshner (2004) attempted to delineate how the analyst's empathic responsiveness can facilitate movement from the realm of the imaginary to the symbolic. With regard to both Kohut and Winnicott, he asserted:

> The analyst's empathic response does not necessarily or exclusively involve compliance with narcissistic wishes but can be seen as a kind of performative communication offering a point of contact with a structural social order. That is, the analyst's words do not simply gratify the patient but enact a form of social recognition of something that was lacking in his early experience and to which he was entitled... Perhaps we could speak of an empathic *point de capiton*, in which a specific intersubjective interaction links the subject to a symbolic order. (pp. 41–42)

Following Kirshner, the Winnicottian holding environment might thus be understood as the establishment of a form of social order that can serve to open the horizon of the symbolic.

In a 1960 letter to Winnicott (Lacan, 1987), the French analyst stated,

> And yet how I do feel myself supported by and in agreement with your inquiries, in their content and in their style. Does not the "transitional

> object," all of whose merits I have shown to those close to me, indicate the site at which precisely, that distinction of desire in relation to need is marked. (p. 78)

In this assertion, Lacan recognized that Winnicott had detailed the phenomenology of the child's transition from a position of imaginary oneness and wholeness, powerfully structured by (the denial of) need, to the beginning of a relation toward mother and a world structured by symbolism, language, and the dialectic of desire.

As is well known, Winnicott emphasized the role of play in both child development and in the clinical situation. Play is the stage on which transitional phenomena come to appear and through which symbolism becomes possible. The play space itself can thereby function to synergize the play of the signifier (of language), dramatically enriching the dialectic of analytic discourse and facilitating the register of full symbolic speech that, in an early seminar, Lacan (1953) proposed as the goal of psychoanalytic discourse. In the context of the frequent polemical tone of much psychoanalytic writing, particularly in regard to technique, scant attention has been paid to the theoretically integrative function of the analyst. No single theoretical perspective, no matter how comprehensive or powerful, can encompass the full complexity of an individual or a particular patient. Nor can one theory provide a ready answer for all technical decisions, particularly over the expanse of a long and difficult treatment. As Greenberg (2003) observed, "There are too many good analysts (of all theoretical persuasions) doing too much good work and learning too many new things for any of us to close our minds to the contributions of others. The vitality of psychoanalysis will always depend on our openness to mutual influence" (p. 359). Unquestionably, it is a significant challenge to work from a primary theoretical point of view yet to remain open to the insights and heuristic value of other theories without stumbling into a posture of confused and unfocused eclecticism.

In the clinical material that follows, I endeavor to demonstrate how I allow my technical approach to be informed by an integration of two disparate theoretical points of view: those of Winnicott and Lacan. During the course of my training and clinical practice the empathically focused, child-developmentally derived clinical holding environment of Winnicott (1960) and to some extent the similar self–self-object matrix of Kohut (1977) have come to inform my work, particularly with more disturbed patients. At the same time, Lacan's (1953) insistence that the unconscious is structured like a language, as well as his differentiation of the imaginary universe of narcissism from the possibility of symbolic discourse and exchange (1955), has radically informed the ways I listen to patients and how I respond to them. Rather than opposing these theories, I have increasingly attempted to integrate them. In my clinical work, I have continued to grapple with both points of view and have written from a Lacanian (Gorney, 1978,

1982, 1988a, 1988b; Gorney & Muller, 1988) as well as Winnicottian and Kohutian perspectives (Gorney, 1979, 1994, 1998).

Particularly with more troubled patients, I begin the treatment by employing a flexible and responsive Winnicottian frame that holds the patient in care, long before the place of the unconscious can begin to be articulated in speech. Through establishing a setting of safety and security, I endeavor to permit the voice of the Other eventually to emerge, as it inevitably will, and to be heard and responded to. It is my experience that the articulation of desire, the place of the Other, linguistic links to the unconscious, and the possibility of symbolic discourse, as conceived by Lacan, require a climate of security and safety in order to become useful parts of the treatment. It is here that the empathic awareness of Winnicott can allow us to create a reliable transitional therapeutic environment, one within which the profound theoretical and clinical insights of Lacan can be most precisely observed and technically employed.

In the clinical material that follows, I hope to illustrate how Winnicottian conceptions of transitional phenomena, play, and holding, which informed my technique, eventually facilitated the emergence of Lacanian signifiers, the beginnings of symbolic exchange, and the patient's articulation of his long hidden desire.

CLINICAL MATERIAL

"I am extremely pleased with the results of this analysis," stated Mr. D., at the end of his fourth year of treatment. "If you have no objections, I would like to set a termination date exactly 6 weeks from today. I have decided to accept that business proposition in California, and I shall need to be moved within 2 months."

While I had no "objection" exactly, I did have many misgivings. The patient had entered treatment at the age of 25, beset by low self-esteem, feelings of social and intellectual inadequacy, chronic obesity, and an inability to form intimate relationships. Mr. D. had been born in Israel but had spent his childhood and adolescence in another country, having been adopted at the age of 6 weeks. His father, a wealthy and powerful Jewish industrialist, had used his money to arrange for the Israeli adoption, after it had become clear that his wife was unable to conceive. The patient grew up in great material luxury as the only son to one of the wealthiest families in a small developing country. While he claimed that he had lived like "a prince," with every material whim indulged, his inner life was unremittingly lonely and tormented. His adoptive mother was described as depressed, unavailable, and extremely passive, whereas his adoptive father was described as controlling, grandiose, sadistic, and sociopathic.

Mr. D. left the country in which he was raised to attend a well-known American university and, doing the bare minimum to get by, emerged unaffected by the experience. He then spent 3 unfocused years working for business associates of his father here in this country. His proudest achievements on entering analysis after this period were his ownership of a red Porsche, his $5,000 computer system, and his penthouse condo—all bankrolled by his father. Mr. D. entered analysis to "find my own way," as he said, and to escape the financial and emotional control of his father. Although the patient himself did not complain of being isolated, what was particularly notable was his extreme emotional impoverishment; he had no close friends, he felt bored and empty most of the time, and his sexual life consisted of occasional passive encounters in his car with prostitutes. In regard to this aspect of his life, he did not foresee that analysis would be of any particular benefit, nor did he particularly wish it to be. He was resigned to being a loner and living in what he called a "black hole."

The "black hole" emerged within the consulting room and therapeutic relationship during the first 2 years of analysis. Mr. D. alternated between making very concrete requests for advice, solutions to his problems, or medication and lengthy periods of heavy, uncomfortable, unrelated silence with rigid, frozen withdrawal. His few words were entirely in the form of complaints; he seemed completely cut off from his desire. One day, on lying down on the couch, Mr. D. rested the back of his hand on his forehead (a common gesture for him) and said, "I have a request to make. You notice that I keep putting my hand on my forehead when I lie down. That's because I have poor eyes and am very sensitive to glare. The light from the floor lamp behind my head has been bothering me ever since I first started using the couch. Would you mind if I got up and turned it off?" I immediately got up out of my chair, turned the light off, and said, "I hope that this now will be more comfortable for you." For the next 6 months I turned off the lamp just prior to Mr. D's session every time that I saw him. The "black hole" continued unabated. Then one day shortly after he lay down on the couch, Mr. D. began (for the first time) to weep. The weeping turned into sobs and he said, "I can't believe it. Every time I come here I say to myself, 'Will he have remembered it again today? Will he have turned it off?' My heart is pounding when I ring the bell. I am pacing in the waiting room. And then when I come in, I see that you have remembered. I can't tell you how much it means that you remember."

This consistent enactment of Winnicottian holding enabled Mr. D. to begin to emerge from his "black hole," and he began to use his treatment as a basis on which to make some concrete changes in his life. Yet, I had misgivings 4 years later when he announced his plan for termination so that he might pursue a business opportunity in California that promised to be extremely lucrative. Even though the patient had finished an MBA, had severed some of his financial connections with his father, had lost a considerable amount of weight, and was well onto the fast track in his career, his inner experience and his personal relationships, including with me, continued to be enormously restricted, so I was concerned about a premature termination.

On one level, the analysis seemed to have had major impact; Mr. D. was now highly motivated and goal directed. He was confident and competent in his dealings with the world and no longer felt apathetic and impotent in his work life. On another level, however, it seemed as if little had been accomplished. The patient continued to be unable to remember any dreams and persistently claimed not to have a fantasy life, and his personal relationships remained superficial and fragmentary. Indeed, he had kept a remarkable distance from me during the analysis, seeming to use me as a benign, stable alternative to his father and attempting to employ me as a sounding board and role model to facilitate the development of his career. Throughout, he stubbornly resisted all efforts on my part to explore transference (which he persistently denied) or to interpret his rigidly hidden emotional life (which he claimed was nonexistent).

For this reason, I expressed my misgivings to the patient regarding his proposed termination plan but told him that I would not make an "objection," leaving that sort of response to the domain of his father. Persistent interpretations of his continuing rejection of all forms of emotionally salient living, inability to engage in genuine dialogue with me, and his refusal to examine his inner emotional life continued to fall on deaf ears. He reiterated his satisfaction with the manifest results of the analysis, and, at his request, a termination date 6 weeks hence was set between us. The next 2 weeks, however, saw a marked change in the patient's affect and in the content of the sessions. Instead of being detached, he was gripped. Instead of discussing the details of his business plans, he told me for the first time of the late-night cybersex in which he had been compulsively engaged for over a year. Adopting the alias "King Stud," he repetitively enacted the fantasy of having his erect organ admired, touched, and sucked.

After a week of excitedly describing these activities, Mr. D. arrived late for a session. This was most unusual; he was never late, always arriving compulsively ahead of time. He apologized and informed me that he had been walking to the session, early as usual, but on impulse decided to visit a palm reader and "spiritual advisor" on seeing her sign on the street. The reading had taken longer than expected. Mr. D. reported with excitement that this Gypsy woman had told him he would achieve "great financial success" and that he was no doubt descended "from royalty." Even though he had never before believed in any aspect of spiritualism, he felt that there was great truth in what the reader had told him. Despite repeated inquiry on my part, the patient denied any relationship between either the cybersex or the visit to the spiritual advisor and our impending termination date.

Two days after he had come late for his appointment, Mr. D. missed his first session in the entire treatment without giving prior notice. He arrived for our meeting the next day appearing unusually calm and cheerful. He did not apologize for having missed the session. Rather, he stated that he had had a "wonderful experience" the previous day and recounted the following tale. A few hours prior to the session, he had felt "horny" and begun leafing through the *Yellow Pages* under "Massage." A particular ad caught his eye for a massage parlor with "a good address." Utterly forgetting his analytic hour, he went to this establishment and found it to be very posh, decorated like "a palace." Mr. D. had never been to a massage parlor before and was delighted that he got to choose the woman he wanted from among several presented to him. She took him to a private room, gave him a bubble bath in a Jacuzzi, towel dried him, massaged him with baby oil, and performed oral sex. He left feeling "on top of the world," "totally relaxed," and "in a state of bliss" and was not even upset when he realized that he had forgotten his session with me.

Since such feelings and behaviors were most out of character for Mr. D., I asked him what it was about this particular advertisement in the *Yellow Pages* that had so captivated him. He said that he really did not know, other than the "good address," since it was one of numerous such ads on the page. I then handed him a copy of the *Yellow Pages* and asked him to show me the exact ad. As we sat together side by side on the couch, I read, "Monarch Studio. Where you are treated like a King! Where you will come again and again ... For attended bubble baths and showers." In the upper left-hand corner of the ad was a bejeweled crown. The address was only two blocks from my office.

Knowing Mr. D's extreme resistance to interpretation, I decided to suggest cautiously the following possibility: "You have not yet expressed directly any feelings about our upcoming termination. Yet, the cybersex, the palm reader, and the visit to the massage parlor must all be a means of expressing through action the real meaning to you of leaving me." Mr. D. then began to tell me the following story. Throughout much of his lonely childhood and adolescence, his one source of comfort and attachment was the family dog, named Rex. The two of them were inseparable companions. When he left his family's home at age 18 to come to America for college, his one regret was leaving Rex behind. Shortly after Mr. D.'s departure, Rex became inconsolable, moody, and highly aggressive. After a few weeks, the patient's father gave an order to a servant to shoot the dog. When Mr. D. reached this point in the narrative, he began to cry. I then said to him, "When Louis XIV would leave Paris and travel to Versailles he did not have to leave anyone behind. His wife, his children, his staff, his ministers, and his entire court traveled with him, because he was, after all, the king. Our ending now threatens you with abandonment. Perhaps you fear that what became of Rex will also befall you. But if you were born of royalty and were a king, like in the cybersex or with the palm reader or in the massage parlor, you could exercise your *birth right* [I said this with emphasis] and never have to leave anyone important behind." Mr. D. then began to speak of his childhood preoccupation with his specialness as a Jew, particularly growing up in a country where few Jews lived. He had imagined himself connected by blood to the ancient Kings of Judea, tied to them through his own birth in Israel. He then recalled the story told to him of how he had been brought hidden in a basket by his real mother and sold to his adoptive parents in a secret meeting held in their suite in the King David Hotel.

I said, "Your mother sold you for money, as if the money was worth more than you. At 6 weeks you lost your birthright, and now, since you have set the 6-week ending with me, the pain and terror of abandonment returns again. Since you are not really a king, nor am I really in your court, you cannot take me with you. But you do have the power of keeping me with you as long as you need me, if you decide to stay here." Mr. D. then modified his plans and agreed to remain in treatment for "a while longer." This term extended into 2 more years of highly productive analysis, during which he managed to sever all remaining financial ties to his father. He became less grandiose and isolated, began to date a few appropriate women, and engaged with me in a more open and spontaneous manner during sessions. Upon termination, 2 years later, Mr. D. was manifestly more relaxed, had developed a keen sense of humor, and had become engaged to a woman, who seemed to complement his other new life choices. Although in certain ways his life had become more manifestly conventional, he still retained an ongoing yearning to be special and a taste for thrills and excitement. He had fully emerged from the "black hole" and was now ready to engage with the uncertainties of vital living.

DISCUSSION

In the conception of Lacan (1955), the ego is understood as the locus of *mèconnaissance* (misunderstanding), constituting the fundamental alienation of the subject from the unconscious and the dialectic of desire. The Lacanian ego is precipitated through the child's misidentification of himself with reflected images, deriving from both specular and interpersonal experience (Lacan, 1949). Over time this ego becomes ossified and rigidified in accord with these externally derived reflections, resulting in an alienated subject, caught up in an imaginary world of images and increasingly cut off from the realm of desire, the unconscious, and the symbolic. In the case of Mr. D., access needed to be gained to the previously unnamed domain of the symbolic for this individual to begin to lay claim to his long-buried desire.

From the perspective of Davoine and Gaudillière (2004), in their contemporary Lacanian research on trauma, the symptom is a marker pointing toward a *place*—a nexus of catastrophe, destruction, and trauma occurring in the past but relived inescapably in the present. The symptom both masks and begins to communicate the mute pain and terror of this as yet unsymbolized location. The unsymbolized trauma comes to haunt the subject while at the same time forbidding free access to its individual, familial, or social history. It is only when this place of trauma can be named and inserted into the symbolic order of language that the trauma can be remembered, not relived repetitively as if it were branded or carved into the subject's very being. When the catastrophe inhabiting the place of the real (the unsymbolized) can be brought into a "social link" through the dialectic of symbolic speech in a human relationship, the trauma can be remembered, spoken, eventually integrated, and, even, for long periods, usefully repressed or forgotten. This field of symbolic language is entered through the inscription of a name or word that functions as a signifier. How to facilitate the emergence of such a signifier, in speech or, perhaps at first, in gesture, within the psychoanalytic situation is at the center of Davoine and Gaudillière's clinical concerns. This was the clinical challenge most at stake in the treatment of Mr. D.

For Mr. D., access to the unsymbolized traumatic place was gained through the emergence and delineation of a critical signifier, "King," and its associated signifying chains. According to Lacan, the signifier can function as a "nodal point" in the subject's discourse, binding together numerous strands of unconscious material, much as an upholstery button (*point de capiton*) gathers together yards of fabric. When the signifying chain can be unraveled via resonant listening and intervention by the analyst and inserted into a social link (Davoine & Gaudillière, 2004), then the voice of the Other may be heard. As signifying chains expand through metonymy and metaphor, the patient's discourse becomes more evocative and resonant. For Mr. D., a critical signifier first announced itself in the name "King Stud" during cybersex. It was then elaborated metonymically through the Gypsy woman's assertion that he was descended from "royalty" and next in the selection of "Monarch Studio—where you are treated like a king." Finally, it was elaborated in memories of the dog "Rex."

We continued to inscribe, in the social link of the analytic space, Mr. D.'s early traumatic journey, which now became an increasingly complex and resonant narrative. My eventual interpretation of his long-standing wish to be a king to exercise his "birthright" exposed the metaphorical function of a whole range of regal signifiers. This then enabled Mr. D. to address at last the trauma of his adoption and loss of connection with a fantasized maternal paradise. Like Moses, he had been cast adrift in a basket, alone in the world, looking for the Promised Land. However, just as for Moses, the completion of his quest eluded him. As the trauma surrounding his birth and subsequent development was further elaborated through interpretation, Mr. D. was finally able to relinquish his current version of a lifelong unconscious fantasy—namely, that the Promised Land was now to be found in the material riches of California[1]. No longer experiencing himself as nobility on an endless journey, Mr. D. was ultimately able to settle down within the consulting room, where he could have his genuine needs for (symbolic) caretaking fulfilled by his relationship with me and remain within the "holding environment" (Winnicott, 1960) of the treatment until its authentic completion and his healthy departure into independent life.

Early in treatment, Mr. D.'s ossified ego and unspoken, dissociated, and traumatized state threatened to engender a psychotherapeutic impasse. It was at this juncture that my consistent adoption of a nonverbal, Winnicottian "holding environment" helped establish the basis for the eventual emergence of transformational linguistic signifiers. The patient's early failure to thrive within the therapeutic setting immediately indicated to me that the deepest level of trauma was infantile and preverbal in origin. Consequently, I attempted to maintain a broadly empathic, nondemanding ambiance in which it became possible to respond to some of Mr. D.'s traumatically conflicted needs through symbolic gesture and disciplined enactment (Gorney, 1998). Indeed, it was my repeatedly remembering to turn off the offending lamp that enabled Mr. D. to begin to speak of his traumatic past.

The establishment of a climate of understanding and safety created the possibilities of establishing "transitional space" and "potential space" (Winnicott, 1953) within the consulting room. Through receiving a reliable maternal provision (holding) that engenders confidence, the child (or in this case the patient) can begin to play in the transitional area where reality and fantasy are kept usefully blurred. Within this area, the possibility of potential space emerges. This is critical in treatment because it is within the zone of play as it opens up that the creative expression of the signifier may first be heard. For the child, potential space is at root transitional; it is an intermediate zone of experience that bridges the gap opened up by the growing separation–individuation of the child from the mother. It is a space separating a state of fantasy and fusion from one of actuality and separateness, and it is in this gap that the child's play can begin—his first efforts at "creative living." These efforts do not take place wholly inside a fantasy of fusion with the mother, nor are they wholly separate from her. Rather, creative play occurs within an undefined potential space where symbols can emerge and where the child can increasingly define and individuate him or herself. As Winnicott (1967) writes, "In favorable circumstances the potential space becomes filled with the products of the baby's own creative imagination" (p. 102). This unfolding process triggers the infant's capacity for increasing efforts at symbolic representation. Moreover, immersion in potential space involves a certain type of affective experience, one of vitality, aliveness, and

[1] This fantasy may represent the *objet a* of Lacan (1973)—a fantasy of restoration of that which has been lost. I have not elaborated this perspective here in this chapter, but it is, no doubt, relevant to the vicissitudes of Mr. D's desire.

play (Bram & Gabbard, 2001; Gorney, 1998). Reliable environmental provision facilitates the entry into potential space, which, according to Winnicott, then provides the basis for all subsequent cultural experience and creativity.

Within the treatment, it was only after Mr. D. became able to employ the analytic relationship as a transitional space that he could generate and play with the important signifiers deriving from his experiences with cybersex, the Gypsy fortuneteller, and the massage parlor. This form of play within potential space immediately brought vitality and aliveness into the analytic relationship. More importantly, it opened up a place for the symbolic where full elaboration of the emerging signifying chain could occur.

For Winnicott, early play is the stage on which transitional phenomena first appear. The analyst endeavors to put play into the relational system of the treatment so that the patient can be, even momentarily, dislodged from his frozen, imaginary objectifications. It is at this moment that the signifier may assert its voice and come eventually to be heard. In the analysis of Mr. D. a major signifier was identified by the analyst to open up a transitional field of play within the formerly rigidified analytic setting. The transitional space itself functioned to synergize the play of the signifier, thereby dramatically enriching the dialectic of the analytic discourse. At first glance, Mr. D.'s efforts at play (e.g., in the cybersex or massage worlds) might have seemed symptomatic, perverse, or, most likely, forms of acting out and resistance. Instead, by being heard as initial efforts at play, the possibility of creativity was evoked within the potential space of the treatment. It was here finally that a Lacanian perspective could be used to enable the linkages in the signifying chain to reveal themselves. Consequently, from the perspective of technique, the patient's developing a capacity for play is not identical with the play of signifiers inherent in symbolic communication. Rather, creation of the play space is a necessary precondition for these signifying processes to become manifest in a clinically accessible sequence.

To return to the original proposition of this chapter, differing theoretical and clinical psychoanalytic perspectives need not oppose or negate each other. Rather, multiple points of view can be employed synergistically to enhance and facilitate each other. In particular, I have attempted to demonstrate how creation of a Winnicottian holding environment and a subsequent openness to an emergent transitional play space on the part of the analyst may facilitate access to the symbolic. As a point of linkage between Winnicott and Lacan, it can be asserted that the play of signifiers and the signifying chain itself occurs within transitional–potential space. As Kirshner (2004) observed, it may be useful to regard Winnicott's contributions as "a bridge" to Lacan. Transitional phenomena, the importance of which was early on recognized by Lacan, are themselves efforts at bridging. The transitional bridge between fantasy and reality, between the imaginary and symbolic, can be seen as the place where the self can come into being. It is on this bridge that Winnicott and Lacan meet and facilitate each other.

REFERENCES

Bram, A. D., & Gabbard, G. O. (2001). Potential space and reflective functioning. *International Journal of Psychoanalysis, 82*, 685–699.

Davoine, F., & Gaudillière, J. B. (2004). *History beyond trauma* (S. Fairfield, Trans.). New York: Other Press.

Gorney, J. E. (1978). Resonance and subjectivity: The clinical application of Lacan. *Contemporary Psychoanalysis, 14*, 246–273.

Gorney, J. E. (1979). The negative therapeutic interaction. *Contemporary Psychoanalysis, 15*, 289–237.

Gorney, J. E. (1982). The clinical application of Lacan in the psychoanalytic situation. *Psychoanalytic Review, 69*, 241–248.

Gorney, J. E. (1988a). Reflections on impasse. In P. C. Hogan (Ed.), *Criticism and Lacan: Essays and dialogues on language structure and the unconscious* (pp. 147–151). Springfield: University of Illinois Press.

Gorney, J. E. (1988b). Intervention in transference. *Ornicar? Revue du Champ Freudien, 46*, 53–80.

Gorney, J. E. (1994). On limit and limit setting. *Psychoanalytic Review, 81*, 259–278.

Gorney, J. E. (1998). Twinship, vitality, pleasure. In A. Goldberg (Ed.), *The world of self psychology: Progress in self-psychology* (Vol. 14, pp. 85–106). Hillsdale, NJ: The Analytic Press.

Gorney, J. E., & Muller, J. P. (1988). The master-slave relation in psychoanalytic impasse. In J. D. Montgomery & A. C. Greif (Eds.), *Masochism: The treatment of self-inflicted suffering* (pp. 142–165). New York: International Universities Press.

Greenberg, J. (2003). Forward. *Contemporary Psychoanalysis, 39*, 353–359.

Kirshner, L. A. (2004). *Having a life: Self pathology after Lacan.* Hillsdale, NJ: The Analytic Press.

Kohut, H. (1977). *The restoration of the self.* New York: International Universities Press.

Lacan, J. (1949). The mirror stage as formative of the I as revealed in psychoanalytic experience. In *Ecrits: A. Selection* (A Sheridan, Trans.) (pp. 226–280). New York: Norton, 1977.

Lacan, J. (1953). The function and field of speech in psychoanalysis. In *Écrits: A Selection* (A Sheridan, Trans.) (pp. 30–113). New York: Norton, 1977.

Lacan, J. (1955). The Freudian thing, or the meaning of the return to Freud in psychoanalysis. In *Écrits: A Selection* (A. Sheridan, Trans.) (pp. 114–145). New York: Norton, 1977.

Lacan, J. (1958). The direction of the treatment and the principles of its power. In *Écrits: A Selection* (A. Sheridan, Trans.) (pp. 226–280). New York: Norton, 1977.

Lacan, J. (1960). Letter to Winnicott. In *Television* (J. Mehlman, Trans.) (p. 78). Cambridge, MA: MIT Press, 1960.

Lacan, J. (1973). *Seminar XI: The four fundamental concepts of psychoanalysis* (J.-A. Miller, Ed., A. Sheridan, Trans.). New York: W. W. Norton & Company, 1978.

Luepnitz, D. L. (2009). Thinking in the space between Winnicott and Lacan. *International Journal of Psychoanalysis*, *90*, 1–25.

Rodman, F. R. (1987). *The spontaneous gesture: Selected letters of D. W. Winnicott*. Cambridge, MA: Harvard University Press.

Winnicott, D. W. (1953). Transitional objects and transitional phenomena. In *Through paediatrics to psycho-analysis* (pp. 229–242). New York: Basic Books, 1958.

Winnicott, D. W. (1960). The theory of the parent-infant relationship. In *The maturational process and the facilitating environment* (pp. 37–55). New York: International Universities Press, 1965.

Winnicott, D. W. (1967). The location of cultural experience. In *Playing and reality* (pp. 95–103). New York: Basic Books, 1971.

Chapter 4

Vicissitudes of the real

Working between Winnicott and Lacan

Mardy Ireland

> A baby is an instinctual being living all the time on the brink of unthinkable anxiety.
>
> Winnicott (1962, p. 57)

> The umbilicus of a treatment is the question of desire and how it is trapped in its birth or its movement.
>
> Lacan (1954, p. 167)

These two quotes and the relationship between them frame the topic and question of this chapter: Can we envision a model of contemporary analysis in which practitioners work in a middle channel between the contrasting approaches of Jacques Lacan and Donald Winnicott? To date, the work of Green (2005), Kirshner (2004), Ireland (2003), and Luepnitz (2002) represents variants of psychoanalytic practice that derive from the work of both men. Luepnitz (2002, 2005, 2009) described what she sees as this increasing phenomenon in terms of the metaphor of a new middle school in psychoanalysis.

To further elaborate this middle pathway, this chapter focuses on the polyvalence of the word "real" and what it means for psychoanalytic work. To do so I will take the register of the real as defined by Lacan (1953b, 1978) and juxtapose it with Winnicott's (1956, 1959) notion of how one becomes and feels real—letting the introductory quotations provide the contextual background. Two case vignettes will then be offered as a means to flesh out this theoretical juxtaposition. Finally, it will be suggested that the dialectical tension between the developmental thrust of Winnicott and the structural approach of Lacan can be partially resolved through the creative coupling of their different uses of the term real.

WINNICOTT'S BECOMING AND FEELING REAL

To feel alive and real was foremost in Winnicott's (1956, 1958) mind as the aim of an analysis, because for him it constituted the essence of being human. Feeling real, he said, is in the experience of being "saturated with the color of one's own internal objects" (1958, p. 34) That is to say, in the theater of one's own mind there ought to be a full company of "good" to "not so good" players that provide the necessary grounding and texture to one's sense of self and of others. For Winnicott (1956), the infant subject's developmental ability to establish a feeling of being real depends on the provision of care by a good enough primal object/mOther (I use the spelling/neologism *mOther* to incorporate the roles of the object, language, and the Other in the symbolic language mother). This provision consists of a quality of presence by the primal object (described as primary maternal preoccupation) that he believes enables adequate holding and handling of the infant such that something fundamental in the infant's need and emergent self is seen. This in turn sets the next stage for object presenting. Throughout the period of provision it should be said we are not talking about perfect attunement but conditions of optimal failure. It is in noting this necessary presence of optimal failure or lack that Lacan's work potentiates and complements Winnicott's notion of "provision."

Provision can be reframed via Lacan as an adequate weaving of the Real, Imaginary, and Symbolic registers by the primary object who gathers together the diverse manifestations of the incipient infant subject, thereby setting the conditions for his/her emergent subjectivity. First, maternal provision must be Real in terms of providing adequate sensory dimensions of care and handling of an infant. Second, provision also includes the Imaginary in terms of the ways mOther draws on her own fantasies to hold her infant in reverie and to attune herself to the infant's emotional needs and emergent desires. Finally, the good enough mOther's role must always include the Symbolic insofar as mOther (as well as father) must reserve a separate place in her mind for the infant as a subject in the process of becoming who will take up his or her own unique place in society—a place that may, or may not, reflect a parent's wish. If this symbolic aspect of maternal provision is missing, the infant will remain psychically stuck in imaginary identification, whereby the child remains identified with what he or she imagines the mOther wants or needs the child to be. As André Green (1999b) concluded, Winnicott gives the analyst the best working coordinates for establishing "the minimal conditions for symbolization" (p. 311).

In other words, all three Lacanian registers of experience must exist within good enough maternal provision for infants to be brought fully into the symbolic realm so that they can mine the gap being carved in them by the symbol. By this I mean that if the real, symbolic, and imaginary registers of experience as described by Lacan are not adequately woven or knotted together within the subject of the mother herself, the provision she provides will never be "good enough." Likewise, only with good enough provision (which takes place within the real of bodily experiences) can the mOther's symbolic interpretation (e.g., as she speaks with the infant) meet the infant's very real needs. Then, the gap between what the symbol can represent and what it leaves outside "in the real" can come to function as a potential space for creativity or desire to be filled by the infant in his or her own way. Basic to Lacan is the crucial point that the desires that humanize and create meaning spring from the fundamental lack in the subject. Without adequate maternal provision, however, this gap remains as a catastrophic hole in a developing body-ego or psychic envelope that cannot contain a symbolic identity. Basic psychic survival then becomes primary. For many of these individuals or subjects, desire can be discovered only later within the provision of an analytic (or perhaps other) reparative relationship.

What is real for Lacan can be defined as what resists the grasp of the symbol and cannot be circumscribed by language. The Real suggests the realm of the impossible or impossible to conceive, of which death is a paradigmatic example. Lacan's (1958) somewhat cryptic statement of what it means to be human—"Life has only one meaning, that in which desire is borne by death" (p. 277)—suggests that to be truly human is to welcome the gain of desire and to accept the loss inherent in being a symbolic subject. It is because of such subjection that we are the only creatures with consciousness of our impending death. Each person is given calibrated degrees of freedom to pursue their desire and shape a singular life and death through the gift of language. The Winnicottian caveat to Lacan is that to creatively sustain desire in the face of impending death requires individuals first to establish a psychic place in which they feel real. Lacking this, there is only potential psychic catastrophe in every experienced gap in the self—something against which the subject must strenuously defend. This crucial issue returns us to Lacan's introductory quote—"The umbilicus of a treatment is the question of desire and how it is trapped in its birth or its movement" (1954, p. 167).

Metaphorically speaking, the symbolic net functions as a container in which much of the Real of unmediated experience will be wrapped, leaving the remaining elements of the Real to exist as it were in the holes of the net. From a Lacanian perspective, these parts of the (biological) Real are experienced as the ongoing background pulse of the drives. Lacan named this remainder the *objet a*, which he considered the cause of human desire (see Chapter 6). Contact with the Real can also be approached through momentary lapses of consciousness—whether from intense pleasure, pain, or moments of traumatic rupture of self or relationship. Perhaps this concept of the Real can help us understand Winnicott's (1962) baby as an "instinctual being living all the time on the brink of unthinkable anxiety" (p. 57). Winnicott describes the emergence of the infantile subject from a process of maternal mirroring in which the infant's body-ego or psychic envelope is first coconstructed (similar to Lacan's imaginary). In a complementary manner, Lacan emphasizes how the incipient infantile subject must be successfully gathered together by the mother as Other, the representative of the symbolic order who brings the infant into the symbolic net through her interpretations of infantile need and her ideas of the place the child will take in the family and society. While these symbolic interpretations by parents establish a foundational alienation in human infants between the Real and the newly emerging symbolic subject, the paradox is that when children become actual speaking subjects within the symbolic order, they will then depend on these linguistic signifiers to articulate and hold their personal identity.

When the symbolic netting of the mother–infant relationship is not adequate, various psychopathologies suggesting Winnicottian failures of formation of a self can occur. Under these psychic conditions, individuals may develop the experience of a lurking, ever-present disaster into which they might fall or perhaps a feeling of an endless, yet each time unexpected, series of catastrophes that somehow has to be survived. Life then is about survival and not about living with a desire that has been constituted within the gaps of the symbolic net and free to generate movement. As Winnicott (1956) says, "Failures at this level [of development] are not felt as maternal [or parental] failures but as an annihilation of the infant self" (p. 304). He says further:

> Good enough environmental provision in the earliest phase enables the infant to begin to exist, to have experience, to build a personal ego, to ride instincts, and to meet the difficulties inherent to life. All this feels Real to the infant who comes to have a self that can eventually even afford to sacrifice spontaneity, even to die. On the other hand, without the initial good-enough environmental provision, this self that can afford to die never develops. The feeling of real is absent and if there is not too much chaos the ultimate feeling is of futility. (p. 304)

In other words, analysis cannot approach the question of the infantile kernels of the Real as the cause of desire in such individuals without providing a "lived experience" (Winnicott, 1960) within the analytic relationship in which this landscape of "too much Real" can be transformed by the process of symbolization.

At this intersection of Winnicott and Lacan lies the clinical truth that in cases of inadequate maternal provision psychoanalysis must involve the work of reinscribing patients into a symbolic framework at the foundational level where language first becomes embodied. This is a quilting point, as it were, between the theories of Winnicott and Lacan. The analytic work of inscription will hence be within the area of the unrepressed unconscious or Freud's (1915, p. 148) area of "primary repression." At this level, Lacan introduced the hypothesis that language is composed of discrete letters that exist in the real as the raw material foundation of language and speech (Lacan, 1953b, 1955, 1956, 1972). He invents the word *lalangue* (1972, p. 126) to designate a language that includes the Real of the letters themselves and the imaginary world of fantasy that attaches to them. *Lalangue* is different from, but underpins, the paternal language of linguistic meanings of culture. The letters of the body as Lacan speaks of them inhabit us as libidinal and traumatic sources expressed in emotional tones of voice, rhythm, and musicality of speech, which strike and stir us. The letters that are libidinal bodily traces become imaginatively elaborated in later infantile fantasies of desire. Lacan is mistakenly rendered as conflating language with the symbolic when he has in fact underlined the importance of both the Real and Imaginary aspects of language as well.

From a Lacanian perspective, Bion's (1962a) notion that human beings invariably seek their "emotional truth" may refer to the bedrock of how each psyche and mind have been etched from the body in the Real by the primary object bringing the Otherness of language to it. "Good enough" provision at this stage of infantile development is crucial and makes symbolic paternal language and speech ultimately matter. And only when language can truly matter is it possible in Lacan's terms for speech to become an act of creation (1953, 1954). I have argued that for some individuals a reinscription must happen in an analysis because there has been some form of psychic catastrophe in the initial infantile encounter (Ireland, 2003). Sometimes an analyst can bring language anew to the Real of residual trauma in its original etching in such a manner that the patient can gain a feeling of being real where previously has been mainly deadness or terror. At her best, an analyst can sometimes do this if she is able to hear the patient's call for what has been missed and can then respond.

CLINICAL VIGNETTES

The case vignettes that follow draw attention to the necessity of an adequate capturing of the Real by both the Symbolic and Imaginary registers in the process of becoming human. I believe, as well, these vignettes express the polyvalence of the word real as I have been describing it in a middle stream between Winnicott and Lacan. Each case in a different way illustrates how a patient's subjective experience of not feeling real is intimately related to an early life history in which the Real has been insufficiently woven by the Symbolic and Imaginary registers.

Lacan (1955, 1964) said it, but others have described it similarly as well—psychoanalysis is the treatment of the real by the symbolic. Simultaneously however, Lacan (1964) also stressed that something real in the analyst is always needed to enable the analysand's process of becoming more capable of following the movement of his desire. Winnicott and those of the Middle School of British psychoanalysis would add to Lacan that the person of the analyst matters—meaning the "realness" in the coloration and configuration of the analyst's own inner object world. Thus, the significance of the subjectivity of the analyst, something real in both Winnicott's and Lacan's senses of the word, comes into play in every analysis but may be more salient with deeply disturbed patients or when working with infantile mental states.

Case vignette 1

A patient whose history was an agonizing illustration of severe infantile trauma came to me several years after her former analyst had traumatically ended a prior analysis. Two earlier treatments had also ended badly. As she said, "I know I do something, but I don't know what it is that makes this happen." Ms. X.'s father had murdered her mother in her presence when she was a few months old, and the two of them (patient and her mother) were not found for a couple of days. Later she experienced severe childhood physical and sexual abuse in a foster home.

In the second year, a pivotal moment occurred—a moment to which we returned various times during analysis. She told a dream in which her abusive foster brother came to my office with her. I would not let him in entirely, but their hands were fused so she had to sit on one side of my door and he on the other. My hand was on the door holding it nearly closed. (As one might expect, I came to appreciate the word *hand* as an important signifier.) I then gave her a letter opener with a "serrated edge" and said she had to cut herself free, because I could not do it for her. The letter opener seemed an evocative and enigmatic object. Then I said in the dream in an ironic tone, "And now would be a good time to dissociate." The topic of dissociation had come up quite often in our sessions. She said we both laughed in the dream when I said that, and indeed we laughed together in the moment when she reported this part of the dream. This shared laugh, I believe, discharged intense anxiety related to the violent situation as well unconscious recognition of how absolutely necessary dissociation had been to her survival. She then used the letter opener in the dream to cut her hand away, leaving a small flap of skin taped to the door so that her brother could feel it on the other side of the door. (We might ask what this flap is about.) So one source of much of her childhood trauma was now at the analytic door for the first time. While on one hand she was now safely inside my office, she also realized its opposite—she was trapped. And she remained scared because she realized he would still be there when she left her appointment.

After a particularly long silence in this same session in which I could feel her inner conflict in the form of there being a thick storm cloud in the room between us, she said she felt she should tell me something but felt afraid to because of what it might mean to the future of the analysis given her past treatment experiences. She had been unable to get online the day before, and after many attempts she called the Internet service provider for assistance. In the course of the consult, she discovered that she had been repeatedly typing the wrong password. She said to me, "I had been typing your name, Ireland, instead of another name I use as a password that starts with the same letter. It's the name of the man who killed my father—I mean who killed my mother. I don't know why I said that. I don't even know why I use that password. It makes no sense really."

Actually, it made sense on at least two levels when we were able to return to her dream. In this story the letter that was meant to be opened in her dream could be opened—or as Lacan (1955) would say, the letter always arrives at its destination. Her father had psychically killed himself as well as her mother that day, and from that moment he was no longer available as a symbolic father to give her a viable last name and place within his family or society. He gave her only a letter to call her own, yet this served as an animating kernel of her being. Neither did she have an adoptive father to offer his name, only a foster father who failed to protect her from a physically and sexually abusive foster mother and brother. She had recognized in her repetitive entry of my name as a password her nascent hope in the analysis—which may be why she had not wanted to tell me of the incident. Could she actually use me as a password to the wider "web" of the world of others? Having had this hope in analysis raised before with disastrous results, she was left terribly afraid. We might speculate that were her analyst to become truly important, someone would have to be killed. Perhaps for this reason the imaginary transference was thick and terrifying for me as well.

From a different vertex, I addressed the intensity of her hope and dread of a repetition by saying that, while it was true she had been using my name, at another level, the first and most important letter of my name also began her father's name and thus belonged legitimately to her as well. I went on to say that the importance of the letter "I," with which began my name, was in fact *given to me* by her and not stolen from me as she may have felt it to be. (She had concern about "stealing" things from me. I kept in mind Winnicott's thought that the child who steals is at least letting you know he still carries hope for the object world having something of value.) Every time she made that mark, she was reminded that she had her own place to take up in the world. While she needed a helping hand to reach it, the place was hers. On another level, "I" was also a word that told us that there was a person inside her who longed to be able to use the word "I" and to speak freely of her own desires. She wanted to speak without the terror of a violent reprisal—a violence she had lived with growing up and, at moments, was afraid would spring from me as well.

My understanding is that this incident was not all about the imaginary analyst in her mind (her fantasies of who I was) or even the analyst as a new real external object to be used in Winnicott's best sense. Instead, it was very much about the constituent elements of a symbolic net, its letters (which exist in the Real), and words (signifiers existing in the Symbolic) that I, as her analyst in the symbolic transference (as Other), stood for and was holding for her to make use of in her own way and in her own time to become and feel more real. In other words, in holding Lacan's three registers in mind in regard to the letters and words of the dream, I am being mindful of several things. There is a need for the imaginary transference to have its play in the field of idealization as well as destruction. I am aware that my presence as a real, benign, and new object will be necessary for her to be able to psychically modify a violent imaginary inner object world. I am aware that the letters of my name, in so far as they are also hers, locate real animating kernels of her own desire in me that she must take up in due time. In speaking to her having a legitimate place in the symbolic order, I am occupying the position of the Other who affirms the rights to desire, responsibilities, and limitations of any symbolic identity, including my own. In being mindful enough of all these things, there can be hope that her analysis will enable her to become a more real and alive subject of her own desire.

Case vignette 2

This second clinical example further illustrates Lacan's notion of a material, corporeal basis to language. Serge LeClaire (1998) fleshes out this idea by speaking about an inscription of letters on the infantile body during moments of mother–infant care. As the mother speaks while handling the infant, a corporeal experience of the difference between pleasure and unpleasure becomes registered. This is part and parcel of the process of the mother–infant couple coconstructing a body-ego (in the Imaginary) from a purely biological body (in the Real). In this process one letter could be said to mark the infant's body for *jouissance*, making a gap between the infant's biological and psychic body, whereas a different letter will be associated with the object that later comes to fill that gap. Because these letters exist in the Real, carried by such things as the tone, cadence, music, and cacophony of a speaking voice, rather than residing purely in the symbolic register of words and signifiers, they will always evoke visceral impact. Such visceral effects are unique to each person, although, because language is shared culturally, there may be transpersonal inscriptions as well. Under the circumstances of "good enough" provision, these infantile inscriptions can become a person's unique formula of *jouissance* around which fantasy will wrap itself to give desire its changing forms (Lacan, 1963–1964). Symbolization does not entirely capture (nor will it ever capture) the whole of a human being's experience. One definition of *jouissance* is what is uncaptured by language and therefore lives as leftover energy remaining in the body.

What Lacan emphasizes and LeClaire (1998) elaborated in his metaphor is that there is always a double inscription of language in the human being. One inscription of language concerns the conscious level of linguistic meanings that can be repressed or not. But elsewhere, there is always another inscription that consists of a series of letters in the Real insisting within and underpinning a person's discourse. LeClaire even suggested that if it were possible to string together and speak or sing these letters in a particular emotional tone, the result would be to plunge individuals into a state of ecstasy or trauma since this is their own unique equation of *jouissance*.

Ms. G. first came to the outpatient clinic where I worked when she was in her early 20s after being mugged. The work was relatively ego supportive and lasted only a few months. Over the years, I saw her only intermittently. In 2003, I noted two dreams from these visits that seemed to indicate directions for further work. In Dream 1, she and I were in a game of finding a baby, but when we found the baby someone who is dead was holding it. She also told me at this time that she had periodic dreams in which a baby was dead. Dream 2 was "something about words."

It was not until Ms. G. (now in her 40s) returned again in 2004 that a different kind of work became possible after I was able to make a pivotal interpretation about her not wanting to repeat her mother's life. At this time she committed to an increased frequency of sessions leading to a schedule of five times a week.

The degree of dissociation or blankness Ms. G. harbors inside her is not as easily explained as in the first case vignette. The patient has experienced series of somatic symptoms—vertigo, headaches, stomachaches, and panic attacks—whose intensity has threatened to end the treatment at times. Intense anger has also come close to cutting off the analysis when there has been felt emotional contact between us, and her silences, which can feel deadly or full of terror, evoke fear in me that the treatment will come to a dead end suddenly and without warning. The sudden breaking off of relationships with others is where *jouissance* in a symptom seems the most evident. There is a flash of pleasure in establishing a separate omnipotent existence before she inevitably disappears into blankness and deadness. Precariousness of this sort dominated the first year's work and continued to occur in moments in the treatment for several years.

For Ms. G., speech has been a hollow conveyer belt of communication, not one of a living creative material from which a life can be sculpted. Despite a large frozen inner landscape of the Real, at the end of the second year of analysis I could see tendril beginnings of possible transformation of this landscape in certain drawings she did. She began drawing in the second year of analysis, and it is noteworthy that she had never done any artwork before as an adult, although she had bought art supplies that remained unused. I believe that the fact that I was a psychologist–art therapist who later trained as an analyst with Winnicottian and Lacanian sensibilities, and later returned to analysis, was critical to the patient being able to settle into her working analysis. This I believe speaks to something real in me that was unconsciously apprehended by the patient but that took time to ripen.

One drawing of interlocking puzzle pieces was especially evocative (Figure 4.1). From one vertex, this drawing had a psychotic quality in its rigidity of form. Yet, from another perspective, it could be seen as a first attempt to bring form to something that had always been unspeakable. "Thinking through everything all the time" (represented by the upper left section of flesh-colored puzzle pieces) was juxtaposed, she said, to the newer "feeling parts" of her whose silent voices began to show up in her dreams—feelings she is ambivalently trying to listen to (represented by the section on the right side of the drawing of multicolored puzzle pieces). The feeling pieces are trying to move toward a thinking side, she said. But in the middle between the two sides is the "emptiness" or blankness (represented by all the black puzzle pieces) that is either being changed by the two sides coming to meet or alternatively will swallow all the pieces up. She was unsure what would happen. In the midst of the black emptiness were two white puzzle pieces that only confused her by their being there. I wondered if they could be representing she and I and how we were in the soup of it all. A second puzzle drawing appeared a year later (Figure 4.2). This drawing showed more movement of colored pieces within the black background, and the drawing was much less rigid in its quality. She was anxious about

Figure 4.1 Puzzle No. 1.

Figure 4.2 Puzzle in Transit.

not knowing what the puzzle pieces were making but also was excited. This transit of one drawing to the other over a course of a year lent support to the hypothesis that the first drawing was evidence of her crossing a threshold regarding moving from the Real into representation of her experience.

The lively dreams of this patient have served to guide her in life and to compensate for the quality of deadness that often characterizes her waking life. For example, rather quickly her dreams translated our interactions in the analytic hour into the language of her work so that we could share a vocabulary and begin to construct a new set of signifiers and point of reference. Dead caretakers and babies in her past dreams evolved in the second year to occasional dreams of children or adolescents whom she knew to be parts of herself following her around but could not speak. The earlier dream fragment of something about words evolved into a dream of her lying on a table with someone tending to her body with words. This suggests to me that we are indeed living an experience in the analysis (as Winnicott might say) where language and speech are being re-founded (as Lacan might say). The following session occurred several months after the first puzzle drawing toward the end of the second year of treatment. It is the fourth session of the week coming after several days of severe physical and emotional panic that seemed to calm down only after talking in detail about possible unfelt feelings and unknown thoughts about an upcoming meeting with someone. This meeting was probably more like a "date," one she "looked forward to" yet also wanted "to run away from screaming."

PATIENT: I am not feeling panicked again today.

ANALYST: How do you feel?

P: Pretty good really. I had another dream that was sort of schoolish. [She had what she called a "schoolish" dream the day before about the importance of learning something.] In the dream you and I were talking about words—I mean all kinds of things about words. You were talking about the difference between words, about the difference between thinking words and speaking them, about the sounds of letters and parts of words, about the spaces between the words, and how you can take smaller words out of the bigger words. [She might have even said more things but this is what I could get down.]

A: And the feeling tone of the dream?

P: I was very interested in all of it. There was just a lot to think about all that.

A: In part at least your dream seems to be filling out what we were talking about yesterday when you said that the panic subsiding seemed to have to do with how we were talking about your anxiety about your upcoming meeting with John but that it was hard to explain how talking worked to help. The way I would put it was something like we drew a circle somehow around the anxiety and that helped.

P: But why do I even get the panic? That is the other side of the question for me.

A: Well it is the other side, something like when you or me or anyone has very big feelings that cannot be expressed somehow in words or fantasies. It fills our whole body and mind up in a panic. Given what you have inside you from your family experience you simply have no language really for many feelings you have, and then there is the emptiness.

P: Yeah, that's another thing about the dream. You were talking about the feelings that are around words—that is, how you can hear, see, and feel a word. I do think that part of the panic was about your being away on the weekend even though it didn't change anything about our meeting on Friday. [The day after Thanksgiving, when I was going to be away]

A: Well, we have some time before then and we can see what we can do talking about it before then. [I am not sure how long the ensuing silence was or what was happening on either side of the couch, as if I fell into a gap of dissociation for some time and then emerged.] How did the dream end?

P: I was writing things down to think about them. There was an O and I together. And then I wrote the word "let."

A: Any associations to these letters or the word? Hmm, Oi. [Like the Jewish expression of distress] Or let's see, what are these letters and words trying to tell us about you?

P: Like the O and I were a little separate but I wrote them together. And yet may have been part of a bigger word but I don't know what.

A: So this is a loose association perhaps but I am thinking that when you lose the link with me—when I am gone away on the weekend—it can be like you feel flushed down the t*oi*let.

P: [Laughs a laugh of recognition here] I am thinking that there may have been a T and an R I wrote too. And I am thinking of O and I as meaning on and off in electronics or, you know, it could be a binary language of zeroes and ones like in computers. Maybe also the t, r—letter and the e-mails I have been writing

A: An I and a one. Both. If you think about it as you as being on and off what comes to mind?

P: I was just running through it. It is a programming language, and John is a programmer. [As is she, but in a different field] It is all things that are in black and white—there are no shades of gray.

A: Well, then, perhaps you can make gray by letting [playing here with the word of the dream] relationships be both on and off and not like all those rules you have operated by before. You are either all the way in a relationship and then lose yourself and have to cut it off or you are all the way out and then feel lost and alienated.

P: I am going back to the dream now in my head and thinking of the feelings around the letters and paying attention to what the O feels like .... It seems like such a bizarre dream, but I must somehow know its importance if I can dream it .... One of the other things you were telling me in the dream was about the feeling impact of the words that I say on someone else, especially regarding the on and off difference. I can get that it [how words are used] needs better balance not just for me, for but others too.

A: Yes.

P: You know, I can sort of get the idea of it.

A: And, the idea isn't enough; you have to live it a bit—especially here.

P: Well, how do you get the gray if you only have something like scalding water and ice cold water—it is so hard to work with.

A: Yes, but if you take a small amount it isn't so catastrophic—a little on and a little off—perhaps say about time—and maybe timing.

P: But these are such extreme categories [the scalding and ice cold or submerged in relationship vs. no relationship], and I would want them to change from such extremes.

A: True, they are extreme categories, and you would want them to change, and I think where this is most evidently beginning to happen is here in this relationship.

P: Ah, you mean like you go away but you always come back.
A: Yes. And it's time to stop.

Session discussion

There is a descending movement in this session from the level of linguistic meaning drawn from her dream to particular letters residing in the Real that appear in the dream (Lacan, 1953b, 1955). Freud (1900, 1919) was the first to note in his discussion of the dream of the burning casket that the Real is inside as well as outside of us. A shift in register occurs after both the patient and myself fall into a gap of dissociation immediately following her mention of an upcoming break. Then there is a lived experience of moving from dissociation to a reunion with the first appearance in the treatment of a bit of transitional play; I attempt to speak in this session to how language is inscribed on more than one level. That is to say, I address part of what I can hear in the letters themselves and in the signifiers and words that could emerge from them. For example, at a Symbolic level, the O could represent the circle of talking that helped her panic subside; however, the O also exists at the level of the Real—as a toilet of psychic annihilation she seems to experience whenever our link becomes an unbearable gap during some, but not all, separations. There is also the imaginary play between us as she begins to fantasize about the O as off and I as on and the imagined categories of cold and hot water and how these experiences resound in her.

Not spoken about in this session but thought about are other associations to the letters that may be of use in the future. For example, is the I near the O referring to how often she lives perilously close to psychic obliteration? Also, given that the letter O is the first letter of her last name, is this a transference comment of her how she is now placing herself (as the O) closer to me (*I* being the first letter of my last name) in the work? Is the I also a word signifying the position in a sentence in which she could inhabit more fully the desire (or the O) she approaches by becoming more able to say, "I want"? Only time and more speaking would tell.

This chapter initially posed the question of whether a model of psychoanalysis can be envisioned that puts the differing approaches of Winnicott and Lacan into useful dialectical play. This question has been answered affirmatively by offering two examples of thinking and working in this middle channel. Specifically, the polyvalence of the word "real" in each theory places these two analysts in a complementary and supplementary relationship to one other that enables psychoanalytic work. In each case vignette I presented the Real aspects of language (i.e., Lacan's *lalangue* or letters of the body) and the relative capacity for a sense of feeling real (Winnicott's elaborated inner object world) in the context of the role the primary object (or analyst) has in bringing symbols to inscribe infant (or an analysand's) experience. Last, in each clinical example I noted that both Real (Lacan) and real (Winnicott) aspects of the analyst—in other words, the signifier of her or his name as well as the individual real letters of our names, the real traumatic and animating kernels resident at the heart of our being, the particularity of our own inner object world—are also always working elements in the analysis, even when we may be unaware of their facilitating, inhibiting, or negative effects. It could be said then that it is in the vicissitudes of the real between Winnicott and Lacan that every analysis finds and takes its place.

REFERENCES

Bion, W. R. (1962a). A theory of thinking. In *Second thoughts* (pp. 110–119). New York: Jason Aronson, 1967.

Bion, W. R. (1962b). *Learning from experience*. New York: Basic Books.

Bion, W. R. (1963). *Elements of psychoanalysis*. London: Karnac Books, 1984.

Bion, W. R. (1967). *Second thoughts*. London: Karnac Books.

Bion, W. R. (1970). *Attention and interpretation*. London: Tavistock Publications.

Bion, W. R. (1992). *Cogitations*. London: Karnac Books.

Freud, S. (1900). *The interpretation of dreams*. In J. Strachey (Ed. & Trans.), *The standard edition of the complete psychological works of Sigmund Freud* (Vols. 4 & 5). London: Hogarth Press, 1949.

Freud, S. (1915). Repression. In *Standard edition of the complete psychological works of Sigmund Freud* (Vol. 14, pp. 146–158). London: Hogarth Press, 1949.

Freud, S. (1918). From the history of an infantile neurosis. In J. Strachey (Ed. & Trans.), *The standard edition of the complete psychological works of Sigmund Freud* (Vol. 17). London: Hogarth Press, 1949.

Freud, S. (1919). The uncanny. In J. Strachey (Ed. & Trans.), *The standard edition of the complete psychological works of Sigmund Freud* (Vol. 17, pp. 219–256). London: Hogarth Press, 1949.

Green, A. (1999a). *The fabric of affect in psychoanalytic discourse*. London: Routledge.

Green, A. (1999b). On discriminating and not discriminating between affect and representation. *International Journal of Psychoanalysis*, *80*, 277–316.

Green, A. (2005). *Key ideas for contemporary psychoanalysis*. London: Routledge.

Ireland, M. (2004). *The art of the subject: Between necessary illusion and speakable desire in the analytic encounter*. New York: Other Press.

Kirshner, L. (2003). *Having a life: Self pathology after Lacan*. Hillside, NJ: The Analytic Press.

Lacan, J. (1953a). The agency of the letter in the unconscious or reason since Freud. In *Ecrits: A selection* (B. Fink, Trans.) (pp. 146–178). New York: W. W. Norton & Company, 1977.

Lacan, J. (1953b). The function and field of speech and language in psychoanalysis. In *Ecrits: A selection* (B. Fink, Trans.) (pp. 30–113). New York: W. W. Norton & Company, 1977.

Lacan, J. (1955). Seminar on the purloined letter. In J. Muller & W. Richardson (Eds.), *The purloined Poe: Lacan, Derrida, and psychoanalytic reading* (pp. 28–54). Baltimore, MD: John Hopkins University Press, 1988.

Lacan, J. (1958). The direction of the treatment and the principles of its power. In *Ecrits: A selection* (B. Fink, Trans.) (pp. 226–280). New York: W. W. Norton & Company, 1977.

Lacan, J. (1960). The subversion of the subject and the dialectic of desire in the Freudian unconscious. In *Ecrits: A selection* (B. Fink, Trans.). (pp. 292–325). New York: W. W. Norton & Company, 1977.

Lacan, J. (1963–1964). *Seminar XI: The four fundamental concepts of psychoanalysis* (J-A. Miller, Ed., A. Sheridan, Trans.). New York: W. W. Norton & Company, 1978.

Lacan, J. (1953–1954). *The seminar of Jacques Lacan, Book II: The ego in Freud's theory and in the technique of psychoanalysis* (J.-A. Miller, Ed., S. Tomaselli, Trans.). Cambridge: Cambridge University Press, 1988.

Lacan, J. (1959–1960). *Seminar VII: The ethics of psychoanalysis* (D. Porter, Trans.). New York: W. W. Norton & Company, 1992.

Lacan, J. (1955–1956). *The seminar of Jacques Lacan III: The psychoses* (J. Miller, Ed., R. Grigg, Trans.). New York: W. W. Norton & Company, Inc, 1993.

Lacan, J. (1972). *On feminine sexuality, the limits of love and knowledge: The seminar of Jacques Lacan, Book XX: Encore* (J.-A. Miller, Ed., B. Fink, Trans.). New York: W. W. Norton & Company, 1999.

LeClaire, S. (1998). *Psychoanalyzing: On the order of the unconscious and the practice of the letter*. Stanford, CA: Stanford University Press.

Luepnitz, D. (2002). *Schopenhauer's porcupines: Intimacy and its dilemmas*. New York: Basic Books.

Luepnitz, D. (2005). Toward a new middle group. Paper presentation at the American Psychoanalytic Association Spring Meeting, Washington, DC.

Luepnitz, D. (2009). Thinking in the space between Winnicott and Lacan. *International Journal of Psychoanalysis, 90*, 957–981.

Winnicott, D. W. (1956). Primary maternal preoccupation. In *Through pediatrics to psychoanalysis* (pp. 300–305). New York: Basic Books.

Winnicott, D. W. (1958). The capacity to be alone. In *The maturational processes and the facilitating environment* (pp. 29–36). New York: International Universities Press.

Winnicott, D. W. (1959). Classification: Is there a psychoanalytic contribution to psychiatric classification? In *The maturational processes and the facilitating environment* (pp. 124–139). New York: International Universities Press.

Winnicott, D. W. (1960). The theory of the parent-infant relationship. In *The maturational processes and the facilitating environment* (pp. 37–55). New York: International Universities Press.

Winnicott, D. W. (1962). Ego integration in child development. In *The maturational processes and the facilitating environment* (pp. 56–63). New York: International Universities Press, 1965.

Winnicott, D. W. (1963). Communicating and not communicating leading to a study of certain opposites. In *The maturational processes and the facilitating environment* (pp. 179–192). New York: International Universities Press.

Winnicott, D. W. (1969). The use of an object and relating through identifications. In *Playing and reality* (pp. 86–94). London: Tavistock, 1971.

Chapter 5

Applying the work of Winnicott and Lacan

The problem of psychosis

Lewis A. Kirshner

The theme of this volume is the possibility of a psychoanalytic therapy that can move between two seemingly incompatible theories of personal mental life: D. W. Winnicott's model of a self, born in the context of a pediatrician's notion of good enough mothering, and Jacques Lacan's conception of the subject, with roots in phenomenology and linguistics. In this chapter, I focus on their contributions to understanding and treating psychosis, reviewing some of the important concepts they introduced and applying them to clinical material with a paranoid patient. I approach their respective positions as in some ways complementary, in others more dialectically opposed, pointing to ramifications beyond the two authors to wider trends within contemporary psychotherapeutic practice. Juxtaposing Winnicott and Lacan in this way can help us see the problems of our current methods and concepts more clearly and contribute to enlivening and enriching our work with more troubled patients.

While we know that classical psychoanalytic technique is not usually helpful with psychotic patients, much useful therapeutic work can still be done. At present, however, we do not have a very good model for how to conduct this treatment. Partially because of failed or overambitious attempts to treat schizophrenia, for example, with psychoanalysis, current clinical practice in North America has become limited with rare exceptions almost exclusively to pharmacotherapy. Reconceptualizing the therapeutic task as supporting the subjective coherence and identity of patients may offer a productive direction. While the terms *self* and *subject* have different etymologies and been used in contradictory ways, as Luepnitz discusses in Chapter 1, I take the position that for Winnicott and Lacan, at least, they can be seen as complementary attempts to get at the same ineffable object: subject and self not being "things" that can be defined or specified but ways of speaking about persons. Rather than an entity with a fixed character or definition, they refer to a continuous process of creating and sustaining a subjective position—a successive series of figurations of meaning that define the self.

In working with neurotic patients, questions of the stability of the self and of subjective coherence usually remain implicit as a stable background for the treatment process (although they can emerge with insistence around important moments in the analysis), but they are crucial in addressing more disturbed patients. A painful instability of self, lack of subjective continuity, problems of identity, and even the very notion of being a separate subject are problems frequently present in borderline and psychotic conditions. These patients can be regarded as manifesting a psychopathology of separation and loss of the primary object that accompany the birth of the self. The term *subjectivation*, introduced by Lacan (1945), addressed this process. Although clearly referring to the process of becoming a separate subject, subjectivation is nonetheless a difficult concept to define and harder still to conceive how it might be accomplished in treatment.

Although we cannot determine a precise moment of origin, we can approach the process of subjectivation developmentally, from its earliest beginnings in infancy. Especially for the psychotic patient, the tenuous, preliminary steps toward the birth of the subject may never have been superseded by more durable structures or external supports, so that a constant upheaval at the source, as it were, comes to dominate the clinical picture. The organization of self for these patients is brittle and unstable, and their subjective experiences are exceptionally fluid and unpredictable. For this reason, the clinician lacks a consistent partner or interlocutor in the therapeutic work. Although some tentative forms of therapeutic alliance are possible in certain instances—for example, appealing to the rational abilities of the paranoid patient—the shared pursuit of insight (already problematic in the neurotic) is not a realistic objective for treatment, making it almost futile to seek an ally in the borderline or psychotic ego. For this reason, developing a clinical setting that fosters the continuity of the self or the creative growth of a separate subject represents an alternative technical approach.

Winnicott, with his notion of regression to the point of earliest environmental failure, took the possibility of a reconstruction or rebirth of self quite literally. Or perhaps he simply avoided differentiating the notion of self as metaphor for an ongoing and indeterminate process like subjectivation from the fiction of a substantive entity inside the person. Winnicott's ambiguity about the nature of self had the advantage of incorporating the familiar experiential duality of an enduring inner sense of selfhood alongside a constantly shifting subjective identity. That is, we feel ourselves to remain the same person, while experiencing ourselves differently at different moments, in varied affective and intersubjective contexts and in changing states of need and desire. Though certainly aware of this problem, Lacan considered that the notion of self endorsed an erroneous belief in a unified or whole subject, which he opposed by a portrayal of subjectivity in constant interplay with other subjects and engaged in an impossible effort to resolve an intrinsic split. I do not believe that Winnicott endorsed a naive conception of a whole self, although he may have slipped in this direction in his clinical objectives.

From the many places in which Winnicott spoke about the birth of the self I will focus on two principal texts: "Transitional Objects and Transitional Phenomena" (1953), and "Mirror-Role of Mother and Family in Child Development" (1967), both included in the volume *Playing and Reality* (1971). Lacan wrote about analogous phenomena in his first major paper on the Mirror Stage (1949), the basic elements of which were included in his presentation "Some Reflections on the Ego" presented on May 2, 1951, in London at the British Psycho-Analytical Society, subsequently published in 1953. Whether Winnicott was present is not known, but he did mention Lacan's concept of the mirror in his own paper on the subject. For his part, Lacan was also quite interested in Winnicott's concept of the transitional object, commenting on it several times in his Paris seminars and arranging for the translation and publication of the paper in the journal he directed, *La Psychanalyse*. I regard the thinking behind both authors' papers as tied closely to the important problematic of the origins of the subject.

TRANSITIONAL OBJECTS AND TRANSITIONAL PHENOMENA

Winnicott began his paper by drawing attention to the baby's use of what he called "the first not-me possession," which starts with the newborn infant's fist-in-mouth activities and leads eventually on to an attachment to a teddy, a doll, soft toy, or to a hard toy—the familiar "transitional object." These objects and phenomena belong, he wrote, to the realm of illusion in that they are given meaning well beyond their actual existence as playthings. The realm of illusion creates an area of play and provides the basis for the child's initiation of creative experience of the world. Winnicott made it clear that we are dealing here with a yet unexplored developmental step beyond simple oral satisfaction, beyond the drives and objects of the classic Freudian oral stage. He then suggested areas for further study of the transitional object, of which I will stress two as particularly relevant to psychosis: the nature of the object; and the infant's capacity to recognize the object as "not-me."

I take the phrase "the nature of the object" to mean what kind of notion or representation of the other person is involved in the infant's way of relating to her. Much confusion is involved if we do not have firmly embedded in our thinking that the so-called object is an evolving representation of another person in the mind that amalgamates subjective wishes, beliefs, and expectations with more or less accurate perceptions of actual words and behavior of the other. The object is therefore partly imaginary, partly symbolic, and partly real (and thereby also related to play; Feinsilver, 1989). In this sense every object is transitional—partly found in the world, partly an invention of the subject. The nature of the object varies within and between individuals from an almost totally idiosyncratic or bizarre representation of the other to a fairly accurate or consensually recognizable version. In the former case, we are dealing with what Winnicott called a subjective object—that is, one perceived as identical with what the infant or patient imagines it to be. This conception is quite similar (perhaps a developmental precursor) to Fonagy's term "psychic equivalence" (Bateman & Fonagy, 2004), which he used to describe a primitive form of thinking in which subjective thoughts are taken as an accurate view of reality. Fonagy showed how this mode of cognition is prevalent in borderline patients, especially under conditions of danger, and made it a cornerstone of his mentalization model of treatment. Of course, the extreme of the subjective object is the delusion, in which the basis for the interpretation of external reality (referring to social and interpersonal reality, not to the real as such) can be quite bizarre or illogical, in contrast to the usual plausibility of perception in Fonagy's patients.

Later, Winnicott (1953) went further to say that a person who attempts to make us validate his subjective objects as real is psychotic:

> Should an adult make claims on us for our acceptance of the objectivity of his subjective phenomena, we discern, or diagnose, madness. If, however, the adult can manage to enjoy the personal intermediate area without making claims, then we can acknowledge our own corresponding intermediate areas, and are pleased to find examples of overlapping, that is to say, common experience between members of a group in art or religion, or philosophy. (p. 241)

Here, Winnicott proposed that in addition to the familiar notion of an inner psychic and an outer objective reality to describe a person a third component was needed: that of "an intermediate area of experiencing, to which inner reality and external life both contribute" (p. 230). This transitional area of experience will not be not challenged by others provided that no claims are made on its behalf that require their assent or participation. He characterized it as a realm of illusion and "a resting-place for the individual," who struggles with the perpetual problem of discriminating what is subjective from what is objective, what is imagined from the reality of an intersubjective situation. It is an intermediate state between what he called the baby's initial inability and ultimate ability to accept reality and "objective perception."

Later, Winnicott used the metaphor of transitional space to describe the intermediate area of experiencing. Within this space, transitional phenomena can occur, and the familiar transitional object like the baby blanket or teddy bear can be invented. Winnicott insisted that while the transitional object appears to the observer to come from external reality, this is not the case for the baby; neither does it come from within the child (it is not a hallucination). From here, he stated, transitional phenomena become diffused normally over the area of culture to overlap with the sharable illusions of others. Lacan's (1956) snappy response to this conception, in his seminar on object relations, was that the British give everyone the right to be mad. He then acknowledged that this state of affairs seems, in fact, to reflect a general truth.

As illustrated by his ironic comment, Lacan was much more questioning than Winnicott or the British theorists in general about the nature of the object. He was not a naive realist about objective reality. At the same time, it is not clear that he shared with Sigmund Freud and Winnicott the questionable notion that the object is first created or hallucinated by the infant's wishes. Unlike them, he did not believe in the concept of primary narcissism or a merger of infant and mother, out of which the subject must, as it were, give birth to itself by separating private from objective reality, subject from object. He was, however, concerned with differentiating imaginary object relations from symbolic ones. Crucial to this distinction was the entry of the infant into language, which provides the infant's identity as a named being in a human world governed by symbolic operations that define his or her place. Lacan's symbolic order maps the cultural world of social reality. The imaginary object, on the other hand, exists as a mental construction or fantasy, not unlike Winnicott's subjective object, in close relation to the subject's wishes. It was the notion of a continuum from subjective to objective, governed by reality testing as an ego function, that Lacan attempted to revise. For him, imaginary and symbolic coexisted as discrete domains of experience, both woven together with the unknowable real. What seems to the subject as objective reality always partakes of an admixture of fantasy.

One of Lacan's criticisms of ego psychology was its pretension that analysts could be a reasonably objective judge of reality and were thereby entitled to impose their supposedly more realistic egos on the ego of the patient. This is a complicated issue that has obvious relevance to treatment of psychotic patients. In contemporary practice, many analysts want their patients to acknowledge them realistically as the person they really are, as though interpreting the transference and defenses could strip away the illusory distortions and reveal the true person inside. For Lacan, this notion of an essential identity would be the real illusion. On the other hand, clinical experience has led Lacanians (e.g., Fink, 2007) to stress the danger of symbolic interpretations to psychotic patients in favor of a concrete, "reality-oriented" approach. Uncovering associations for their links to other signifiers, for example, can open quickly onto an unmediated void, as these patients lack a basic symbolic inscription as subjects.

In reading Winnicott's seminal paper on the transitional object, one becomes aware of a slippage between his notion of the first not-me object as an anthropomorphic thing—a blanket given certain human qualities—and the construction of the human object itself. He took up this aspect of development in papers dealing with Margaret Klein's model of the depressive position that emphasized the role of primitive aggression. As Phillips (1988) outlined, Winnicott modified Klein's schema by proposing a developmental path culminating at what he called the stage of concern (Winnicott, 1963). In his paper on object usage (1969), he argued that the infant's "ruthless" attitude toward the mother, with its experience of destructive aggressivity, could lead toward a full awareness of her survival (if met by her nonretaliatory acceptance). She is then placed outside the infant's "omnipotent control," existing separately. Various types of failure of this process were also described. Acknowledging the other's existence as not-me (if such a progression actually occurs) is only the first step in a developmental process fostering awareness of the thoughts and feelings of the other. Apart from mentalization capacities, the ability to form reciprocal relationships with objects depends on cultural knowledge and consensual validation (to avoid the appearance of madness). We also note that actively psychotic patients can believe (and fear) in the reality of their destructiveness of others and the world despite repeated observations of their survival.

THE MIRROR FUNCTION IN WINNICOTT AND LACAN

Winnicott's formulation of the Mirror-Role of mother and family (1967) did not owe much to Lacan's paper on the Mirror Stage, although he must have been familiar with it. The focus of his exploration was different from Lacan's, centering on the mother's facial expression while she is being scrutinized by the infant. The quality of the maternal face as a mirror for the infant is what mattered to him, whereas for Lacan the visual gestalt of the image in the actual mirror carried the major significance. Nonetheless, the conclusions of the two men are not entirely dissimilar. Both saw the mirroring process as foundational for establishment of a self, albeit with different implications.

Lacan was early to see the active gaze of the infant as having the quality of a basic drive. Infants, who quickly perceive that their satisfaction and pleasure depend on the presence of the mother, have in-born means of attempting to reach her. The cry and the gaze are probes into the world seeking a response from the mother and, by receiving it, quickly establish a circuit that ties desire to the presence of the mother. This would seem to have influenced Lacan to emphasize, as Winnicott did, the internalization or psychic inscription of the circuit from infant to mother and back to infant as the basis for self-awareness. Yet in the mirror stage, he chose to limit his argument to infants' fascinated and excited discovery of their own image. For Lacan, infants discovered themselves in a false form (the image) that served to found the ego through the realization, "this is me." Up until this virtual moment, the neurologically undeveloped child has only a presumably disorganized and fragmentary sense of its own being. In the mirror, it see a complete shape. Of course, for Lacanians the mother herself can serve as the identificatory mirror object. We need not dwell on this issue; the important point is infants' self-discovery in a visual image.

For Winnicott, anticipating the vivid evidence of the importance of active maternal mirroring subsequently filmed on videotape by infant researchers, children learned about their existence through reading their effect on the mother's facial expressions. Being seen, infants could come to feel that they also (like the idealized mother) truly exist. Moreover, the memory traces of this experience install a representation of the object—of a good, loving object—that becomes a resource for children at times of maternal absence. In this precise sense, the mirror role of the mother is the source of a subjective experience of self gradually acquired by infants. Failing this response, however, as Winnicott outlined, children are thrown back into a kind of mechanical perception of the other; a deadness sets in that may deprive them of a sense of being real. The origins of psychosis, for Winnicott, lay in this original deficiency, which is for all intents a preverbal one, whereas the mechanism of foreclosure, the crucial pathogenic operation for Lacan, occurs at a subsequent phase. Winnicott's incipient self is anchored in an already intersubjective process that bodes well for the infant's future connection with the world of others. Lacan's imaginary ego only creates a gap, henceforth unbridgeable, between the subject and a false self.

CONCEIVING OF PSYCHOSIS

The great German psychiatrist Karl Jaspers (1997) proposed that the phenomenon of psychosis involved two dimensions: (1) the history of the patient's reactions to lived experiences that are readily understandable; and (2) an unknown change in function in which something new either of psychological or organic origin occurs and which manifests itself by a series of primary disturbances. These primary disturbances might consist, for example, of an awareness of troubling noises, feelings of being targeted, or presentiments of danger. Jaspers wrote that the patient cannot easily pinpoint the starting point for these changes, suggesting the difficulty of determining the dividing line between disease and normality over the years preceding the outbreak of a delusional process. Lacan used Jaspers' work extensively in his doctoral thesis of 1932, *De la psychose paranoïaque dans ses rapports avec la personnalité*, which concerned the case of a paranoid woman he named Aimée, after a character in a novel she had written. Certainly, Jaspers' model seems to fit a fairly typical clinical presentation of psychosis. That is, once one comes to know the patient, a part of the content of his psychotic beliefs appears as understandable as any person's way of thinking, yet another aspect of the presenting symptoms remains strange and inexplicable.

Lacan's early writings on psychosis reflected his growing interest in psychoanalytic ideas about the ego and its relations with external objects, for example, as developed in Freud's paper "Some Neurotic Mechanisms in Jealousy, Paranoia and Homosexuality" (1922), which Lacan translated into French in 1932. Two other important papers of the same period of Freud's thinking, "Group Psychology and the Analysis of the Ego" and "The Economic Factor in Masochism," were also important for Lacan in his attempts to understand delusions of persecution and jealousy (see Julien, 1985). The patient presented in his thesis, Aimée, had attacked a well-known actress, Mme. Huguette Duflos, because of feelings of persecution. She had at first idealized the actress but later felt ridiculed by her playing a role that, she believed, had been modeled by the author of the play, Pierre Benoit, on Aimée herself. Lacan's own contributions to a theory of psychosis at this point were rather slim, based on the familiar notion of finding meaning in the symptoms but adding, in Aimée's case, at least, a self-punitive aspect to the paranoia. She was striking at herself, Lacan concluded.

Lacan's doctoral thesis struggled with Freud's complicated ideas about bonds of love, identification, and projection as they move back and forth between the ego, superego and ego ideal, and the love object. Freud showed how these identifications and projections can shift, so that one's ego or superego can be modeled after the object. A libidinal relationship of self-love (or hate) could then be internalized, as in some forms of masochism or narcissism. Reciprocally, these dynamics could be reexternalized in the form of an object relationship characterized by love, persecution, or jealousy. For Freud and many analysts after him, paranoid delusions could be directly attributed to unconscious conflicts about homosexuality (Frosch, 1983). This concept has been challenged with the evolution of psychoanalytic theory, and one has the frequent impression reading case material that the theory dictated this interpretation in advance. As Lacan saw, the problematics of the ego that were central to Freud's thinking did not explain the specificity of paranoia, but he used this model to decipher the autobiographical meanings of his patient's psychosis.

At a second phase of his work, marked by his paper "Notes on a Question Preliminary to Any Treatment of Psychosis" and his seminar on psychosis, Lacan (1966) took up the relationship of language and the signifier to these disorders. The key question at this point in his development revolved around the determination of the subject by language, with a devaluation of the roles of identification and projection emphasized earlier (as imaginary constructions). He now criticized the value of understanding meaning in the patient's symptoms but instead emphasized the existence of an unknown, unconscious structure that determined the delusional beliefs. The analyst's understanding, in Lacan's thinking, represented an imaginary reaching for a complete depiction of the person that short-circuited the impersonal operations of language and the symbolic order. The psychotic discourse, he proposed, came in some sense from outside the subject, carrying an enigmatic message, "a hieroglyphic," to be deciphered by the analyst.

What psychiatrists usually call projection was redefined by Lacan as the effect of a profound inner failure of primary repression, which he posited as the basic defect in psychosis. To describe this mechanism, he adopted from Freud the term *verwerfung*, which he translated into French as foreclosure (forclusion). Freud had used this term to describe a form of defense different from repression in that its object was repudiated or expelled from psychological structure and thereby was treated as if nonexistent. Although Freud did not make much use of the term *verwerfung* in his work, Lacan found justification for his interpretation in the Wolf Man case. Freud had written that what is foreclosed from psychic reality can appear in external reality, as not being a part of the subject, just as the Wolf Man's visual hallucination of his finger cut off was interpreted as an effect of his repudiation of castration. In the famous case of Senatspresident Schreber, Freud (1911) stated, "It was incorrect to say that the perception which is suppressed internally is projected outwards; the truth is rather, as we now see, that what was abolished internally returns from without" (p. 71).

Lacan elaborated his notion of foreclosure in terms of a primary refusal of the structuring "Nom-du-Père,"[1] the metaphoric "name of the father," a kind of primary repression that breaks the fantasy of dual union with the mother and engages the nascent subject on the rails of the symbolic order of language and culture. While complex in its details, the Nom-du-Père basically represents the infant's awareness of a third position beyond the mother–child dyad for which the actual father stands and that is concomitant with the assumption of speech and learning of a name. One might say in Winnicottian terms that it signifies a structural obstacle to sustaining the fantasy of a subjective object, like of an undifferentiated relation with the mother.

What seemed to be at stake for Lacan, as for Winnicott, at this stage of early psychic life was a process of separation as a self or subject from the mother–child relation. Subjectivity for both began with a fundamental loss. Freud regarded this primal loss as the impetus for a lifelong search to refind the lost object in normal human relationships. The theory proposed by Lacan was that an ineffable sense of loss accompanies the emergence of a new world of symbolic forms that links the subject to a cultural world of extraindividual meaning and, in various ways, covers over the existential emptiness of individual existence. By failing to take this subjectivizing step into the symbolic order—that is, by using the mechanism of

[1] The expression *Nom-du-Père* puns on the very similar sounding phrase *Non-du-Père*, "the no of the father," which states the first symbolic law or prohibition.

foreclosure—the future psychotic was condemned to face a void without access to the laws of cultural structure that provide symbolic representation to the unmasterable excitement (*jouissance*) of the existential real. The psychotic then lives, as it were, without a true unconscious (which involves repression and other mechanisms like the pleasure principle that enable the subject to remain within the limits of the cultural framework) but remains in an unmediated relationship with the real of the drives.

At this point, we can see a possible convergence between Winnicott and Lacan around the notion of the origin of the psychotic subject: in Winnicott's case, a failure of the primary object to enable the birth of a self in transitional space; in Lacan's, a kind of inaugural refusal of conventional meaning. For Winnicott, the result was a one-sided development of the subjective object and the phenomenon of certainty that he said characterized madness. More precisely, the inaugural failure involved a primal breakdown in which a deficiency of the maternal function in infancy left a kind of basic fault at the level of transitional space that could later become the nidus for a psychosis. We could say that the notion of a zone of transitionality as the condition for human social existence invokes a necessary acceptance of the intrication of all subjective phenomena, including having a separate self, with the other. Lacan, too, referred to the attitude of certainty typical of the psychotic, which he attributed to the lack of a true unconscious that could be structurally transposed onto the position of the analyst (in the place of the Other[2]) in the transference. That is, neurotic patients seek the unconscious symbolic meanings of their existence, which they imagine they can learn from their analyst (in the place of the Other). Psychotics do not attribute knowledge to their transference Other in the same way. So for both Winnicott and Lacan, in different ways, the problem of an impaired linkage of the subject with first the mOther and then other subjects was fundamental to understanding psychosis.

THE CASE OF MRS. GOOD

With this background, I turn to the case of a patient, Mrs. Good, to explore the application of these ideas. She was a 37-year-old, unhappily married woman who sought treatment at the encouragement of her physician. At her initial visit, she recounted a complicated story that began a few months earlier when she felt an attraction to an unknown man at her health club, in itself not a disturbing experience to her, although she had never been unfaithful to her husband. On that occasion, leaving the exercise area, she encountered a female acquaintance, Mrs. Austen, whose reactions to her—specifically the

[2] The Other is the term Lacan used to refer to the field of the symbolic—the generalized other. For the infant, this dimension can be considered equivalent to the mother herself, sometimes written as mOther.

look she saw on the woman's face—indicated that this woman must be having an affair with the man and was angered by her intuition of Mrs. Good's interest. What my patient reported actually observing was a cold nod of nonrecognition, as though a refusal to acknowledge their connection.

Mrs. Austen was not an unimportant figure to my patient, as she was a published author and leader of a literary group from which Mrs. Good had formerly sought acceptance. She was, herself, an aspiring writer. After their chance encounter, she became aware of a series of strange coincidences suggesting that she was being followed around town. This inaugurated the "enigmatic" change in reality noted by academic psychiatrists to characterize the onset of psychosis. After her initial disconcerting experience at the gym, things seemed to change for Mrs. Good. She was being followed and watched, and people seemed to be signaling her. The strange incidents multiplied until she became certain that she was in danger and developed panicky feelings that led her to seek help.

The threat she felt increasingly took the form of being arrested on false charges. Changing health clubs helped temporarily, but soon afterward she thought she saw the same man in the new parking lot and later drove past Mrs. Austen collecting her children at a nearby elementary school. Subsequently, on hearing another woman refer to someone being stalked, she wondered if she herself might be suspected of stalking those children. Her trips around the town were accompanied by a number of familiar vehicles, and she noticed people making gestures that seemed to refer to her. This grew more frightening to her, especially as she felt a lack of support from her husband, who was growing impatient with her fears.

What Mrs. Good saw on her trips to the market or sports club were observable facts—the cars, familiar faces, people holding cameras. They made sense to her as part of a coherent structure—a plot to catch her in an apparent crime. Her perceptions were organized internally by a belief system she had about her neighbors and herself that involved ostracism and jealous vindictiveness, based on an impression she may have given of sexual interest in the other woman's lover. Despite many internal contradictions and nonsensical aspects of this explanation, Mrs. Good held firmly to it, was convinced of it, and wanted to persuade me of its truth, wishing me, as Winnicott says, to "share an illusion that is not my own" (p. 3). Winnicott (1971) called this "a hallmark of madness," and, indeed, the woman was paranoid, proving the adage that all that remains to the psychotic is his or her ability to reason.

Freud (1922), in his paper "Certain Neurotic Mechanisms in Jealousy, Homosexuality, and Paranoia," stated that sufferers from persecutory paranoia:

> ... take up minute indications with which these other, unknown people present them and use them in their delusions of reference. The meaning ... is that they expect from all strangers something like love. But these

> people show them nothing of the kind; they laugh to themselves, flourish their sticks, even spit on the ground as they go by—and one really does not do such things while a person in whom one takes a friendly interest is near. One does them only when one is quite indifferent to the passer-by, when one can treat him like air .... The paranoiac is not so far wrong in regarding this indifference as hate, in contrast to his claim for love. (p. 226)

Of course, we immediately suspect that Mrs. Good's demand for love was implicitly directed toward Mrs. Austen, if we do not fall into the error of immediately equating her desire with homosexuality. Triangular conflicts like the one Mrs. Good described are ubiquitous and produce jealousy and narcissistic rage but not delusions. It was the structural position that Mrs. Austen occupied that made the situation so powerful.

With respect to Winnicott's point about the capacity to recognize the object as "not-me," Mrs. Good clearly knows that the people she sees lead independent lives from her as separate beings. She is not like a schizophrenic patient who declared of a television character that "he is me" or like a normal toddler who cries when a playmate falls down, both classical illustrations of blurred or unformed ego boundaries, the phenomenon of "transitivism." The identification with the object, we might say, is less complete in Mrs. Good's mind. The people in her story remain external to her, and everything she describes comes from what she saw or heard in the real world. Perhaps this grip on actual people and events is what has kept her from losing all touch with reality, for example, hallucinating or showing bizarre, regressive behavior. We might say that she presents a narrative of ordinary life that is rational up to a point but extremely implausible.

The concept of reality testing is often applied to psychotic thinking, but this can be a misleading term. It might be more accurate to say that for Mrs. Good reality and fantasy were a single thing, without any blurry, intermediary transitional area of illusion. There seemed to be no important distinction for her between one realm and the other, as there would be in a neurotic, who is concerned to separate the subjective element from accurate perception and recognizes that most experiences involve a mixture of these. Although Mrs. Good's perception of others seems largely illusory, what may be more important than this external judgment of "reality" is her own certainty and lack of curiosity about her own mind. Winnicott's depiction of a transitional space between the self and the real object creates a difficulty by seeming to place the problem at the level of perception of the real rather than that of the subject's self-awareness. Lacan knew to avoid this problem by recognizing that the object relationship is always shaped by unconscious fantasy. We might then modify Winnicott's list of developmental tasks by adding to it the subject's capacity to recognize the object as partially "me." The other person is *my* object, partially my own creation. Winnicott (1953) restricted the expanding realm of playful, healthy illusion "to the arts and to religion and to imaginative living, and to creative scientific work" (p. 97), implicitly endorsing a brand of psychoanalytic objectivity (reality testing) that analysts no longer claim. We should rather understand the transitional realm as expanding over all of human experience, every feature of which retains its irreducible quota of subjectivity.

In Lacan's seminar (1956–1957) dedicated to the theory of the object relation, all interpersonal reality is in this sense transitional, the object always existing in connection with a fantasy—like the transitional object itself, partly found, partly created. From here, the neurotic subject can try to work out the "me" part of his perception of the other from the "not-me" part, the subjective from the if not "objective," which in the realm of human relations may be an impossible determination, then at least from the consensual, observable, and evidentiary. How much of what I feel or believe about the other's behavior and intention is my own fantasy? This distinction can be quite difficult to make, as Winnicott stressed. He wrote, "This matter of illusion is one which belongs inherently to human beings and which no individual finally solves for himself or herself" (p. 14). Perhaps for this reason normal or neurotic subjects usually confine the painful and frustrating effort at resolving illusion to a limited number of important relationships and either keep most remaining impressions of others private or shares them only with people who will agree with them.

The intrinsic problem of determining the accuracy of intersubjective perception is a powerful argument against analytic certainty. Our inability to *know* supports Lacan's position against analysts making interpretations about meaning, which are inevitably based on countertransference attitudes and preconceived ideas of how neuroses are caused and, for that reason, are notoriously variable across any group of clinicians. Nonetheless, analysts can help patients improve their capacities to understand their subjective perceptions more deeply, and, in fact, this is what much of psychotherapy is about. The important developmental issue is to acknowledge the omnipresent subjective or transitional aspect of all perception and to eschew certainty. The model of mentalization therapy developed by Bateman and Fonagy (2006) addresses this problem by helping patients think better about what goes on in their minds and in the minds of others.[3] Lacan made the logical but often overlooked point that mentalizing implies awareness that our perceptions are structured unconsciously and that we need to speak about them to someone else to have access to their meaning. For the psychotic, lacking a symbolic unconscious, this access is unavailable and perception remains in the real.

[3] Their research focused on application of this therapy to patients diagnosed with borderline personality disorder, but the process can be generalized to many other patients.

To restate the problem of Mrs. Good from the perspective of mentalization, the impairment she demonstrates is not so much about perceiving objective reality as about seeing herself as responsible for constructing her perceptions. She seems to lack an important step in awareness of her own subjectivity. From this point of view, excessive conviction that one's current beliefs coincide with reality, independently of any consensual validation, represents the diagnostic sign of psychosis. Could Mrs. Good be helped to place her present-day beliefs about reality in the context of her own life history, of which they are certainly a product, as Jaspers (1997) advocated? This was the approach taken by Lacan in his medical thesis of 1933 about paranoid psychosis in relation to the personality, previously regarded by French psychiatry as a form of organic disorder. His central contribution in that work was to recognize the connection between psychotic breakdown and the life experience of the patient—a variation on Jaspers (see Cox-Cameron, 2000, for an illuminating discussion of this relationship). We will see how far this perspective takes us in making sense of Mrs. Good.

Some clinicians make the mistake of attempting to show patients like Mrs. Good the errors of their thinking, which they call "reality testing." The inference is often made that the psychotic has a weak ego that can be supplemented by the healthier one of the analyst. From this vantage point, one might point out that it is unlikely that people would go to such lengths to entrap her, especially over such a minor incident as the one in the health club. Moreover, she has no real evidence for her theory. Her husband, for one, has relentlessly pursued this path of argumentation. In this effort, he behaved like a trainee who attempted to refute a paranoid man's belief that a diagnosis of posttraumatic stress disorder (PTSD) in his medical record was being suppressed so that he could be discredited as a psychotic by the authorities. The record was obtained, and no diagnosis of PTSD or anything like it could be found, but the patient was not persuaded. A further level of delusional explanation was of course required to deal with the new evidence, but more important was the anger the patient felt at being disbelieved by his therapist, whom he soon fired. Experience teaches us that confronting denial is not a useful technique with psychotic patients, who give every evidence of having a paradoxically strong ego, not open to doubt.

Mrs. Good naturally wanted my response to the verdict on reality declared by her husband. I already knew that his approach had reduced her to hopeless tears and that she now felt even more alone and helpless and was contemplating divorce. If we try to imagine how Winnicott might have reacted to her, we might ask first, as he did, what type of subject (patient) are we talking about? He considered three kinds, of whom the third represented the failure to form a personal self. In this person, early environmental failure has produced a sense of futility about life and a false self. The central therapeutic issue for such a patient, he proposed, does not involve conflicted wishes or desires but unmet need. For Winnicott, this patient in analysis enters a regression in which the therapist is not a pretend parent or a transference object, as she might be for a neurotic subject, but a real object on whom she literally depends. "Holding" then became a powerful metaphor for Winnicott's approach to meeting basic early needs, and he was prepared to accept the level of demand involved without attempting to question it. The American analyst Arnold Modell (1976), while strongly under the influence of Winnicott, described the regressive transference as occurring in the transitional space of necessary illusion. It is as if the therapist becomes the mother in a way that must not be interpreted or questioned—that is, in the manner of a transitional object.

Winnicott applied his model in the case of Margaret Little, who has written about her experience as a patient in a moving memoir (Little, 1985). As she described, he literally held her and made interpretations and interventions in which he seemed to consider her a helpless infant. There are other examples of his willingness to gratify his patients' dependency wishes or, perhaps, needs, which may have presaged the mothering approach taken in much current practice—and not only with borderline or psychotic patients. Little's autobiographic report acknowledged her unique transference to Winnicott but also stressed what she conceived as a real relationship with him. Her understanding of their relationship as real speaks to another confusion in today's practice, namely, the conceit that the therapist can or should strive to become a real person to the patient, a notion that carries an essentialist belief in the unified subject—a whole self. Of course, the therapist is a "real person" to the patient, but only in the sense that all object relations have a transitional quality, part subjective, part coming from the object. It is around these issues that Lacan can be quite helpful, reminding us once again that transference and countertransference are imaginary constructions that permeate all relationships (although I believe the term *transitional constructions* is more accurate).

With Mrs. Good, I took the position that I had no way to know what was true and what was not in her perception of the world. Thinking of Winnicott, I answered her queries about her husband's rejection of her beliefs by saying that I supposed her assessments like everyone's were a mixture of facts and her own interpretations of them. Since she raised the question, I concluded privately that she was still maintaining a fragile transitional space in which the border between accurate perception and private fantasy remained important. To challenge her too much might produce something akin to what Winnicott called an impingement, an intrusion that collapses transitional space and forces the child into a defensive withdrawal or compliant adaptation to the mother with consequent construction of a false self. Indeed, Mrs. Good gave many indications of having lived a false-self existence as a good child conforming to her family's and husband's expectations. Her facade of conventional adaptation had been broken only on a few occasions, as I learned, by serious assertions of her will that had led to ruptured relationships and attempts at new beginnings. In her current situation, she was living in her husband's town in his former home, not far from his ex-wife and child whom she helped entertain. They had a minimal social life with neighbors, but she had made only one real friend, now married and unavailable. The couple shared an interest in music but otherwise lived fairly separate lives. Mrs. Good's unhappiness had surfaced 2 years earlier when they saw a couples' counselor. Mr. Good then acknowledged his controlling behavior, and the therapist encouraged his wife to undertake more activities on her own. Out of this had come her joining the writing group to which the woman who was to figure so prominently in her delusions belonged.

Mrs. Good seemed grateful that I did not take a firm position about what was real, and she could acknowledge, like many paranoid patients, that her explanation did not seem realistic. Also like them, she was frightened and alone in her delusions and seemed to seek a nonjudgmental listener to whom she could talk openly. Expressing a willingness to listen to these patients is often an important intervention. This reassuring connection, however, only brought out the importance she attached to her beliefs, suggesting as Freud proposed that they solved a problem by covering over the loss of ties to real objects. Despite signs of improvement in her daily functioning, Ms. Good continued to have episodes of extreme apprehension when she felt in danger. She proposed moving elsewhere to escape her persecutors, but her husband found this solution unreasonable. Perhaps, she was looking to refashion her life by breaking out of the trap she experienced and to reconstitute her premorbid state of relatively coherent mental functioning. Finally, after an angry confrontation in which she revealed her fears of being harmed, as well as some self-destructive thoughts, her husband brought her to an emergency room. The psychiatrist there told her she was having a psychotic episode and was suffering from delusions. She was hospitalized voluntarily and was a compliant patient taking medications until the time of her discharge a few days later. She told me she almost believed her doctor, but when she drove off with her husband she noticed a familiar blue car following them.

With respect to Winnicott's remarks about dependency, Mrs. Good came faithfully to her appointments two and three times per week, seemed eager to confide delusional beliefs, and discovered that her enormous anxiety about the imagined persecution and danger began to evaporate when she boarded the train to come to my office. In my experience with paranoid patients, this positive involvement in treatment usually is accompanied by a magical transference in which the idealized therapist is endowed with special wisdom or power. These attributions may prop up the fragile narcissism of the paranoid subject who feels so at the mercy of alien forces. The patient may then feel safe enough to tolerate a partial regression toward, if not Winnicottian absolute dependency, at least the state of being cared for. On the other hand, regression to psychotic helplessness usually requires the support of a hospital setting and may not serve a useful purpose (Frosch, 1983).

Mrs. Good's idealizing transference enabled her to use the treatment situation as a support and to speak more freely. Eventually, she became more frankly depressed as she confided her loneliness in the marriage, the emotional distance she felt, and her feeling that she functioned basically to support her husband's lifestyle. Yet she also reflected that he was a kind person, and she acknowledged loving feelings toward him, much like her reaction to her own father, revealing a degree of preservation of object ties that stood in the way of further decompensation.

Lacan's aphorism about therapy was to pay attention to the text, not the psychology of the author. He meant that one should attend closely to what the patient actually says, not attempt to interpret what she might mean. From this position, the therapist can hear certain words and expressions that stand out and seem to call for further inquiry, like Mrs. Good's comparison of her husband to her father. This line of associations can be explored within the flow of the session, not in the question-and-answer format typical of the contemporary psychiatric interview, which seeks information, not personal meaning. With this approach, Mrs. Good began to diverge from recounting the details associated with her feelings of persecution and to fill in significant gaps in her history.

Mrs. Good's "healthy" transitional space was occupied by her writing; she had hoped to become a novelist (it was interesting that her mother had once won a local award for her writing). In fact, she had had one short story published. In that story, a little girl felt shunned in school because she was one of two Roman Catholics in her class of Southern Baptists. Like Mrs. Good, she was not religious. The child sought solace from her mother, who reassured her that she was a good person despite her difference from the majority. The girl realized that she had to find ways to enjoy herself at school without being part of the group; she was like "an apparition on the playground." She then had a minor accident, which isolated her more. During this period she occupied herself by writing and performing a play, which concerned an eccentric neighbor who had gone mad and become a menace to people. The narrator of the story described playing the several roles of the dangerous madman, the sheriff trying to capture him, and the therapist who eventually healed him. Of course, Mrs. Good saw the similarities between her fictional character and her own childhood, but this did not lead to insight about her delusions. The presentation of her life history made her story more intelligible to me but also reinforced Lacan's conclusion in his seminar on the psychoses that delusional thoughts are not determined by the usual neurotic process of expressing the repressed through symptoms. If the persecutory thoughts were a metaphor for her past, this fact in no way explained them.

On the other hand, the close connection between the plot of Mrs. Good's story, the split selves of its main character, and the indication of an identification with her mother (through writing) suggested another hypothesis. Rather than an attempt to make sense of her past traumas or to tell a story of her subjective predicament as a form of sublimation, Mrs. Good may have written to create a life—that is, to create a fictional self in place of a lack. In this way, her story should not be interpreted but should be taken as a kind of self-contained reality.

In a late seminar, Lacan (1975–1976) attempted to reformulate his prior conception of psychosis as a failure to sustain the metaphoric knot that holds together the domains of real, imaginary, and symbolic that constitute the subject. He proposed that a fourth term, which he called *le père du nom*, a father of naming, as it were, could supplement this defect of the triadic knot. He invented a name, the *sinthome*, to describe a use of language that affords direct expression of *jouissance*, of a pleasure in the real, rather than the classical *symptôme* that functions as a compromise formation indirectly conveying an unconscious and unrealizable desire for *jouissance*. Lacan interpreted the writings of James Joyce as an example of this creative process of naming—writing not to communicate or to be understood but to cohere as a subject of *jouissance* (see Aubert, 1987). During this period, he was revising his approach to the nature of the psychoanalytic cure, moving from a linguistic model based on the signifier to a more abstract topology (the borromean knot). His exposition hinted that everyone might require a supplement of the father's name, some dependency on the word of the father, to avoid madness (Julien, 1991). In this sense, his invention of the *sinthome* may represent Lacan's attempt to theorize (and reappropriate) Freud's influential notion in the Schreber case that psychotic manifestations are restitutive after normal libidinal object ties have been lost; they are not symbolic of a repressed unconscious but refer only to themselves. Be that as it may, the clinical problem of how to stabilize a patient's effort at self-cure remains.

More often than Lacan may have seen, the psychosis can represent a traumatic disruption in the past. Mrs. Good's depiction of her isolated childhood hinted at early trauma of which I had no direct evidence. I was interested in her fictional character's accident as a representation of a traumatic event and, on inquiry, learned that Mrs. Good had experienced two significant injuries, but much later in life. In the first, she was hit by a car while riding her bicycle and was very seriously injured. This occurred at a moment when she was about to pursue a romantic relationship with a man she had recently met. He visited her in the hospital, but, after a second accident several months later, when her car was hit from behind, causing facial injuries, he seemed reluctant to make a commitment. Someone whom she considered her closest friend at the time commented to her, "There are no accidents in life." Mrs. Good felt blamed by this remark, broke off both relationships, and left her job to continue her recovery in another city. She told me that a therapist there "saved her life" by telling her that the two incidents were only a "terrible coincidence."

The story of these life events and her subsequent therapy is another example of the problem with reality so characteristic of paranoid patients. Real and imaginary are telescoped so that there is no transitional space to play with possibilities but only a deadly trap from which escape is impossible. "No accidents" meant that what happened in the real represented her wish and responsibility. She had no interest in exploring her possible contribution to the accidents as one might routinely expect in neurotic patients. Perhaps for this reason, the authority of a therapist who could redefine reality as "terrible coincidences," a paternal naming, as Lacan suggested, was decisive in her recovery. Certainly, searching for the meaning of this or other experiences was not helpful for Mrs. Good.

Mrs. Good recounted similar stories of betrayal by men as well as by female friends, all of which sounded credible, although reflecting her naiveté about people, vulnerability to injury, and a powerful sense of being an outsider. She described a subsequent setback when she broke off another relationship and moved away after concluding that her partner had lied to her about a weekend trip. Women friends also played a role in this painful betrayal by taking his side. Yet she displayed resilience, reestablishing herself in a new town where, a few years later, she met her current husband. An important factor in her attraction to this relationship was the presence of his young son for whom she felt compassion after his divorce.

As a child, Mrs. Good confided, she had terrible nightmares about things happening to her younger brother (by 2 years) that made her feel guilty. She had even wondered whether her ostracism by children at school was because she was a sinner, a bad person—hence her mother's reassurance. When upset, she had been permitted to lie down at the foot of her parents' bed. There was not much cuddling or holding. Mrs. Good provided other examples of the theme of guilt, and she could see that in many instances she had felt responsible irrationally for things she had not done. In one incident, working as a cashier as a young teenager, she feared that a discrepancy in the receipts might point to her having stolen the money. She put her own savings in the cash register to make up the difference, but the next day when the manager discovered the missing bills in a drawer Mrs. Good was afraid to say anything and lost her money. She did not tell anyone about this. I was struck, on one hand, by the outpouring of associations to her sense of badness and guilt and, on the other, the little interest she seemed to take in making these connections to her current fears. Again, her apparent free associations were not the product of a symbolic elaboration of signifiers giving access to the unconscious (as in a neurotic), which could be interpreted, but the repetitive expression of a drive-saturated "real" in which she lived. They expressed not feelings of guilt or forbidden wishes but perceptions of a fused imaginary–real in which she was imprisoned.

I did comment, however, on the similarity between Mrs. Good's mother and Mrs. Austen, the woman in real life whom she guiltily believed she had offended, both writers as she aspired to become. Her account of their contacts was suggestive to me of Winnicott's discussion of the relationship between the transitional object and the mother. He commented on the psychic death of the object, describing how the transitional object depends on an internal representation of the mother, which, in turn, is tied to the availability of the actual mother. If the mother is away for too long, the inner object may fade and, with its disappearance, the attachment to the transitional object may also be lost. From this perspective, we could infer that the tenuous presence of an internalized good object representation of her mother was undermined by Mrs. Good's inability to make a relationship with the idealized mother substitute, Mrs. Austen.

Another possible outcome of maternal absence was proposed by Winnicott's former teacher, Melanie Klein (1952), who observed that loss or frustration of wishes for love can evoke a hateful, bad inner object via a cycle of projection and introjection of aggressive wishes, which she emphasized (see Winnicott, 1955). The concept of an aggressive instinct and its vicissitudes has played a role in psychoanalytic theories of psychosis, especially in terms of a hypothetical fusion and defusion of libidinal with aggressive drive energies, but this notion was not much used by Winnicott or Lacan. Winnicott did refer to a lack of instinctual fusion in his paper on classification (1959), but his main emphasis there was on the environmental provision that makes this process occur. Psychosis in his view was better approached in terms of regression and a need for a repair of an early maternal deficiency than as an instinctual phenomenon, which he saw as clearly secondary. When he did speak about psychic death and annihilation, as in his story of the woman patient toward the end of his article on the transitional object, the threat was the result of a rupture and separation, not the unbinding of instincts as Klein advocated. In another example dealing with the danger of separation, Winnicott hospitalized Margaret Little during a summer break for fear she would commit suicide. In neither case, however, did the frustration and anger of these women over being left appear to have been taken up.

In general, the role of aggression as an innate drive in psychosis was not emphasized by Winnicott or Lacan. If we view these Freudian terms as metaphoric, however, rather than as part of a psychoanalytic biology of dubious validity, we might find an equivalent conception in Lacan's hypothesis of *points de capiton*, or quilting points, which bind or suture language to fixed symbolic meanings and to a consensual social reality. Lacan stated in his seminar on the psychoses (1955–1956) that psychotics lack these stable ties, so that the signifier cannot be stabilized in its movement, nor can the imaginary identifications of the self cohere. A threat of fragmentation of the self (of the ego, Lacan would say) releases aggression. This aggressive response leads to attempts to create new signifieds to stabilize identity, like delusions of persecution—not internal fragmentation, but "something is being done to me." Perhaps this interpretation of the subject's perception of hostile forces arrayed against her can provide an alternative way at looking at the phenomena of instinctual defusion or its Kleinian version of projective identification of bad internal objects onto others. Delusions provide a meaning (signifieds) that stabilize the slide toward a meaningless real.

It can be difficult to address a paranoid patient's anger, except in its reactive form of defensive and indignant postures in which there is not much owning of the aggression. As noted already, Freud and Lacan criticized the concept of projection of aggression as a defense in favor of a change in the psychic organization of perception. They proposed that psychotic patients directly experience a poorly differentiated environmental other that is inimical and exclusionary toward them, hence the importance of providing holding and safety to mitigate the omnipresent danger. To feel anger is to exist as a subject of emotion, the center of an affect that is carried internally. On the other, naming an affective state for a patient may have value in recognizing a potential subject who could have a symbolic relation to the other. The act of naming, apart from Lacan's conjecture about a *père-du-nom*, can have binding effects, providing definition to a confusing inner state, provided that it uses language at a less highly charged level.

In Mrs. Good's case, I commented on her being hurt by the cold look of nonrecognition from Mrs. Austen and the indifference of others, hoping to provide a scaffolding of meaning linked to her story. The therapeutic problem again was that for her the look was in the real, not a subjective perception that could be elaborated. Winnicott's article on the Mirror Stage explored situations in which the baby fails to get back a response to his scrutiny of the mother, a situation that has been extensively explored by infant researchers since the research by Edward Tronick on the still face paradigm (Tronick et al., 1978). He filmed infants playing with their mothers, who were instructed to let their faces go blank at a certain moment. What he then observed was a breakdown of the previous playful rapport between mother and baby, signs of distress, and a withdrawal or turning away. Tronick's data supports Winnicott's idea that when the mother "reflects her own mood or, worse still, the rigidity of her own defenses" (1967, p. 112) the baby perceives only her face, not a mirror. "Perception," he wrote, "takes the place of that which might have been a significant exchange with the world" (p. 113). Clinicians are familiar with patients who constantly scan their faces and are exquisitely sensitive to lapses of attention caused by momentary distraction or preoccupation. They may ask the therapist if he is bored or make negative inferences about his feelings for them based on a perceived lack of responsiveness. Mrs. Good did not seek eye contact, but she did insist on tape recording our sessions and told me she listened to them repeatedly. As I did not notice her bringing up aspects of their actual contents, I wondered whether she was trying to hold onto me via the voice, which Lacan saw as a drive of the baby equivalent to the gaze.

In Winnicott's terms, we could say that a baby deprived of healthy mirroring reverts to "object relating" rather than "object using." For Winnicott, object relating meant conceiving of the object only in relation to subjective needs, not interacting with the object as a separate person—not what we call today an intersubjective relationship. The "significant exchange" of which he spoke in his article implies the communication of personal meanings or signifiers that form the basis of a personal self through intersubjective dialogue, and he carried this analogy from infancy over to psychotherapy. He wrote, "Psychotherapy is not making clever and apt interpretations; by and large it is a long-term giving back of what the patient brings. It is a complex derivative of the face .... if I do this well enough the patient will find his or her own self, and will be able to exist and feel real" (1967, p. 117). Indeed, much of his clinical contribution had to do with helping patients who did not feel real and for whom not being seen left them vulnerable to psychic disintegration and depersonalization.

Mrs. Good tried to revive her fading feelings of connection with her husband by appealing to him to move away to a new place and to take her side against the malevolence of Mrs. Austen. Because she could see that he was making efforts to hold onto her and said he loved her, she made efforts to maintain their relationship in a transitional space by trying in her therapy to separate feeling abandoned by him from a more balanced assessment. Over time, however, a split between her compliant false self adapted to his reality and a more genuine private self seemed to dominate the picture. There was no intermediate zone where she could explore other possible expressions of herself or the relationship besides submission or rejection. This either–or choice led to feelings of sadness and defeat with a sense of repetition of past disappointments. Perhaps in response, she made strenuous efforts to connect with her distant family. Her mother, curiously, seemed dismissive, but her father showed compassion and hinted that he could understand her feelings of marital estrangement through his experience of his own and his parents' marriages. Unable to confront her husband directly, Mrs. Good announced a plan to visit her family, confiding that she might not return, although she was afraid to tell him so. Her only option, she told me, was to pick up stakes and start a new life as she had done in the past.

Once back at her parents' home, Mrs. Good kept up contact with me by telephone. She presented a confident front, reporting that the strong acceptance she received from father and sister was very comforting to her. After several weeks, her husband informed me that she was initiating divorce. She wrote me to say she was feeling well and was no longer bothered by fears of being followed. She was grateful that I had stuck by her during that difficult period. She subsequently found a new job and, against my suggestion, reported she did not think she would need more help. I understood that she had repeated a familiar path to recovery from rejection and object loss.

DISCUSSION

Mrs. Good was able to recover, at least temporarily, from her psychotic episode, as she apparently had done in the past. The episode had a connection to her life history that became rather obvious, as her fictional story shows. But this history, while helping to explain some of her vulnerabilities and defensive style as well as suggesting a repetitive element of failed identification with her mother, did not enable us to understand why she became ill rather than an unhappy neurotic. The precipitating event offers a suggestive clue to her underlying deficit, namely, the blank look on Mrs. Austen's face at the club. The incident was glossed over by a pseudo-Oedipal, triangular configuration; Mrs. Good was attracted to another woman's man. Yet the Oedipal side of her character seemed quite undeveloped and may have represented a fantasy of womanhood or a false self based on imaginary identifications with her mother or other female figures. The traumatic element in the event seemed to be the rejection and nonrecognition by Mrs. Austen. My attempt to supply words for this experience in a climate of recognition and holding was intended as reparative or as enabling Mrs. Good to use her capacities for self-repair, not to heal the basic defect.

Why should such an injury have precipitated psychotic developments? Winnicott (1952) hypothesized an infantile trauma of deficient mothering before organization of a self (which may have biological determinants). He saw the phenomenon of breakdown in terms of regression to the point of environmental failure (1954). I have linked this precocious trauma to a fragility of transitional space, which can collapse, telescoping imaginary and real when a mental link to the primary other cannot be maintained. For his part, Lacan also hypothesized a very early deficit with his notion of foreclosure (*forclusion*). In his paradigm, something at a primal stage of development interferes with the symbolic elaboration of early experience. There is no *nom-du-père*, or intervention of a third, to oppose a fusional fantasy or a state of living in a world of subjective objects. Lacking access to the symbolic use of language, the subject is consequently burdened by a slippage or loss of meaning and a concomitant closeness to the real. Because of limited capacity to elaborate the drives and impulses toward others in the symbolic register, she cannot mentalize her experiences in the world. They do not enter psychic life where they can be elaborated and processed but remain as parts of an incomprehensible reality.

For the potential psychotic subject, then, affectively significant life events are not endowed with personal meaning but have an opposite desubjectifying effect. Because her construction of reality is fragile, both in terms of subjective identity and the nature of her relation to objects, she is at risk of ego fragmentation and flooding by depersonalized bodily experiences when faced with rejection or frustration of needs and wishes. Loss of object ties is followed by delusional efforts at restitution of symbolic investments. Yet this description does not explain the source of the fundamental defect, except to call on the biological predisposition. Although we have learned some ways to treat the paranoid patient, the question preliminary to treatment of psychosis raised by Lacan in the *Ècrits* does not yet have a satisfactory answer.

REFERENCES

Aubert, J. (Ed.) (1987). *Joyce avec Lacan*. Paris: Navarin Editeur.

Bateman, A., & Fonagy P. (2004). *Mentalization-based treatment for Borderline Personality Disorder*. Oxford: Oxford University Press.

Cox-Cameron, O. (2000). Lacan's doctoral thesis: Turbulent surface or founding legend? *Psychoanalytische Perspectieven*, 41/42.

Feinsilver, D. B. (1989). Transitional relatedness, containment and the transference neurosis. *International Review of Psychoanalysis*, 16, 433–444.

Fink, B. (2007). *Fundamentals of psychoanalytic technique: A Lacanian approach for practitioners*. New York: W. W. Norton & Company.

Freud, S. (1911). Psychoanalytic notes on an autobiographical account of a case of paranoia. In J. Strachey (Ed. & Trans.), *The standard edition of the complete psychological works of Sigmund Freud* (Vol. 12, pp. 1–84). London: Hogarth Press.

Freud, S. (1922). Some neurotic mechanisms in jealousy, homosexuality, and paranoia. In J. Strachey (Ed. & Trans.), *The standard edition of the complete psychological works of Sigmund Freud* (Vol. 18, pp. 221–233). London: Hogarth Press.

Freud, S. (1924). Neurosis and psychosis. In J. Strachey (Ed. & Trans.), *The standard edition of the complete psychological works of Sigmund Freud* (Vol. 19, pp. 149–156). London: Hogarth Press.

Frosch, J. (1983). The role of unconscious homosexuality in the paranoid constellation. In *The psychotic process* (pp. 62–109). New York: International Universities Press.

Jaspers, K. (1997). *General psychopathology, Volumes 1 & 2* (J. Hoenig & M. W. Hamilton, Trans.). Baltimore: Johns Hopkins University Press.

Julien, P. (1985). *Pour lire Jacques Lacan*. Toulouse: Éditions Ères.

Julien, P. (1991). Le *manteau de Noé*. Paris: Descleé de Brouwer.

Klein, M. (1952). Some theoretical conclusions regarding the emotional life of the infant. In *The writings of Melanie Klein* (Vol. 1, pp. 61–93). London: Hogarth Press, 1975.

Lacan J. (1933). *De la psychose paranoïaque dans ses rapports avec la personnalité, suivi de premiers écrits sur la paranoïa*. Paris: Editions du Seuil, 1975.

Lacan J. (1940–1944). Le temps logique et l'assertion de certitude anticipée. Écrits, Paris: Seuil, 1966.

Lacan J. (1945). Le temps logique et l'assertion de certitude anticipée. *Les Cahiers d'Art*, 1940–1944, 32–42.

Lacan J. (1949). The mirror stage as formative of the function of the I. In *Écrits* (A. Sheridan, Trans.) (pp. 1–7). New York: W. W. Norton & Company, 1977.

Lacan J. (1953). Some reflections on the ego. *International Journal of Psychoanalysis*, *34*, 11–17.

Lacan J. (1955–1956). *The Seminar, Book III: The psychoses* (R. Grigg, Trans.). London: Routledge, 1993.

Lacan J. (1956–1957). *Le Séminaire, livre IV: La relation d'objet*. Paris: Seuil, 1994.

Lacan J. (1966a). Notes on a question preliminary to any treatment of psychosis. In *Écrits* (A. Sheridan, Trans.). New York: W. W. Norton & Company, 1977.

Lacan J. (1966b). The mirror stage as formative of the function of the I. In *Écrits* (A. Sheridan, Trans.) (pp. 1–7). New York: W. W. Norton & Company, 1977.

Lacan, J. (1973). *Les quatre concepts fondamentaux de la psychanalyse* (*Le Séminaire, livre* XI): 1964, Paris: Seuil.

Lacan J. (1975). *Le Séminaire, livre XI: Les quatre concepts fondamentaux de la psychanalyse*. Paris: Seuil.

Lacan, J. (1975–1976). *Le Séminaire, livre XXIII: Le sinthom*. Paris: Seuil, 2005.

Lacan J. (1993). *The Psychoses: The seminar of Jacques Lacan, book III: 1955–1956* (R. Grigg, Trans.). London: Routledge.

Lacan J. (1994). *La relation d'objet (Le Séminaire, livre IV)*: 1956–1957, Paris: Seuil.

Lacan, J. (2005). *Le sinthom (Le Séminaire, livre XXIII)*: 1975–1976, Paris: Seuil.

Little, M. (1985). *Psychotic anxieties and containment: A personal record of an analysis with Winnicott*. Northvale, NJ: Jason Aronson, 1990.

Modell, A. (1976). The holding environment and the therapeutic action of psychoanalysis. *Journal of the American Psychoanalytic Association*, *24*, 285–308.

Modell, A. (2000). *Other times/Other realities*. Cambridge, MA: Harvard University Press.

Phillips, A. (1988) *Winnicott*. London: Fontana Press.

Tronick, E. Z., Als, H., Adamson, L., Wise, S., & Brazelton, T. B. (1978). The infant's response to entrapment between contradictory messages in face-to-face interaction *Journal of the American Academy of Child & Adolescent Psychiatry*, *17*, 1–13.

Winnicott, D. W. (1952). Psychoses and child care. In *Through paediatrics to psycho-analysis* (pp. 219–228). New York: Basic Books, 1975.

Winnicott, D. W. (1953). Transitional objects and transitional phenomena. In *Through paediatrics to psycho-analysis* (pp. 229–242). New York: Basic Books, 1975.

Winnicott, D. W. (1954). Metapsychological and clinical aspects of regression within the psycho-analytical set-up. In *Through paediatrics to psycho-analysis* (pp. 278–294). New York: Basic Books, 1975.

Winnicott, D. W. (1955). The depressive position in normal emotional development. In *Through paediatrics to psycho-analysis* (pp. 262–277). New York: Basic Books, 1975.

Winnicott, D. W. (1959). Classification: Is there a psycho-analytic contribution to psychiatric classification? In *The maturational processes and the facilitating environment* (pp. 124-139). London: Hogarth Press.

Winnicott, D. W. (1963). The development of the capacity for concern. In *The maturational processes and the facilitating environment* (pp. 73–82). London: Hogarth Press.

Winnicott, D. W. (1967). Mirror-role of mother and family in child development. In *Playing and reality* (pp. 137–138). London: Tavistock, 1971.

Winnicott, D. W. (1969). The use of the object and relating through identifications. In *Playing and Reality* (pp. 101–111). London: Tavistock, 1971.

Winnicott, D. W. (1971). *Playing and reality*. London: Tavistock.

Chapter 6

The object between mother and child

From Winnicott to Lacan[1]

Alain Vanier

In a lecture he gave at the French Institute in London on February 3, 1975, Jacques Lacan was trying to make clear that what he himself called the *objet a* was the same thing Donald Winnicott called the "transitional object." Already during the 1960s, Lacan spoke of Winnicott as someone whom he appreciated and liked the most of all Anglo American psychoanalysts. He would even argue that he discovered the *object a* in the transitional object, although we must say that *object a* is not *exactly* the transitional object: at the very most, it is one of its incarnations, but I would go as far as to say its generalized concept. This is what I would like to examine now, focusing on Lacan's comments concerning the mother–child relation.

On November 28, 1956, during his seminar on "The Object Relation," Lacan referred to Winnicott's article "Transitional Objects and Transitional Phenomena," published in its first version in 1953 (after a 1951 conference at the British Psychoanalytic Society). Lacan underscored the oscillation of illusion–disillusion observed between the mother and her child and insisted on the workings of transitional objects, of which, he said, it is impossible to say "on which side they are situated in the dialectic, reduced and incarnated between hallucination and the real object" (Lacan, 1956–1957, p. 35). These objects are therefore imaginary. However, his reference to Winnicott serves here specifically to introduce what was at the time Lacan's main concern, "the object lack." He was interested in the fact that it was not possible to found "any genesis of reality based on whether the baby has, or does not have, the breast" (id., p. 125). The frustration of *jouissance* may perhaps trigger a second burst of desire, but it certainly does not lead to the constitution of an object. When discussing the transitional object, we cannot therefore speak of reality or unreality: for Lacan, transitional objects are half real, half unreal.

The transitional object is a clinical discovery made by Winnicott. It is a tertiary object existing between the mother and the child, objecting to the dual relationship. At first, Lacan identifies it with the *Fort-Da* spool

[1] Translated by Kristina Valendinova.

(Lacan, 1958–1959); that is, he does not situate it as directly linked to weaning, a process he considers to be traumatic only for the mother. Next, he identifies the transitional object with the thumb—the first object of *jouissance* other than the breast—an object that is not permanently there but nevertheless remains within reach (Lacan, 1967–1968). A subject functions at the beginning on the level of the transitional object, which commands it. In this way, the object is neither real nor illusory.

Let us first notice that Winnicott insists on this intermediate zone, on the fact that we are dealing with a "not-me object," which at the same time does not belong to the other. The object covers a hollowed-out space that is necessarily created. It is not Lacan's (or Sigmund Freud's) lost object: the purpose of the transitional object is rather to *be* lost—hence all the little dramas that occur when it is misplaced, something mothers spend so much time trying to keep from happening. The transitional object is the commemoration of a lack. We might say that it gives lack the meaning of a loss (Vanier, 2006).

Second, we should also note that Winnicott stresses that he is not so much interested in the object itself but in the use one makes of it—"the use of the object," as he says. The English "use" can very well be translated by the French *jouissance*, a complex term that on one level means "enjoyment." Lacan proposed the term *jouissance* to designate the satisfaction derived from the use of the desired object. But the difficulty lies precisely in that this satisfaction, which we should think of as total and impossible, presupposes an object that has been fundamentally prohibited. Indeed, the Freudian Oedipus implies that the subject has only one object of complete satisfaction—the mother—and that this object is forbidden. All other objects provoking desire will be substitutes of this first object and can be only partially satisfying. We must therefore make a distinction between satisfaction and *jouissance*. In addition, *jouissance* seems to contradict the pleasure principle by corresponding to a rise in tension rather than to its return to the lowest possible level. The concept of *jouissance* is therefore not unrelated to Freud's death drive as articulated in *Beyond the Pleasure Principle* (1920g).

Not all forms of *jouissance* are impossible for humans, however, and Lacan restated the concept several times. On one hand, there is what he called *phallic jouissance*, a possible yet limited enjoyment available to the subject within the confines of the pleasure principle. On the other hand, he indicated the possibility of a *jouissance* beyond language, which he named the *jouissance of the Other* and which he opposed to finite phallic enjoyment. The limit of phallic *jouissance* depends on the signifier: this is why Lacan considered castration (as a symbolic operation) the only means of access to this possible enjoyment. The complex term *jouissance*, therefore, starts off from a purely legal meaning, in the sense that we might, for example, speak of someone having a usufruct over a property, a right limited by the interdiction to diminish its capital. In Lacan's definition, the *object a* is a fragment, a remainder of this fundamentally impossible *jouissance*.

Winnicott later differentiated between object relating and object usage and finally wrote that children are "addicted" to the transitional object or rather that the mother expects them to become addicted to it. We can see here that the object is tied to another kind of pleasure in *jouissance* (another kind than drive gratification or the pleasure principle). Indeed, because the first dealings which children have with the primordial Other must pass through the body, these transactions are the first instances of *jouissance*, dividing the body organ by organ, orifice by orifice, and remaining bound to the signifiers that are transmitted during these first exchanges and that will remain inscribed on their body.

In the beginning, Lacan labeled the *object a* with the initial of the *other* (lowercase *o*—in English we should say "object *o*"), which is to be found in the realm of the imaginary. But it was—at the start—also located as an object belonging to the mother, as one of those objects that appear for children when, due to her inadequate response, she is dislodged from her initial place by the articulation of their demand, by the circuit of demand. This displacement of the actual from perfect mother, which occurs as the realization of something lacking in her, restores a place for the so-called big Other (capital O). Lacan says it also carries with it the objects belonging to the mother. For Lacan, the drive is linked to language and to the effects of demand on need. The satisfaction it brings is not unrelated to the reactivation of the dimension of loss, which means that its movement can only repeat itself. That is, with each satisfaction the drive is reactivated, since its satisfaction is also a disappointment, unable as it is to recover the first object. Within this perspective, the first mother is symbolic. As a privileged form of the real, she is both present and absent, present against a background of absence. She is the one who will process and symbolize the game of *Fort-Da*. In the game of the infant's demand, as well as in the succession of oral and anal losses the subject will encounter, the first symbolic mother gradually fulfills her role by dispersing herself into these objects.

However, quite soon the *object a* ceases to belong to the mother, as Lacan draws a line between the breast and the mother's body, between the specific object and the mother. Children always lose something of themselves in this transformation. Once the object has been dropped, let go of, it is-much like the transitional object—neither of oneself nor of the other. The *object a* is neither the other nor the phallus, except in fantasy. Rather, it is a semblance (of what was lost), caught in a movement of metonymy of which the phallus (as figure of completion) is the horizon. Strictly speaking, it is not the partial object. It is designated as the object of desire, and, to quote Lacan (1960), "it receives its function from the Symbolic." He writes:

> This means that as a partial object it is not only a piece, a spare part of the device imagining the body, but from the very beginning an element of a structure, and—if we can put it this way—it is a part of the deal in

> the game being played. Having been selected among the appendices of the body as an index of desire, it is already an exponent of a function .... (p. 682)

Thus, the object is no longer only imaginary. It detaches itself and from the very beginning has its place in the symbolic, as the *cause* of desire but not its object. It is "the index finger raised toward an absence" (p. 682). Absent as it is from the mirror image, it is what the libido, entrenched in the narcissistic image, invests. Nor is it only symbolic; since it cannot be reduced to a signifier, it cannot be symbolized. It is the residue of the very operation of symbolization, what is left from the division of the subject and its emergence. The *objet a* is what escapes being captured by the signifier. While it causes desire, it is not itself aimed at by desire. It is not an empirical object but an object of logical consistency that is occasionally incarnated in the partial objects, yet it is not only them. The symbolic gives *objet a* the coordinates of its function, but these are not what it *is*, since it cannot define itself. Lacan says that it provides an access to the real but at the same time screens it. When this moment occurs, the *object a* can be located as real. The *object a* is "fit to symbolize the central lack expressed in castration and at the same time to mask it, since it is evanescent and punctuated and leaves the subject ignorant of what is beyond appearance" (Lacan, 1964, p. 73).

Lacan goes on to refer to the four occasional substances, which are in this case those four facets of the *object a* distributed according to demand and desire, polarized by castration "which is the whole weight of the function of the *objet a*. It is impossible to articulate the object *a* without this reference" (Lacan, 1971, p. 450). We should note that the link to demand and desire implies what Freud called fixation (1905d).

Seen from another angle, *object a* is articulated through *jouissance*, if only as a drive. It represents the object of the partial drive as contingent, since it is basically always missed by the drive, which thus continues to reactivate itself. This is why it is best to understand Lacan's "*plus-de-jouir*" (surplus enjoyment) with the equivocal French word *plus*, meaning both "*manque à jouir*" (lack of enjoyment) and the return of *jouissance* via fantasy. Although language (the symbolic) cancels out *jouissance*, the body does not become completely empty of it. There is a return, an insistence from the residue of *jouissance*—the *a*—through fantasy, which then becomes one of the crucial stakes of psychoanalytical treatment. Fantasy acts as a screen against the real pursued in the sexual nonrelationship (again, within the symbolic operation of the pleasure principle), in which case the *object a* of fantasy regulates *jouissance*.

The three facets of the *object a* in Lacan's teaching—the object as imaginary, then symbolic, and finally real—are here merely sketched out. They correspond to a series of moments in the psychoanalytic cure, which the very movement of Lacan's teaching espouses and describes, not as a model of a type of treatment but rather as an x-ray of the treatment of a type (namely, the type Lacan) insofar as this treatment can be generalized beyond the singular case. These conceptual shifts therefore not only accord with a work of theoretical clarification but also bear witness to the manifestations and the aftereffects of psychoanalytical treatment as well as to the effect of freeing which this treatment brings. And here we should keep in mind that the aim of psychoanalytical treatment is connected to the position of the analyst. Analysts work from what they were able to get out of their own analysis; the status analysts give to the object is thus of the utmost importance. Analysts' own analysis enables them to handle transference without identifying with the figures it brings into play. From their analysis, they have obtained knowledge of what has become for them, by the end, their analyst. The analyst, for Lacan, gradually assumes the place of the *object a* in the analytic cure, the movement of which will show the object's function as the cause of desire. One might link this argument to the position of Winnicott (1962), who was able to say that "he always looks forward to the end of each analysis." He added that regardless of the analyst's relationship to the analytic framework, the former is "nevertheless a subjective object for the patient" (p. 166).

Therefore, regarding the position that the analyst occupies in the cure, patients who reveal the place of the transitional object[2] that the analyst holds for them is in contradiction with neither Winnicott nor Lacan. Analysis depends on the position of the analysts, and they are able to hold this position only thanks to their own analysis, an idea Ferenczi (1928) referred to as the second fundamental rule of analysis, one that was equally maintained by Freud. Lacan (1955) defined psychoanalysis as "the treatment one expects from a psychoanalyst" (p. 329). Winnicott's position was not fundamentally different, since he too was able to say that although there is some difficulty in distinguishing between psychotherapy and psychoanalysis, for him the fundamental question was, "Has the therapist had an analytic training or not?" (1958, p. 115).

I would now like to take up two of Lacan's comments that may appear contradictory but that are only paradoxical and can actually help clarify the preceding discussion. In 1967, he concluded a lecture by pointing out that it is important that the mother does not take her child to be the transitional object. Yet, several years later, he remarked that for a woman, a child is *always* the *object a*.

***

A 7-year-old boy comes to my office. He is always scared of being left alone, especially in the evening when he goes to bed but also during the day,

[2] Speaking to her analyst, one patient thus said, "Do you know what I call you? I call you Teddy Bear. Today I said to my friends, I have a meeting with Teddy Bear, etc. It's the name I gave to my first toy when I was a child."

and he has great difficulty allowing his mother to leave. Incidentally, the night before coming to his first meeting, he had a dream that I was stealing his mother. He is always scared of being stolen, of somebody stealing him from his parents and especially from his mother. She tells me that the same morning she left him alone in the car—"for two seconds, just to put a letter in the mailbox"—and he panicked and ran after her because "he was afraid of being stolen." I will not recount the details of the following sessions, but the situation improved rapidly, and, by the third session, he was no longer afraid in the evening. "In bed I can keep myself busy. I play with my stuffed animals now, and I can fall asleep." During the day his fear has also changed. He is no longer afraid of being stolen but that "Mommy will abandon me." This change makes his mother want to speak to me. She tells me that indeed she was very attached to the boy. He used to sleep with her, and she felt touched that he would need her so much when he would come to her bed in the night. She says that in the beginning she could not separate herself from him. She realizes that she had given him a name that reminds her of her favorite stuffed animal from when she was a child. But when he began to walk and especially after he started school, she would sometimes forget him, forget that she was supposed to pick him up, or she would lose him in the supermarket because she was busy shopping and forgot about him. "Is this why," she asks, "he is afraid that I will abandon him? Is he traumatized?"

This mother tells us explicitly that the child occupies for her the place of the transitional object. For her, her son is caught in a process of separation that she herself had never before been able to negotiate. She has always been very "symbiotic," she says, first with her mother and then with her husband. But the child is not a psychotic. With his phobia, he protects himself from what he perceives as his mother's desire to lose him because she is overly attached to him. She is in fact trying to prevent what has already happened—that he let her go. Indeed, weaning was a very bad experience for her. She continued to breastfeed for a very long time and later felt very hurt by the autonomy that the boy attained when he began to walk.

This articulation between separation and the object appears to me particularly obvious in the case of psychotic mothers and their infants. For a time I was in charge of a hospital service that received these mothers and their babies. We know that for these mothers, birth does not properly constitute a separation as such; in other words, the real disconnection of bodies does not constitute a separation in the symbolic sense.

In these relationships, there is a moment that is particularly difficult to negotiate. Winnicott emphasized this in his 1959 article in which he recounted the case of Esther, a patient whose psychotic mother alone took care of her during the first months of her life. After a certain time, the mother began to behave very strangely. After one sleepless night, she began wandering around a field near a canal, watching a former police officer digging. Then she went to the canal and threw the baby in. We will not discuss here—although they are not without importance—both the police agent and that the baby was thrown or dropped, except to notice that "to drop, to let fall" refers to a certain object function of the baby, in the sense in which Lacan calls the child the *object a*. Winnicott referred to this function by saying that if the baby is not held and supported—the concept of holding—it falls "infinitely," which testifies to the particular place the child holds for the mother, compatible with the place the object *a* for Lacan (Winnicott, 1957).

From Lacan's perspective, when the child has the status of the *object a* for the mother, separation is possible only on the condition that this object refers to a lack that is in principle already there for her. This means the mother must assume a third place between herself and the child. Without this indexing there is only real separation, where the object manifests itself as a piece of refuse, as something that must be thrown away because it condensates a limitless, and therefore deadly, *jouissance*. Children can be the *object a* for the mother in the sense that they are a phallicized object. This also means that they are symbolically separate, since the phallus is an operator of separation, an index of lack in the symbolic. The maternal *jouissance* in question therefore implies a symbolic castration, that is, a limit. In the opposite case of a "real" separation, the *jouissance* that concerns the subject is deadly, without limits, beyond the pleasure principle. We can observe this situation in psychosis, where the object is not separated. Lacan even stated that the psychotic has his *objects a* in his pocket, as evidenced by his acoustic–verbal hallucinations. Schreber's main fear was to be left forsaken by his God (Freud, 1911).

We will recall that Winnicott wrote that Esther's mother was able to give the child a good start but that difficulties apparently started when the child sought to become separate from her. For this mother, separation could be accomplished only by a real throwing away and not by a symbolic separation. In fact, during these first months, something of the order of articulation of demand introduces such mothers to the difficult question of otherness. The demand comes only if it has been possible for the baby's crying to become qualified, retrospectively, as a call—that is, if the mother was able to give crying the value of a demand addressed to her.

For this to happen, she must assume a subject in the baby (Vanier, 1989, 1995, 2007). Supposition is not a certainty but rather a belief, an act of faith, an interpretation of this necessary reliability as continued support of being. Supposing a subject implies a place, the place of the Other, from which such supposition can be upheld. The supposed subject is held by the mother, and their combined whole is retrospectively, after the fact of separation, figured as an image of fusion, of symbiosis, an essential part of *holding*. It is in this way that the subject is already there, in the mother, who represents it for herself as separate and, by supposing a knowledge in the child as separate subject, brings it into existence. This position manifests itself for the analyst in the work with autistic children, as is demonstrated in Melanie Klein's analysis of little Dick (Klein, 1930). Meaning is not at first produced by the child, and it returns to the child only if the mother is able to provide it.

Dick was a child treated by Melanie Klein, the son of analysts from the British Psychoanalytic Society. Speaking of his treatment, Frances Tustin said that it was the first cure of an autistic child, well before Leo Kanner introduced the term "autism." Melanie Klein herself said about the case that in the classical analytic situation she interpreted material only when it had been expressed in several different representations. In Dick's case, where the ability to represent the material was lacking, she specified: "I felt obliged to interpret on the grounds of my general knowledge" (1930, p. 246). We go back to a question already raised by Freud, who argued that for the analytic situation to exist, certain psychic structures must already have taken shape and that where they are lacking we must do something else. Klein gave Dick toys—trains, in particular—based on what she knew about his few interests. We recall her first interpretation. She placed a big train, which she called the "daddy train," next to a small train she called "Dick train." She took the train Dick and made it roll toward the station. Then Dick took the train called Dick, made it roll to the window, and said the word "station." Klein interpreted directly, "The station is mommy. Dick is going into mommy" (p. 242). We recall the effect of anxiety that this interpretation incited in the subject. What she did at this moment was to verbalize the Oedipal myth. "She slams the symbolism into him with complete brutality," Lacan commented (1953–1954, p. 81).

It is clear that this case shows a very particular use of theory. It is not an interpretation, because that would require the existence of what Klein's (1930) speech was only trying to create. She started from her theoretical assumptions, and her intervention caused the child to emit his first call, whereas before he had shown no desire to communicate. In speaking to Dick, she presumed a knowledge in his place, a knowledge that supported her theory. She also assumed Dick to be a subject. For these interventions to work, it was of course necessary that there already be something, perhaps a place, something that made it possible for him to hear what she said. We must also assume the existence of another thing, the primordial Other, who must not be lacking and with whom one has begun something, from whom one has received the first mark. Between a mother and a child there is not only care and feeding; there is also *jouissance*, as Freud noted. There is also language, and the two are connected. The early days of life are marked by the mother's coming and going, her absence and presence, linked as they are to the reduction of hunger's returning claim. To this configuration, which always returns to the same place, will be addressed a call, qualified as such by the Other, the core of a demand that appears only in her absence, as we see happen to Dick calling his nanny at the end of the first session (Vanier, 1993).

The child as a subject is upheld by the mother's assumption and is constituted in this way. On the condition of supposing that the child knows—knows, that is, the object that it could demand—the mother is able to transform its screams into a call. Primarily because she assumes there is a demand, she can, retrospectively, interpret the child's screams as addressed to her, as a call that was made to her. It is therefore difficult to situate this first time of the call, recognized as such by the Other, chronologically. We find the same function of the presumption of knowledge again at the heart of the analytic relation in transference but also in all relationships of oneself to another. What disappears in psychosis is not knowledge but presumption and supposition. Instead, there is certainty. Supposition introduces a third dimension into a dual relationship and testifies to its presence.

On the other hand, demand presupposes a different relationship to the Other because of the possibility that something can be detached and circulate as an object of exchange. In the case of some schizophrenic mothers, we see that, among other problems of the identificatory relationship they can have with their babies, feeding is often regulated by the mother's own feelings of hunger rather than the infant's manifestations. When I asked one of these mothers why she did not feed her baby (he was 1 month old and on that day had not been fed for 8 hours), she answered: "But I am not hungry." This situation can be fragmenting for these mothers because they find themselves as if caught up in what introduces itself as a demand to which they are unable to respond, since demand necessitates an object from which one can be separated without being destroyed.

These mothers testify that, for them, separation on the symbolic level and, therefore, the constitution of the object are impossible, as is any transitional space between themselves and the child. The object cannot be established as separate. Separation itself, not having been symbolized, threatens the subject's very integrity and is likely to push her toward fragmentation. The transitional object is an incarnation of the *object a* and the transitional space its manifestation. *Object a* represents the place of the third, just as the transitional object functions as the third element between a mother and a child.

I hope to have somewhat contributed to bringing us closer to "the problems of separation and loss of the primary object that accompany the birth of the self" (Kirshner, 2009, p. 11). In Winnicott's transitional object, Lacan encountered the limit of the possibility to symbolize much earlier than he came to such conclusion himself. Not all is symbolizable. A part of *jouissance* remains, Lacan concluded, and manifests itself as being connected to an object that is inherently nonsymbolizable and that the symbolic can never deal with completely. In this way, in the psychoanalytic situation, in the space where the psychoanalyst and the analysand are "playing," certain objects will appear as if to concretize the transitory endpoints of the cure. I am thinking of two very long-term patients, who carried books around with them, inspired, they acknowledged, by the books in my library. Each of them had procured for himself the works that he had noticed there. For a very long time, these analysands would bring their books everywhere, one unable to finish his, the other keeping it to reread certain passages—real "stuffed animals." The books were, of course, objects of transference with which they got stuck but that also had a signifying value. One of them was Albert Camus's *The Stranger,* and the signifier "stranger" was very important in the patient's own history; the other chose Friedrich Nietzsche's *Thus Spoke Zarathustra,* and for this patient, each of my (rare) words had the value of an oracle.

These are examples of moments of resistance that the movement of the cure will, in most cases, overcome. Without going into details, which would allow us to specify each of these patients clinically, we can reasonably argue that these objects, which were both found and created (since the act of choosing them had the value of creation), assumed their place in the movement of regression instituted by the analytic process. On the one hand, these objects are typically elements that the analysand finds or assumes in the analyst and that support the transference. On the other hand, they also have a defensive function, protecting the subject against what orients the analysis as a process of separation. If we look carefully, we can see that this type of phenomenon is rather common in psychoanalytic cures, where it is often classified as identification with the analyst, something that the cure will gradually undo. But it is not without importance that an object is used as material for the transference. The fact that in my examples the object was a book was telling, especially if one remembers that, for Winnicott (1951–1953), a word naming the transitional object "appears very early." He added, "The name given by the infant to these earliest objects is often significant" (p.). The object is therefore tied to a name. In this case it was tied undoubtedly to the word "stranger" for the first patient and "spoke" for the second, in addition to the figure of the ideal father. These objects functioned as manifestations of *object a*, objects of desire the subject located in the Other. They constituted a defense against what orients each analysis, namely, the "failure" of the Other at the basis of the fundamental movement of disillusion, which the subject nevertheless continues to resist.

REFERENCES

Ferenczi, S. (1928). The elasticity of psycho-analytical technique. In *Final contributions to the problems and methods of psycho-analysis*. London : Karnac, 1994.

Freud, S. (1895). Project for a scientific psychology. In J. Strachey (Ed. & Trans.), *The standard edition of the complete psychological works of Sigmund Freud* (Vol. 1). London: Hogarth, 1966.

Freud, S. (1905). *Three essays on the theory of sexuality.* In J. Strachey (Ed & Trans.), *The standard édition of the complete psychological Works of Sigmund Freud* (Vol.7). London : Hogarth, 1966.

Freud, S. (1911). *Psycho-analytic notes on an autobiographical account of a case of paranoïa (Dementia paranoïdes).* In J. Strachey (Ed. & Trans.), *The standard édition of the complete psychological Works of Sigmund Freud* (Vol.12). London : Hogarth, 1966.

Freud, S. (1920). *Beyond the pleasure principle.* In J. Strachey (Ed & Trans.), *The standard édition of the complete psychological Works of Sigmund Freud* (Vol.18). London : Hogarth, 1966.

Kirshner, L. (2009). Working between Winnicott and Lacan. Paper presented at 46th Congress, International Psychoanalytic Association, Chicago, IL. Unpublished.

Klein, M. (1930). The importance of symbol-formation in the development of the Ego. In *Contributions to psycho-analysis.* London: Hogarth, 1950.

Lacan, J. (1953–1954). *Les Écrits technique de Freud: Le Séminaire, livre I* (J.-A. Miller, Ed.). Paris: Seuil, 1975.

Lacan, J. (1955). Variantes de la cure-type. In *Écrits*. Paris: Seuil, 1955.

Lacan, J. (1956–1957). *La relation d'objet: Le Séminaire, livre IV* (J.-A. Miller, Ed.). Paris: Seuil, 1994.

Lacan, J. (1958–1959). *Le désir et son interprétation : Le Séminaire, livre VI.* Unpublished.

Lacan, J. (1960). Remarque sur le rapport de Daniel Lagache: "Psychanalyse et structure de la personnalité." In *Écrits*. Paris: Seuil, 1966.

Lacan, J. (1964). *Les Quatre concepts fondamentaux de la psychanalyse: Le Séminaire, livre XI.* (J.-A. Miller, Ed.). Paris: Seuil, 1973.

Lacan J. (1967). Allocution sur les psychoses de l'enfant. In *Autres écrits*. Paris: Seuil, 2001.

Lacan, J. (1967–1968). *L'acte psychanalytique: Le Séminaire, livre XV*. Unpublished.

Lacan, J. (1971). Intervention sur l'exposé de S. Leclaire. In *Lettres del'École freudienne, 9*. Paris, 1972.

Lacan, J. (1975). *Entretiens*. London: Institut français. Unpublished.

Vanier, A. (1989). *Mère psychotique et nourrisson*. Lecture at the W.A.I.P.A.D. Congress, Lugano (Switzerland). Unpublished.

Vanier, A. (1993). Autisme et théorie. In *Hommage à Frances Tustin*. Saint André de Cruzières: Audit.

Vanier A. (1995). Contribution à la métapsychologie du temps des processus psychiques. Questions posées par l'observation et la clinique infanto-juvénile. Doctoral thesis (Dir. P. Fedida), Université Paris Diderot—Paris 7. Unpublished.

Vanier, A. (2000). *Lacan* (S. Fairfield, Trans.). New York: Other Press.

Vanier, A. (2006). Mouvements de l'objet. In *Mensuel de l'École de Psychanalyse des Forums du Champ lacanien, 18*. Paris, 2006.

Vanier, A. (2007). Consequences of clinical experience with psychotic mother and their babies. In L. Caldwell (Ed.), *Winnicott and the psychoanalytic tradition: Interpretation and other psychoanalytic issues*. London: Karnac Books.

Winnicott, D. W. (1953). Transitional objects and transitional phenomena. In *Through paediatrics to psycho-analysis* (pp. 229–242). New York: Basic Books, 1975.
Winnicott D. W. (1957). On the contribution of direct child observation to psycho-analysis. In *The maturational processes and facilitating environment*. Madison, CT: International Universities Press, 1965.
Winnicott D. W. (1958). Child analysis in the latency period. In *The maturational processes and facilitating environment*. Madison, CT: International Universities Press.
Winnicott D. W. (1959). The effect of psychotic parents on the emotional development of the child. In *The family and individual development*. London: Routledge.
Winnicott D. W. (1962). The aims of psycho-analytic treatment. In *The maturational processes and facilitating environment*. Madison, CT: International Universities Press.
Winnicott, D. W. (1971). *Playing and reality*. London: Tavistock.

Chapter 7

The space of transition between Winnicott and Lacan

Jeanne Wolff Bernstein

> And yet how I do feel myself supported by and in agreement with your inquiries, in their content and in their style. Does not the "transitional object" all of whose merits I have shown to those close to me, indicate the site at which, previously, that distinction of desire in relation to need is marked?
>
> Jacques Lacan (1990, p. 77)

Jacques Lacan was not known to be terribly complimentary to his fellow psychoanalysts, British and American ones alike. It is all the more intriguing that Lacan would find such complimentary and endearing words to write to Donald Winnicott from his summer residence in St. Tropez on the subject of the transitional object. In contrast to Michael Balint, whom Lacan frequently cited with a great deal of irony in his first seminar on "Freud's Papers on Technique," Winnicott is referenced by Lacan with genuine respect and curiosity. What accounts for this difference, and what was it that captivated Lacan about Winnicott's work, and in particular, about his concept of the transitional object?

Three years before, Lacan commissioned a translation of Winnicott's paper about the transitional object along with Susan Isaac's paper on fantasy for the fifth volume of *La Psychanalyse* in 1959. He cited Winnicott for the first time in his 1956–1957 seminar "La Relation de l'Objet." In the chapter in which Lacan attempted to explain what an object is and what the loss of an object means, he introduced Winnicott as the analyst who describes the function of the mother as absolutely crucial in the apprehension of the child's reality. Lacan explained that Winnicott replaced the dialectics of the impersonal pleasure and the reality principle with the two living figures of the mother and the baby. Lacan (1956) wrote, "We have identified the pleasure principle with a certain object relationship, namely the relation with the maternal breast, while we have identified the reality principle with the fact that the child has to learn how to let go of it" (p. 34).[1]

[1] All translations by the author.

Frustration does become the key for the introduction of the reality principle, since it is the frustration at the mother's breast that becomes its source. With a slight air of irony, Lacan (1956) observed that Winnicott considers the mother's attuned handling of the baby to be of utmost importance for things to go well later on:

> She has to be there precisely in the moment when she needs to be there, in other words, she has to place the real object in the moment of the child's delirious hallucination to make up/fill up for what is not there. From the beginning, there is no room in the ideal mother–child relationship for a distinction between the hallucinated maternal breast which rises into view through the principle of the primary system along the notions we have of it, and the encounter with the real object about which we are talking here. (p. 34)

Unlike Melanie Klein, who, in Lacan's view mistook the "real" object for the material one and built on it an elaborate system of good and bad object relations, Winnicott, in Lacan's estimation, understood the infant's access to the mother's breast to be of an imaginary nature. As the mother gradually frustrates the infant and initiates the decline from a perfectly attuned mother to becoming a good enough mother, the objects with which the infant fills itself up to make up for this loss are imaginary. The lost object can never be found or refound, but the access to the lost object remains illusory. In a subsequent lecture 2 months later, Lacan referenced Winnicott again, focusing on the ways the infant separates from the mother. He argued that Winnicott realized that the infant creates a transitional object to separate from the mother and that it is the frustration with the object that produces the imaginary realm that Lacan had previously described in his 1949 essay on the mirror stage. He commented, "The object, as much as it is created through frustration, leads us to admit the *autonomy of the imaginative production* in its relationship to the image of the body. It is an ambiguous object, which is between the two, where one can neither speak of reality nor unreality" (1957, pp. 126–127).

Unlike Klein, who hypothesized the mother's good and bad breasts as the object of the infant's idealized or persecutory fantasies (based on real experiences of plenitude or deprivation), Winnicott emphasized the infant's separate imaginary creation of transitional objects to have access to reality. Lacan found this Winnicottian conception much more in line with his way of thinking than Klein's good and bad internal objects, because it highlighted the infant's production of fantasy rather than the relationship to the good and bad object. Winnicott's focus on the infant's fantasmatic creation also harkened back to Sigmund Freud's key notion of fantasy from the 1905 *Three Essays on Sexuality*, which had become so instrumental in Lacan's concept of the *fantasm*.

In that early essay, Freud suggested that the sexual drive is not an instinct but a drive whose reality is aberrant, since it cannot be located in either the instinctual or natural realm. Using the oral drive as a model to illustrate the workings of a drive, Freud showed how a particular pleasure unfolds in the infant autonomously, independent of the pleasure of nourishment. Using thumb-sucking (*lutschen*) as an example, Freud (1905) argued that sucking reveals an independent source of pleasure that derives from nourishment but then detaches itself. Thumb-sucking, he wrote, "appears already in early infancy and may continue into maturity, or even persists all through life. It consists in the rhythmic repetition of a sucking contact by the mouth (or lips). There is no question of the purpose of this procedure being the taking of nourishment" (pp. 179–180).

However, Freud quickly recognized that the purpose of nourishment is delayed, because something else installed itself in the activity of sucking, namely, the sexual pleasure that goes along with the intake of nourishment. This idea of delay constitutes, as Toboul (2006) stated:

> A memorable moment in the history of psychoanalysis since this is the first proof of infantile sexuality. The sexual distinguishes itself from a special satisfaction, different from the satisfaction of nourishment. It even supposes a delay of the nourishment activity and produces an autonomy of a new source of pleasure. (p. 3)

After Freud (1905) had firmly established that the need for nourishment is clearly detached from the need for sexual satisfaction, he also argued that no necessary relationship exists between the object and the drive.

> It has been brought to our attention that we have been in the habit of regarding the connection between the sexual instinct and the sexual object as more intimate than it in fact is. Experience of the cases that are considered abnormal has shown us that in them the sexual instinct and the sexual object are merely soldered together (*verlötet*). ... It seems probable that the sexual instinct is in the first instance independent of its object; nor is its origin likely to be due to its object's attractions. (pp. 147–148)

In this pivotal phrase, Freud underscored that no direct relationship exists between the object and the drive but that a *fantasm* installs itself, around which the infant attempts to deal with the loss of the object. Like Freud, Lacan insisted on the concept of fixation and argued that the *objet a* was fixated to something partial; the *fantasm* succeeds in articulating in some fashion how the drive engages the object and functions as the real motor of the unconscious. The aim of the drive is to obtain satisfaction, but not so much through the object as through the *fantasm* attached to the object.

Hence, the subject is intensely fixated on his or her *fantasm* (as perverse, abject, or depressing and humiliating it may be) to avoid losing the fundamental source of his or her unconscious pleasure or *jouissance* attached to the object of the drive.

What interested Lacan in Winnicott's description of the transitional realm between the mother and the infant was that this in between realm is a space of reality and nonreality, of "demiexistence," which Lacan delineated as the imaginary realm. Winnicott described this fused, intertwined, semipsychotic realm as the temporary state of "primary maternal preoccupation" in which the good enough mother starts off with an almost complete adaptation to her infant's needs. Winnicott (1956) remarked:

> I do not believe that it is possible to understand the functioning of the mother at the very beginning of the infant's life without seeing that she must be able to reach this state of heightened sensitivity, almost an illness to recover from it .... The mother who develops this state that I have called "primary maternal preoccupation" provides a setting for the infant's constitution to begin to make itself evident, for the developmental tendencies to start to unfold, and for the infant to experience spontaneous movement and become the owner of the sensations that are appropriate to this early phase of life. (pp. 302–303)

Elsewhere in this central essay, Winnicott (1956) argued that this way of preparing the infant sufficiently for "going on being" was the basis for constructing the ego and that this "early build-up of the ego is silent" (p. 304). Premature impingements on this silent ego build-up lead to traumatic failures and evoke threats of annihilation for the infant. It is only the gradual letting go of the mother, the gradual measured frustration on the part of the mother, that allows infants to separate and form their own subjective position. Winnicott is never quite clear about how this frustration is to occur and how the mother is to separate gradually from her baby. At least in descriptions that sometimes sound like definitive prescriptions for good enough mothering, Winnicott did not think of the figure of the father as one who helps the mother to separate from the infant and whose task it might be to disrupt the mother–infant dyad. Unlike Lacan, who insisted that it was the task of the symbolic father to intercede and to cut the mother–infant dyad so that the infant was not left at the mercy of her maternal *jouissance*, Winnicott left this symbolic task to the mother and, in so doing, reduced the underlying triadic oedipal structure to a binary one. From a Lacanian perspective, the frustration the father creates on behalf of both mother and infant is not seen as threatening but rather as structuring the infant's burgeoning subjectivity.

Luepnitz (Chapter 1) has often remarked on the glaring lack of the role of the father in Winnicott's work. Whether to see the mother–infant relation as a good enough, sensitively attuned dyad or as a triadic structure that is mediated through the fantasy of the phallus has significant implications for the position of the analyst. Winnicott's work, Philips (1988) observed, "was devoted to the recognition and description of the good mother, and the use of the mother-infant relationship as the model of psychoanalytic treatment. He often took for granted that what mothers did naturally, 'what in fact cannot be taught' was a model for the skill of the psychoanalyst" (p. 3). Lacan's insistence that any dyadic relationship is mediated through a third and that the symbolic father exists from the beginning as a major component of the psychic world of the mother and leads to a formulation of the analytic role that is quite different from Winnicott's naturally learned maternal role. Lacan alluded to this different view of the analytic role in the 1956 "L'Acte Psychanalytique," when he stated that the unawareness of the third in object relation theory leads to "an imperialism of identification." "Since you can identify yourself with me, and I can identify myself with you," he wrote, "it is surely the me (*moi*) of us both which is the best adaptation to reality, which is the best model. In the final account, in a pure ideal state, the progress of an analysis turns into an identification with the me (*moi*) of the analyst" (1956, p. 26). Lacan's argument that the analyst not take on the role of the "subject supposed to know," in which the analysand engages him in the transference relationship, stems from his deeply held belief that analysts trained in the object relations model encouraged an identification with themselves as a goal of the cure.

Lacan (1962–1963) resumed his dialogue with Winnicott in his Seminar X, "L'Angoisse" (Anxiety). In this work, Lacan presented his theory of the *objet a* as the object that causes desire rather than being the object of desire. He explained the powerful dynamics of the *objet a* as the object that causes desire and also fascinates and horrifies the subject when directly confronted with it. Here, he introduced the important idea that the *objet a* is a *cessible* (cedable) object or, more true to the French, but worse in its English translation, "give-upable." Interestingly, the French *cessible* can also be translated as "transferrable." Thus, Lacan wrote, "This characteristic of the transferrable object (*objet cessible*) is such an important characteristic of *a* that I would ask you your kindness to follow me in a brief review to see whether this characteristic marks all the forms of *a* that we have enumerated" (p. 362). In this review, he demonstrated that the most critical anxiety for the infant is the moment that the infant has to give up the nipple of the mother's breast. Rather than following Ranks's steps and arguing that the birth trauma leaves behind the most significant traces of anxiety, Lacan believed that the weaning of the mother's breast constituted the most frightening source of anxiety for the infant. Why the weaning, one may ask? He argued, "The most decisive moment in the anxiety involved, the weaning anxiety, is not so much that the breast is missing on a particular occasion when the subject needs it, but rather that the little child gives up the breast to which he is appended, as a part of himself" (p. 362).

Lacan (1962–1963) humbly mentioned that he was not the only one to have observed this crucial moment but that Edmund Bergler had also already stated that "the breast forms part of the nourishing individual, and that he does not find himself, but is stuck onto the mother, as I already told you in an imagined expression" (p. 362). Here Lacan referred to a much neglected book, *The Basic Neurosis* (1949/1977) by Bergler, a Viennese analyst and colleague of Freud, who fell into oblivion after he immigrated to New York in 1937. Bergler essentially regarded masochism as the basic neurosis from which all other neurotic behaviors stemmed. In particular, he asserted that infants want to maintain a blissful, passive existence and hence experience any intervention from the outside as an intrusion that disrupts their omnipotent sense of themselves. In *The Basic Neurosis*, he defined infants' omnipotent wish to make everything part of themselves as "autarchic," as, for instance, when babies go on a hunger strike and wish to starve themselves to death, in cases when no intestinal problems can be discovered:

> Out of sheer consistency, the child would "autarchically" starve to death. This however, is counteracted by the discovery of a new "libidinous pleasure" experienced during sucking. Still there are reasons for the assumption (Freud) that the child conceives of the breast (bottle) as part of his own body, a modified continuation of the autarchic fantasy. (p. 15)

With Winnicott's 1951 paper, "Transitional Objects and Transitional Phenomena," the emphasis shifted away from the autarchic wish itself to the environment that enabled infants to have such an autarchic fantasy. In that paper, Winnicott described the crucial role of the mother who provides an omnipotent illusion so that infants cannot distinguish between internal and external reality. He said:

> The mother, at the beginning, by an almost 100 percent adaptation, affords the infant the opportunity for the *illusion* that her breast is part of the infant. It is, as it were, under magical control .... In another language, the breast is created by the infant over and over again out of the infant's capacity to love or (one can say) out of need. A subjective phenomenon develops in the baby which we call the mother's breast. (pp. 238–239)

However, rather than contemplating the effects of the withdrawal of the breast, Lacan pushed Bergler's and Winnicott's observations to their logical conclusion by arguing that infants are giving up a part of themselves and, in so doing, identify with a lost part of themselves. In other words, if infants have made the mother's breast a part of themselves, they experience the loss of the breast as a loss of themselves and not of the mother. This "transferable object," which Lacan equated with Winnicott's transitional object, led him to the important conclusion that a primordial identification takes place prior to the mirror stage in which infants identify with a lost part of themselves. This constitutes a prespecular identificatory moment for infants, long before they identify themselves with their alienating mirror image and mistake that mirror image for themselves.

Thus, Lacan (1962–1963) reused Winnicott's transitional object not as a means to illustrate the imaginary realm of the transitional object, as he had done previously, but as a means to illustrate how the object becomes a separable, transferable object. In a sense, Lacan remained truer to Winnicott's idea than Winnicott himself when he realized that infants lose a part of themselves. Infants are faced with the object in front of themselves from which they have to separate, and, while they experience that part as a part of themselves, what they let go of has nonetheless a part of the Other embedded in it. This part of the maternal body that infants have to let go of and that infants mistake as part of themselves precedes the constitution of an object and the establishment of infants' subjectivity. This "something" of the body of the mOther precedes the constitution of the subject, and it is around this "transferable" object, which will become the *objet a*, that infants create a basic *fantasm*. This *fantasm* protects them from the initial primary loss, from that part of the Other that infants had mistaken to be part of themselves. Infants lose something of themselves and are now faced with an object that carries something of their body.

Lacan's formula of the *fantasm S* (*barre*) ($ ◇ a) a illustrates how there exists first a circulation between subjects and the part of themselves that they have lost. This constitutes their primary identity before they find in the Other bodily substitutes for the lost part of themselves. Through the circulation of fantasy, divided subjects are hooked onto a particular *objet a*, which is the remainder that has escaped symbolization and thereby been left outside the constitution of the subject in the field of the Other. As we know, subjects are fixated in their cause of desire on this particular *objet a*, which determines how their desire is structured. Harari (2001) summarized:

> The *objet a* does not appear as proposed to the subject, summoned by desire, but, rather, on the contrary, it is what is located in the imaginary, behind as it were, desire itself, causing it .... The *objet a* from behind one's desire, imprints, imposes, and directs the itinerary of desire (pp. 66, 68).

The *objet a* also represents a response to the paradox Freud left behind when he spoke of the lost and partial object. Since the *objet a* is separable, constituted in the primary moment of separation from the mother through which subjects construct themselves, they always refers back to the basic lack that was constitutive of their separate, subjective existence and that produces a partial object. This necessary lack, engendered through separation from the mother's body, pushes children to substitute words or signifiers for her loss, but the meanings that become constructed around this loss produce a remainder that reminds infants as subject to become that something is lacking and forever lost in this moment of symbolization.

In *Ecrits* (1966) and in *The Four Fundamental Concepts of Psychoanalysis* (1973), Lacan played with the Latin root of separation. "*Separare*, separating, ends here in *se parere*, engendering oneself .... One should simply realize that this slippage is grounded in the fact that they are both paired with the function of *pa*" (1966, p. 716).[2] By playing upon the double meaning of separating and giving birth to oneself, Lacan focused on the paradox that the infant gives birth to himself in the moment of separation.

> But what he thus fills is not the lack (*faille*) he encounters in the Other, but rather, first of all, the lack, that results from the constitutive loss of one of his parts, by which he turns out to be made of two parts. Therein lies the twist whereby separation represents the return of alienation. For the subject operates *with* his own loss, which brings him back to his departure. (pp. 716, 844)

Lacan identified four kinds of *objets a*: the gaze, the voice, the feces, and the breast, which serve as memorials of this early loss to symbolization. In that one aspect, the *objet a* functions much like a fetish, which, as Freud (1927) wrote, "...sets up a memorial to itself (the horror of castration) in the creation of this substitute" (p. 154). Unlike Klein's internal object, which has more literal qualities based on good and bad internalized object relations, the *objet a* cannot be found in a relationship. Instead, *the objet a* can be only momentarily apprehended in a gaze, a tone of voice, a smell, or a fleeting sensation, markers of the early primordial loss of a part of the mother's body, mistaken for his own body. In other words, the *objet a* is a compelling marker that pushes the subject to be drawn to substitutes, which hold the potential illusion of fulfilling the constitutive lack, only to be reminded again and again that this lack is not fulfilled.

Lacan (1967–1968) returned one more time to Winnicott in his seminar "L'Acte Psychanalytique." Curiously enough, he was interested in Winnicott's concepts of the true and false selves, even though Lacan rarely, if ever, used the term "self." Yet he posed the question whether Winnicott's true self has some kind of subjective truth embedded within it that comes close to the subjective truth that he is also searching for in an analytic treatment. Lacan

---

[2] Fink maintains in his new translation of the completed *Ecrits* the page numbers of Lacan's original text.

believed that he had found in Winnicott an analytic partner, insofar as both believed that the true subject is installed behind a false being that has to be uncovered and liberated during the psychoanalytic process. For Winnicott, a false self develops when infants going on being meet too many environmental impingements prematurely and then are forced to hide their spontaneous emotions, thoughts, and sensations. A false self becomes created in response to and in compliance with an overly narcissistic or depressive or unavailable mother who for her own selfish reasons cannot be attuned to the needs of the child. Winnicott (quoted in Newman, 1995) commented:

> At the beginning, the mother's adaptation is either "good enough" or not "good enough." In the first case, the mother enjoys, sees and attends without too great a strain. The baby can, omnipotently, *create* the world. The breast is offered in such a way that the baby gets used to the experience of having created it. It's the magic, the essential illusion. In the second case, the mother cannot adapt—so that one might expect the child to die. But the infant lives; only falsely. The clinical picture is of general irritability, feed disturbance and insult. The infant pretends to be enjoying itself. (p. 418)

Lacan translated Winnicott's false self as a "frozen self" that gradually thaws into a true self by the Winnicottian analyst providing a good enough therapeutic environment that gradually helps patients come out of their protective or false shell. In the Winnicottian framework, the analyst encourages a gradual regression to an early environmental state of being in which patients finally have an experience of genuine attunement. In this regressive process, patients' genuine needs and desires are thought to emerge eventually, since they are finally met by the figure of the analyst who creates the space for patients' repressed desires and spontaneous gestures. However, while Lacan finds common ground with Winnicott's notion of a false self, he parts company with Winnicott when it comes to the "true self." In *L'Acte Psychanalytique*, he suggested somewhat mockingly that Winnicott must hide himself as the good enough analyst behind the discovery of the true self. With his emphasis on the provision of a good enough environment, Winnicott held out the possibility that a true self could finally be achieved if the analyst waited long enough and did not overwhelm the patient with premature interpretations. The patient's discovery of a good enough, attuned, and patient analyst held out the possibility that the "frozen self" could be repaired and a true self restored. Not so in the Lacanian world.

From a Lacanian perspective, the goal of analysis does not lie in the discovery of a true self waiting silently to be detected but rather in the unearthing of the *object* a that lies behind the subject and all of its imaginary identifications with the Other that serve to fill up the hole left by caesura from the Other. Instead of filling this void with a better, more attuned Other, Lacan stated that subjective freedom could come only with the acknowledgment of the fundamental lack that was necessary for the constitution of the subject. In the last part of an analysis, patients must come to terms with the idea that their whole subjectivity was constructed through, by, and for an Other, yet this Other (as subjects imagine them to be) does not exist. As this Other falls by the wayside, subjects have to recognize that there is no Other who holds the strings to their being, no Other through whom they can determine their desire. Deprived of all illusory identifications, subjects come face to face with a situation, reminiscent of the primary separation when infants also had to come face to face with a part that infants thought to be themselves. While Winnicott's truth lies in the true self, Lacan's truth lies in the destitution of the subject and the liquidations of all imaginary identifications. Thus, while both started on a similar path, Winnicott, Lacan concluded, returned to an imaginary level of functioning by revealing himself to be the good enough object behind the true self. Lacan (1967–1968) wrote:

> Behind the false self there is waiting what? The true to start up again? Who does not see, when we already have in analytic theory this *Real Ich,* this *Lust ICH,* this ego, this id, all the references already articulated enough to define our field that the definition of this self represents nothing other than as it is avowed in the text with *false* and *true*, the truth? But who does not also see that there is no other *true-self* behind this situation than Mr. Winnicott himself, who places himself there as the presence of the truth. (p. 74)

Lacan maintained that Winnicott, instead of accepting lack as the ultimate truth behind this false sense of being, filled up the hole again and expanded the circle of illusion and disillusionment. While Winnicott offered his good enough being to draw out the true self, Lacan considered the nothingness of his own being the greatest gift he could offer to the Other.

The last officially recorded time that Lacan returned to a close reading of Winnicott's work was in 1967. One is left to wonder why he never commented on one of Winnicott's last pivotal texts, *The Use of an Object*, published in 1968. In this text Winnicott made the paradoxical distinction between relating to an object and using an object. In relating to an object, individuals use the object subjectively and ruthlessly; the object can simply exist as a subjective and imagined entity. In using the object, on the other hand, subjects have destroyed the object over and over again and have placed the object outside of subjects' omnipotent control and projective sphere. Winnicott (1969) stated, "This thing that there is between relating and use is the subject's placing of the object outside the area of the subject's omnipotent control; that is, the subject's perception of the object as an external phenomenon, not as a projective entity, in fact recognition of it as an entity in its own right" (p. 105). In the same paper, he wrote that "we all hope that our patients will finish with us and forget us, and that they will find living itself to be the therapy that makes sense" (p. 103).

Thus, as much as Lacan thought that Winnicott was holding the good enough analyst up as the object with whom the analysand would eventually identify in the end of a treatment, Winnicott might not have been positioning himself, after all, as such an illusory object since he, like Lacan, hoped that the analysand would lose his investment in the figure of the analyst and find his subjective freedom through the destruction of the Other at the end of an analysis.

Lacan was a surprisingly attentive reader of Winnicott and was clearly intrigued by his work. He called him "the excellent author ... the author to whom we owe one of the most crucial discoveries" (1967–1968, p. 72). Unfortunately, the same cannot be said for Winnicott, who did not cite Lacan in his work. Despite their uneven attention to one another, however, I think their works can be compared best to the structure of a helix where separate strands intertwine, then depart from one another, forming a three-dimensional spiral.

Winnicott's transitional object and Lacan's *objet a* constitute one important contact point that influenced Lacan's thinking throughout many years. Yet other points of contact of which Winnicott and Lacan were possibly unaware exist as well. Both, for instance, wrote about the mirror relationship, with Winnicott privileging the mother's containing function and Lacan emphasizing the alienating misrecognition underlying the mirror's completing function. Another connecting point in this imagined Winnicottian–Lacanian helix can be found between Winnicott's intriguing idea that an "incommunicado element" at the center of each person is to be regarded as sacred and most worthy of preservation. In *Communicating and Not Communicating* (1963), Winnicott wrote, "Although healthy persons communicate and enjoy communicating, the other fact is equally true, that *each individual is an isolate, permanently unknown, in fact unfound*" (p. 187). It is as if Winnicott speaks here about the kernel of the real, the very hole in the symbolic texture that is shielded by veils of fantasies and around which the *objet a* circles. With Winnicott in the background, one can better comprehend Lacan's idea of the hole left by primary repression and how it is constitutive of subjectivity. "Primary repression," Verhaeghe (2004) writes, "always implies a failure: something cannot be put into words. This something that remains stuck at another level of functioning as the core of the unconscious, from which it continues to exert an influence" (p. 189). With Winnicott's idea of the permanent isolate that can never be touched, we come to see that both Lacan and Winnicott were not far apart in conceptualizing the central dynamic structure of the unconscious as a hole or gap or as an incommunicado element. Their depictions of a void at the center of human subjectivity permitted Lacan and Winnicott to describe in their own distinct ways the fundamental agonies and anxieties associated with the rawness of the subject's divided existence.

Last, there is the once again surprising encounter between Winnicott's idea that "the clinical fear of breakdown is the fear of a breakdown that has been already experienced" (in Newman, 1963, p. 61) and Lacan's concept that an inevitable loss has already always happened, long before we could become aware of it, and that only through the *après-coup* are we able to recognize the effects of what has already shaped us. This conjuncture becomes especially poignant when we look one more time at the "transferable object." The function of the "transferable object" is to transport something very primary of the identity of the other's body. This "something," which one takes from the Other but which one all along believed to be a part of oneself, stands in for the constitution of the subject. In a way, one could say that the loss one anticipates in the future has already taken place, and it is this loss from the Other (taken as oneself) that has already shaped the hole of subjectivity. Winnicott regularly emphasized infants' absolute dependency on the parent without whose care no infant can survive. In his absolute dependency on an Other, infants hover on the brink of unthinkable anxieties, which Winnicott later identified as terrifying agonies. They are agonies because babies are neither emotionally nor cognitively developed enough in its isolate being to know that there is an Other to mitigate their fears. The terrors of going to pieces and of falling apart or into a void have already been experienced by babies, yet the adult will know them only once they have reexperienced them, not as fears of the future but as fears already lived through in the past.

Even though both Lacan and, as we can now see, Winnicott were aware of the lack that lies at the core of subjectivity, their clinical practices diverged. For Winnicott, it was important to build and provide a "good enough" therapeutic environment so that the subject's true self could slowly unfold and space be created for spontaneous gestures. He was careful not to impinge on his patients and to overload them with transference interpretations. "I think," he commented, "I interpret mainly to let the patient know the limits of my understanding. The principle is that it is the patient and only the patient who has the answers" (in Newman, 1995, p. 398). Nonetheless, he thought that the void patients would eventually encounter within themselves would need to be filled up by a therapeutic figure who invites and accepts their need for regression to a level of need to resume a developmental process that fosters the growth of a true self. By contrast, Lacan, while agreeing with Winnicott's nonimpinging, anti-Kleinian stance, did not place the analyst in a reparative role, but in a "blind" one. It was the analysand's recognition of the internal void and the liquidation of all identificatory relationships that could lead to the liberation of subjects' unconscious desires and, ultimately, to their own subjective truth. In Lacanian child and adult analysis, the question does not focus so much on the goodness or badness of the parental environment but on the position that children hold in the fantasy world of the mother and father. Instead of conceiving of the cure in reparative terms, Lacan saw the acceptance of frustration and of separateness as crucial first steps toward enabling children to internalize the structuring role of the symbolic father as a means of finding their own separate desire.

Imagine a replay of the *Fort-Da* game with Freud's grandson, standing in his crib. This time, Freud, Winnicott, and Lacan have come together to watch Ernst play with his wooden spool in his crib once again. Ernst throws the spool over the edge of the crib, exclaiming o-o-o, which Freud translates into *Fort*. As Ernst pulls the wooden spool back, he pleasurably exclaims *Da*. All three analysts are watching the same play, yet each is privileging a different aspect of the game, converging in the end on a *Rashomon* effect of the *Fort-Da* game. Freud, as we remember, fixes his gaze on Ernst's capacity to symbolize his mother's absence and presence through the appearance and disappearance of the wooden spool, substituting words for the appearance and departure of his mother. Winnicott, we can imagine, expands the circumference of the playing field, casually, but acutely, observing the mother's reaction to and containment of her son's mysterious play. His focus shifts to the wooden spool and the ways Ernst handles it as a transitional object, negotiating the me-and not-me world for himself. Lacan, we can suppose, listens to Ernst's initial speech, translating his sounds of o-o-o and of *da* into melodies of loss and sacrifice rather than tropes of mastery. The acknowledgment of loss, Lacan might argue, is necessary for the child to claim his own subjectivity to speak his own desire in the absence of his object of desire. While Winnicott may focus on Ernst playing out the role of the possessor of the wooden spool, Lacan sees Ernst sliding into his subjectivity by reclaiming the lost object through his words. As Ernst may master the experience of being separated from the object, he becomes subjugated to the symbolic order. In forming the sounds of o-o-o and *da*, the child renders the mother present and in so doing gives birth to the symbol. In the end, it is an absence Winnicott and Lacan are both observing, yet their interpretation of what this loss means for the infant to become adult takes a radically different course, with Winnicott privileging the good enough environment and Lacan emphasizing the subject's necessary alienation into language and the symbolic realm.

REFERENCES

Bergler, E. (1949/1977). *The basic neurosis*. New York: Grune & Stratton.

Freud, S. (1905). Three essays on the theory of sexuality. In J. Strachey (Ed. & Trans.), *The standard edition of the complete psychological works of Sigmund Freud* (Vol. 7, pp. 125–248). London: Hogarth Press.

Freud, S. (1927). Fetishism. In J. Strachey (Ed. & Trans.) *The standard edition of the complete psychological works of Sigmund Freud* (Vol. 21, pp. 149–158). London: Hogarth Press.
Harari, R. (2001). *Lacan's seminar on "Anxiety": An introduction* (R. Franses, Ed., J. C. Lamb-Ruiz, Trans.). New York: Other Press.
Lacan, J. (1956–1957). *La relation d'objet: livre IV*. Paris: Editions du Seuil.
Lacan, J. (1962–1963). *L'Angoisse: Le Seminaire, livre X*. Paris: Editions du Seuil.
Lacan, J. (1966). *Ecrits* (B. Fink, Trans.). New York: W. W. Norton & Company.
Lacan, J. (1967–1968). *L'Acte psychanalytique*. Paris: Association Freudienne Internationale.
Lacan, J. (1973). *The four fundamental concepts of psycho-analysis* (A. Sheridan, Trans.). New York: W. W. Norton & Company.
Lacan, J. (1990). *Television: A challenge to the psychoanalytic establishment* (J. Copjec, Ed., J. Mehlman, Trans.). New York: W. W. Norton & Company.
Newman, A. (1995). *Non-compliance in Winnicott's words: A companion to the work of D. W. Winnicott*. New York: New York University Press.
Phillips, A. (1988). *Winnicott*. Cambridge, MA: Harvard University Press.
Rank, O. (1922). *The myth of the birth of the hero, a psychological exploration of myth*. Baltimore, London: John Hopkins University Press.
Toboul, B. (2006). The object in Freud and Lacan. Unpublished paper.
Verhaeghe, P. (2004). *On being normal and other disorders*. New York: Other Press.
Winnicott, D. W. (1951). Transitional objects and transitional phenomena. In *Through paediatrics to psycho-analysis* (pp. 229–242). London: Hogarth Press, 1982.
Winnicott, D. W. (1956). Primary maternal preoccupation. In *Through paediatrics to psycho-analysis* (pp. 300–305). London: Hogarth Press, 1982.
Winnicott, D. W. (1963). Communicating and not communicating leading to a study of certain opposites. In *The maturational processes and the facilitating environment* (pp. 179–192). New York: International Universities Press, 1982.
Winnicott, D. W. (1968). The use of an object and relating through identifications. In *Playing and reality* (pp. 101–111). New York: Penguin Books, 1975.
Winnicott, D. W. (1989). *Psychoanalytic explorations* (C. Winnicott, R. Shepherd, & M. Davis, Eds.). Cambridge, MA: Harvard University Press.

Chapter 8

Winnicott with Lacan

Living creatively in a postmodern world

Mari Ruti

> To be creative a person must exist and have a feeling of existing, not in conscious awareness, but as a basic place to operate from. Creativity is then the doing that arises out of being. It indicates that he who is, is alive.
>
> D. W. Winnicott (1970, p. 39)

Winnicott's definition of creativity as a matter of feeling alive is deceptively simple. If all that creativity requires is an awareness of existing—and if this awareness does not even have to be conscious or self-reflexive but merely entails an intuitive sense of having a subjective base to operate from—how could we *not* be creative? Yet Winnicott implies that many of us do not feel sufficiently alive to realize our potential for what he calls *creative living*. Or is the problem perhaps that we do not feel alive in the right way? Are there ways of feeling alive that contribute to creative living and others that, though giving us the semblance of a full and vibrant life, in fact frustrate our creativity?

It seems to me that those of us living in the postmodern era are uniquely qualified to ponder this question, for arguably it is one of the hallmarks of postmodernity to make us feel frantically alive—harried, agitated, and overstimulated—while simultaneously leaving us feeling psychically empty and impoverished. Postmodernity, in other words, adds a new dimension to Winnicott's definition of creativity by highlighting that aliveness comes in various forms and that not all of these forms are equally conducive to psychic well-being.

My objective in this chapter is to think about what it might mean to live creatively in the postmodern world. I will do this by bringing Winnicott into conversation with Jacques Lacan—a strategy that might appear somewhat surprising in light of the fact that these two thinkers are usually thought to inhabit opposite ends of the psychoanalytic spectrum. While Winnicott promotes the notion of a True Self that contains the subject's creative potentialities, Lacan insists that the very idea of a "true" self is an unfortunate and misleading illusion. While Winnicott associates inner growth and development with increasing psychic integration, Lacan presents us with a theory of foundational lack and alienation. And while Winnicott recognizes the needs of the ego in the face of environmental insufficiencies, Lacan posits that all schemas that cater to the ego's demands are intrinsically counterproductive because they draw the subject into the kinds of narcissistic fantasy formations that lead it to look for the meaning of its existence in all the wrong places.

There are therefore good reasons to think that the divide between Winnicott and Lacan cannot be productively traversed. Nonetheless, I would like to illustrate that some of the key differences between these two thinkers are more apparent than real. And I would like to do this by showing that both talk about creativity in ways that are relevant to the postmodern cultural moment.

I should say right away that my aim is not to turn Lacan into a relational analyst (which would be impossible) or to turn Winnicott into a (post)structuralist (which would be equally impossible). However, I think that it is safe to argue that while the notion of creative living is usually associated with Winnicott, it is also something that can be found in Lacanian theory, albeit in a very different form. Similarly, I think that it is safe to say that while Lacan is celebrated for giving us one of the first genuinely nonessentialist theories of subjectivity, Winnicott, in his own way, is also quite interested in fluid and open-ended subjectivity.

The stakes of bringing Winnicott and Lacan together are much larger than merely outlining where their theories might intersect. I engage in this exercise in part to counter the idea that poststructuralist (constructivist) theories of subjectivity and psychic life are better at explaining the bleak facts of constitutive lack, alienation, and disenchantment than they are at offering constructive solutions to the contemporary subject's existential predicament. While it is the case, as Peter Rudnytsky (1991) suggests, that constructivist thinkers frequently posit the crisis phenomena of subjective fragmentation and decentering as paradigmatic of subjectivity as such, I would say that they do so not in order to promote a nihilistic notion of what it means to be a human being, but rather to invite us to rethink the meaning of concepts such as agency, creativity, and psychic potentiality. After all, the fact that the self is socially constituted rather than essential—that it is reflective of its placement in a specific sociohistorical setting rather than of a fixed metaphysical kernel of being—does not extinguish its desire for a meaningful life. On this view, questions about the best way to go about our lives, to sustain a robust sense of personal existence, or to cultivate rewarding relationships do not carry any less weight now than they did prior to the inception of poststructuralism. It is just that the answers are likely to be different from those advanced by more traditional philosophies.

My hope is that considering Winnicott with Lacan will deepen our understanding of the fact that the lack of secure ontological foundations—a condition taken for granted by most constructivist critics—does not necessarily prevent the subject from living creatively in the Winnicottian sense. As a matter of fact, I would like to propose that Winnicott, no less than Lacan, suggests that an overvaluation of psychic coherence may stifle creativity. At the same time, I would like to specify right away that I am not interested in fetishizing existential instability in the manner that has become customary in much of poststructuralist theory. I do not think that the lack of stability in itself is necessarily either liberatory or subversive. And I believe that there are kinds of instability—due, for instance, to extreme forms of social or interpersonal trauma—that make it very difficult for individuals to survive, let alone access creativity. My goal here is thus not to celebrate insecurity for its own sake, but rather to ask how we can productively cope with it, living, as we do, in a cultural moment when many of us find it an inescapable reality.

LACAN AND PSYCHIC POTENTIALITY

Let us consider Lacan first.[1] As we know, Lacan's theory of subject formation is premised on the notion of foundational lack or alienation. The transition from the Imaginary to the Symbolic—from preoedipal drives to the collective social space of signification and meaning production—is, for Lacan, a process of primordial wounding in the sense that the subject is gradually brought face to face with its own lack. While the internalization of the signifier brings the subject into existence as a creature of desire (thereby giving it access to a fully "human" existence), it simultaneously reveals that the surrounding world is much larger and more powerful than any individual subject could ever be—that the self is always merely a minor participant in a system of signification that operates quite independently of its "private" passions and preoccupations. In this manner, the signifier shatters the fantasies of omnipotence and wholeness that characterize the emerging ego of the mirror stage. One could, then, say that, in the Lacanian scenario, we purchase our social subjectivity at the price of narcissistic injury in the sense that we become culturally intelligible beings only insofar as we learn to love ourselves a bit less.

It is worth noting right away that one of the things that drives a wedge between Lacan and Winnicott is that while Winnicott regards the ego as what allows the subject to enter into an increasingly complex relationship to the world, Lacan associates it primarily with narcissistic and overconfident fantasies that lend an illusory consistency to the subject's psychic life. Lacan explains that the subject's realization that it is not synonymous with the world, but rather a frail and faltering creature that needs continuously to

[1] The synopsis of Lacanian theory that this chapter presents is based on Lacan's early work rather than on his final seminars (which are more focused on the Real than the Imaginary and the Symbolic).

negotiate its position in the world, introduces an apprehensive state of want and restlessness that it finds difficult to tolerate and that it consequently endeavors to cover over by fantasy formations. In other words, because lack is devastating to admit to—because the subject experiences it as a debilitating wound—it is disposed to seek solace in fantasies that allow it to mask and ignore the reality of this lack. Such fantasies alleviate anxiety and fend off the threat of fragmentation because they enable the subject to consider itself as more unified and complete than it actually is; by concealing the traumatic split, tear, or rift within the subject's psychic life, they render its identity (seemingly) reliable and immediately readable. As a result, they all too easily lead the subject to believe that it can come to know itself in a definitive fashion, thereby preventing it from recognizing that "knowing" one version of itself may well function as a defense against other, perhaps less reassuring, versions.

One consequence of the subject's dependence on such ego-gratifying fantasies is that they mislead it to seek self-fulfillment through the famous *objet petit a*—the object cause of desire that the subject believes will return to it the precious sense of wholeness that it imagines having lost.[2] In this scenario, the subject searches for subjective meaning outside of itself, in an object of desire that seems to contain the enigmatic *objet a*. Lacan's goal, in this context, is to enable the subject to perceive that this fantasmatic quest for secure foundations is a waste of its psychic energies. His aim is to convince the subject that the *objet a* will never give it the meaning of its existence but will, instead, lead it down an ever-widening spiral of existential dead ends.

How, then, does the Lacanian subject find meaning in its life? Lacan's answer is that it is only by accepting lack as a precondition of its existence—by welcoming and embracing the primordial wound inflicted by the signifier—that the subject can begin to weave the threads of its life into an existentially evocative tapestry. It is, in other words, only by exchanging its ego for language, its narcissistic fantasies for the meaning making capacities of the signifier, that the subject can begin to ask constructive questions about its life.[3] For Lacan, there are of course no definitive answers to these questions. But this does not lessen the value of being able to ask them. The fact that there is no stable truth of being does not prevent the subject from actively and imaginatively participating in the production of meaning.

Lacan implies that it is precisely because the subject can never attain the truth of its being—because it can never achieve a state of transparent

[2] Here it is worth noting that the blissful state of plenitude and *jouissance* that the subject pursues is always necessarily a retroactive and purely fantasmatic construct designed to conceal the fact that no such primordial condition of unmitigated enjoyment ever existed.

[3] As Lacan (1975) explains, "The aim of my teaching, insofar as it pursues what can be said and enunciated on the basis of analytic discourse, is to dissociate *a* and A by reducing the first to what is related to the imaginary and the other to what is related to the symbolic" (p. 83).

wholeness—that it is driven to look for substitutes that might compensate for its sense of lack; it is motivated to invent figures of meaning that can, momentarily at least, ease and contain the discomfort of alienation. In this paradoxical sense, rather than robbing the subject of its inner richness, lack is the underpinning of everything that is potentially innovative about human life.[4] Indeed, it is possible to envision the intricate productions and fabrications of the human psyche as vehicles through which the foundational lack of existence assumes a positive and tangible form. This in turn suggests that the subject's ability to dwell within lack without seeking to close it is indispensable for its psychic vitality. As a matter of fact, such dwelling within lack could be argued to be the greatest of human achievements, for it transforms the terrors and midnights of the spirit into symbolic formations, imaginative undertakings, and sites of delicate beauty that make the world the absorbing and spellbinding place that it—in its most auspicious moments at least—can be.

It is thus because the subject lacks that it is prompted to create, and it is through its creative activity that it manages, in an always necessarily precarious manner, to withstand its lack. In this context, it is important to specify that the translation of lack into creativity is not a matter of dialectical redemption in the sense of giving the subject the ability to turn negativity into a definitive form of positivity. The subject's attempts to name its lack are transient at best, giving it access to no permanent meaning, no solid identity, no unitary narrative of subjective constitution. Any fleeting state of fullness or positivity that the subject may be able to attain must always in the end dissolve back into negativity; any endeavor to erase lack only gives rise to new instances of lack. This implies that the process of filling lack must by necessity be continually renewed. It cannot be brought to an end for the simple reason that the subject can never forge an object or a representation that would once and for all seal this lack. However, far from being a hindrance to existential vitality, this intrinsic impossibility—the fact that every attempt to redeem lack unavoidably falls short of its mark—is what allows us, over and again, to take up the endless process of signification. From this point of view, lack serves as a fertile kind of emptiness that keeps our subjectivities mobile.

Lacan's rendering of the subject's relationship to the signifier is therefore complex in the sense that although he consistently accentuates the subject's relative helplessness vis-à-vis the larger systems of signification that envelop it, he at the same time suggests that it is only by virtue of its

[4] In *The Ethics of Psychoanalysis* (1960), for instance, Lacan argues that, like a potter who creates a vase around emptiness, the subject fashions a signifier, or an elaborate sequence of signifiers, from the void of its being (pp. 120–121). On this view, the signifier is not merely what mortifies the preoedipal body but also what empowers the subject to move to an existential space beyond mortification by granting it the gift of creativity. For an excellent analysis of this aspect of Lacan, see Silverman's *World Spectators* (2000, pp. 45–49).

membership in the Symbolic Order that the subject possesses the capacity to make meaning in the first place. The Symbolic, in other words, is not merely (or even primarily) a hegemonic structure that coerces the subject into its law but also—as I have endeavored to illustrate—the foundation of its creative potentialities. Lacan in fact insists that though the subject can never master the signifier—let alone the signified—it enjoys a certain degree of imaginative leeway with respect to the signifier. He describes this imaginative leeway as the subject's capacity to make use of the "poetic function" of language (1953, p. 264)—the fact that language by definition perpetuates the radical slipperiness, multiplicity, and polyvalence of meaning. In the same way that Heidegger (1971) connects creativity to the individual's ability to dwell in the world in poetic rather than merely instrumental ways, Lacan envisions creativity in terms of the subject's capacity to take a poetic approach to the world—an approach that is content to play with meaning without attempting to arrest it in unequivocal or transparent definitions.

The fact that (the early) Lacan views the subject's main existential task to be to come to terms with its lack explains in part why he tends to be so brutally dismissive of ego psychology. If Lacan criticizes the attempts of ego psychologists to shore up the subject's egos, it is because he believes that they have gotten things entirely backwards: instead of helping the subject accept lack as constitutive of subjectivity, they intensify its existential confusion by reinforcing its narcissistic fantasies. Lacan contends that such an approach is fundamentally flawed in the sense that it hastens to close prematurely the void within the subject's being rather than to foster the psychic and creative possibilities that arise from its capacity to experience this void. It promises the end of alienation instead of teaching the subject to live resourcefully with this alienation. Such a promise, Lacan suggests, is always deceptive and hollow, in the final analysis leaving the subject worse off than before. The "solution" that ego psychology offers to the subject's sense of lack is therefore, for Lacan, merely the highest manifestation of the problem. It impedes, rather than advances, the subject's potential for creative living.

WINNICOTT AND EXISTENTIAL AUTHENTICITY

Creativity—and the capacity for creative living—is, for Lacan, thus a function of lack. Winnicott, in contrast, theorizes creativity as an attribute of a certain kind of existential fullness, of the self's ability to remain true to itself. It is this word "true" that has historically made it difficult for constructivist thinkers to appreciate Winnicott's version of psychoanalysis because it immediately conjures up the image of an essential self. And indeed, there is little doubt that what Winnicott means by the True Self constitutes a certain kind of essentialism. He connects the True Self to what he calls the infant's "spontaneous gesture"—an innate creative capacity that characterizes human life from its inception. As Winnicott (1960) observes, "The spontaneous gesture is the True Self in action. Only the True Self can be creative and only the True Self can feel real" (p. 148).

Winnicott maintains that the spontaneous gesture is linked to the infant's sense of bodily aliveness. It enables the infant to reach out to the world with a degree of agility. In this manner, it generates the preconditions for the emergence of the psyche as a form of mental organization that is capable of creatively and resourcefully interacting with its surroundings. For Winnicott, the psyche thus comes into being as a kind of extension—or enunciation—of bodily aliveness. In this sense, the Winnicottian True Self as a site of spontaneous bodily energy is "essential" in the same way that the Freudian drives or Nietzsche's will to power are essential. It represents a primary force that makes life, including psychic life, possible.

This manner of formulating the issue may help explain why the Winnicottian True Self is actually in many ways the very antithesis of what constructivist thinkers mean when they talk about a fixed essential self. Winnicott (1960) asserts that there is "little point in formulating a True Self idea except for the purpose of trying to understand the False Self, because it does no more than collect together the details of the experience of aliveness" (p. 148). The True Self thus has no fixed content beyond the fact that it articulates the subject's sense of aliveness. It relates to the subject's spontaneous gesture, but it does not in any way dictate the shape or direction of this gesture. As Adam Phillips (1988) remarks, the True Self "cannot strictly speaking be defined because it covers what is distinctive and original about each person. It is simply a category for the idiosyncratic" (p. 135).

On the most basic level, Winnicott connects the True Self to the subject's capacity to fend off states of psychic rigidity and to experience itself as a creature of potentiality. I use the word *potentiality* here in a loosely phenomenological sense. I like to think of Winnicott's notion of creative living as a psychoanalytic answer to the phenomenological problematic of self-actualization. In the phenomenological context, potentiality is not some predetermined or definable entity, but is rather a characteristic of a self that is always in the process of becoming—that is always in the process of inquiring into the parameters and possibilities of its existence. The phenomenological self thus realizes its potential to the extent that it refuses to settle into a specific conception of what it means to be a human being. In this sense, self-actualization has nothing to do with discovering the fixed essence of one's being but rather with feeding the spark that makes continuous self-renewal possible. Winnicott, I would maintain, has an idea similar to this one about what it means to fulfill one's potential—what it means to live in the world in creative ways.

Like the so-called "authentic" self of phenomenology, the Winnicottian True Self holds itself open to constant reconfiguration. The False Self, in contrast, is immobilized into a dead psychic organization that closes off the future. It is defensive and largely incapable of growth and transformation. Having exhausted its sense of aliveness, it has lost its capacity to pursue its potential. In the severe case, Winnicott (1971a) explains, "all that is real and all that matters and all that is personal and original and creative is hidden, and gives no sign of its existence" (p. 68). In such instances, Winnicott specifies, "the False Self sets up as real and it is this that observers tend to think is the real person." Such a self may function quite effectively on many levels of daily existence. However, it begins to falter when it is confronted by what Winnicott (1960) calls "living relationships"—"situations… in which what is expected is a whole person" (p. 142). The False Self therefore fails to convince in relationships and situations that presuppose a depth and versatility of being. It has lost its ability to meet the complexities of the world in supple and adventurous ways. And it has lost its capacity to be at ease with itself.

Because the False Self has lost its inner elasticity, it finds it difficult to deal with the more unpredictable aspects of life. This is in many ways akin to what Freud describes as the kind of fixity of libidinal energy that leads to the formation of symptoms. A symptom indicates, among other things, that something in the subject's psychic life has become stuck or jammed—that something interferes with the flow of inner energy. Consequently, if the subject falls into self-undermining patterns of predictable behavior—the Freudian repetition compulsion—it is because it is unable to break out of circuits of energy that have over time solidified into stubbornly inflexible patterns. Its psychic energies accumulate and get trapped in symptoms, with the result that these energies remain unavailable for more creative endeavors. In this way, symptoms deplete the subject's inner life and extinguish its creative potential. Likewise, the Winnicottian False Self tends to be caught in its own suffering in the sense that it cannot escape the narrow parameters that it has (unconsciously) set for its existence.

Winnicott stresses that the False Self is an inherently compliant self—a self that passively reacts to the world rather than being able to interact dynamically with, or shape, the world. Although a degree of social conformity is a necessary part of human existence in the sense that we cannot live independently of collective conventions, there is a big difference between ordinary or enabling forms of sociality on one hand and the kind of extinction of aliveness that Winnicott describes on the other. The False Self has lost what both Heidegger and Lacan describe as the subject's poetic relationship to the world. Such a self is no longer able to distinguish its desires from what the collective order determines to be desirable.

Winnicott (1971a) claims that in such a state of false compliance, the world and its details are recognized "only as something to be fitted in with or demanding adaptation. Compliance carries with it a sense of futility for the individual and is associated with the idea that nothing matters and that life is not worth living" (p. 65). "The symptom of uncreative living," in other words, "is the feeling that nothing means anything" (1970, p. 50). Against this backdrop, creative living entails the ability to resist both the seductions and compulsions of conventionality; it means "seeing everything afresh" (p. 41).

THE FACILITATING ENVIRONMENT

Winnicott explains that while each infant possesses the potential for creative living—the spontaneous gesture—this potentiality can materialize only as a psychic reality in the context of a sufficiently facilitating childhood environment. While Lacan, following Freud, views psychic development as a matter of coming to terms with one's insignificance and lack of omnipotence in relation to an always disappointing world, Winnicott portrays the world as at least potentially enabling and satisfying. While Lacan regards subject formation as a matter of separation, differentiation, and disillusionment, Winnicott underscores that it is the infant's increasingly intricate involvement in social networks that allows it to cultivate its capacity for creative living.

Winnicott, in other words, attempts to clarify how the self develops from a state of absolute dependence to relative autonomy without at the same time denouncing its ties to others. In his estimation, the infant does not acquire a self by growing out of its early relationships as much as by learning to participate in such relationships with a greater degree of independence. The infant's encounter with the external world enriches and expands its psychic reality, with the result that its emerging subjectivity "is related to the outer or actual world and yet is personal and capable of an aliveness of its own" (1967, p. 31). Winnicott's account of subject formation is therefore gentler than that of Lacan: instead of separation being the primary motor of psychic life, the infant's identity arises in the context of a nurturing interpersonal space.

Winnicott (1967) thus believes that the gradual integration and consolidation of psychic life requires proper environmental care—what he calls "the magic of intimacy" (p. 31). In stark contrast to Lacan, Winnicott argues that a sufficiently facilitating environment feeds the infant's sense of omnipotence in the sense that it preserves the infant's illusion of having created the world it encounters. Ultimately, the infant obviously has to cope with the recognition that the world exists independently of its creative activity; it has to accept the reality principle. However, Winnicott's point is that it is the infant who has been allowed fully to experience its omnipotence who is best able to tolerate the limitations that the world imposes. This is in part because by the time the reality principle is introduced, the child is already well on its way to being able to symbolize.[5] From Winnicott's point of view, therefore, only an infant who has been raised in an adaptive environment can in turn adapt to the demands of the environment. This means that problems in early intimate relationships—such as lack of adequate support or recognition—can damage the infant's capacity for authentic subjectivity.

The classic Winnicottian example of environmental failure is the mother who fails to be good enough, who fails to meet the infant's needs and fantasies, and who consequently ends up imposing her own psychic reality on the infant. Such a mother does not accommodate, but rather intrudes and impinges, thus extinguishing the infant's spontaneous aliveness. Winnicott goes on to specify that the False Self frequently develops in response to a depressed mother who, unable to recognize the infant, demands the infant's recognition of—and compliance to—her own depressive mood. In this situation, the infant is forced to masquerade liveliness to protect itself against the mother's psychic deadness; the infant reassures the mother instead of being reassured. As Winnicott (1963) explains, "The task of the infant in such a case is to be alive and to look alive and to communicate being alive" (p. 192). Such an infant builds the foundations of its psychic life on the premise of having unfailingly to meet the demands of the outside world, with the result that it may never be able to actualize its potential for creative living.

A lot could be said—and a lot has been said—about Winnicott's obsession with good enough mothering and the kinds of burdens that it places on mothers. The problem is not only that the mother gets blamed for the infant's developmental failures but also that she becomes so powerful that she seems single-handedly to determine the infant's future life and psychic destiny. However, if we let the mother off the hook and think of environmental failure more broadly, Winnicott's theory helps us to understand why it is frequently so very difficult for individuals to maintain spontaneous identities. Certain kinds of environments—oppressive or impinging environments—elicit psychic compliance. They put individuals on the defensive. And they cause individuals to die inside so as to fend off being violated, exploited, or run over by the outside world.

In the contemporary context, one could argue that there is something about the postmodern cultural moment—a moment characterized by

[5] Winnicott's famous concept of transitional objects and phenomena is designed to explain how the shift from omnipotence to symbolization takes place. Through the use of such objects and phenomena, the child rehearses, as it were, the skills necessary for symbolization. As a result, they pave the way for separation, independence, and individuation, providing a safety net for the child's inevitable loss of omnipotence. Inasmuch as they are the basis of symbol-formation, they gradually evolve into the subject's capacity to participate in the cultural life of its society. Health, Winnicott (1960) asserts, is "closely bound up with the capacity of the individual to live in an area that is intermediate between the dream and the reality, that which is called the cultural life" (p. 150). A poverty of cultural life, in turn, is a sign of the False Self.

unrelenting exposure to external stimulation, multiple demands on our time and attention, an accelerated pace of life, a surface-oriented tone of social interactions, and a fragmentation of communal space—that makes it difficult to fend off psychic compliance. On one hand, postmodern culture prides itself on its unprecedented fluidity and versatility—the fact that it allows for a diversity of existential modes to coexist in a heterogeneous space. On the other hand, the ever-accelerating tempo of the postmodern world can overwhelm the subject's psychic life, propelling it into a defensive (and therefore inherently inflexible) manner of living. This is one way to understand why so many of us experience the overstimulating ethos of contemporary culture as numbing and soul-deadening. In a sense, we are never far from the specter of the Winnicottian False Self.

Though Winnicott regards psychic maturity as a matter of sufficient ego integration, he simultaneously underscores that defensive integration—the illusion of impenetrable coherence that marks the False Self—leads to a lack of creativity. He goes on to maintain that creativity by definition implies the capacity to tolerate "nonpurposive" states of being—states of internal unintegration that allow the subject to access a psychic reality that is qualitatively different from the one that sustains everyday existence. Creativity, in other words, calls for the subject's ability to surrender its habitual psychic boundaries to allow nonhabitual modes of thought and being to emerge; in this sense, it is only by relinquishing the ordinary that the extraordinary can be discovered. As Winnicott (1971b) explains, "It is only here, in this unintegrated state of the personality, that that which we describe as creative can appear" (p. 64). The inability to allow oneself to experience such moments of disintegration—an inability that both defines and debilitates the False Self—makes creativity impossible. As Winnicott (1967) states, "Organized defence against disintegration robs the individual of the precondition for the creative impulse and therefore prevents creative living" (p. 29).

Winnicott's theory of subjectivity is thus subtle in the sense that it posits psychic integration as a precondition for unintegration. In other words, if Winnicott privileges early developmental processes that allow the subject to attain a greater degree of integration, it is because he believes that unintegrated (nonpurposive) states of being can be attained only by a psyche that feels secure enough momentarily to surrender its sense of mastery. Integration is therefore important not because it gives the subject a coherent sense of being but, quite the contrary, because it makes the subject feel sufficiently protected to be able to relinquish its coherence. A subject who has experienced a reassuring degree of psychic integration trusts its environment enough to be able to relax its vigilance vis-à-vis the world. From this perspective, the point of psychic integration is to enable the individual occasionally to undo that integration.

The fact that Winnicott regards the capacity for psychic unintegration—for formless experience—as a precondition of creativity explains why he places such a strong emphasis on playing as a free-floating activity that is momentarily liberated from the demands of psychic coherence. This is also why Winnicott likens the clinical practice of psychoanalysis to playing. Like playing, free association facilitates the emergence of unintegrated states of being. As such, it is capable of fostering what Winnicott (1967) describes as the subject's "tingling" (p. 31) sense of being fully alive.

Winnicott's choice of play as a metaphor for psychoanalysis points to a very particular understanding of what analysis is supposed to accomplish. Envisioning analysis as a practice of play makes it impossible to conceptualize the analytic process as an attempt to stabilize the self into a definitive identity or way of being. The similarities with phenomenology are once again startling: because the notion of play privileges the endless process of becoming over the stasis of being, it by necessity advances an open-ended model of subjectivity. The "play" of free association cannot aim at fixed subjective truth but merely gives the individual access to a provisional kind of self-knowledge—the kind of self-knowledge that could be argued to be creative precisely to the extent that it is inconclusive.

Analysis—as a form of play that pursues psychic enrichment without demanding truth—facilitates a distinctive process of becoming a person. It underscores that self-constitution is never a linear project but activates diverse modalities of subjective reality. It asks the subject to recognize that insofar as the present is always influenced by the past, and insofar as the future is always a fantasized component of the present, existence inevitably takes place on multiple levels at once. And it employs narratives—or narrative fragments, more properly speaking—to highlight the fact that life histories are always full of ruptures, uncertainties, contradictions, and inconsistencies. These kinds of narratives thrive on the ambiguity of language, making possible the emergence of a distinctive voice that is potentially powerful enough to transform a life—to reinvent a personal story—without at the same time asserting mastery. Indeed, it may well be that what is most important about such narratives is that they give the subject access to the mobility of language, for the mobility of language is what, in the final analysis, allows for the mobility of being. In this sense, the playfulness that Winnicott privileges can only be activated by language. In Lacanian terms, one might say that analysis injects poetry (the poetic function of language) into the subject's otherwise prosaic existence.

Insofar as Winnicott believes that it is play that gives the subject access to its True Self, he, like Lacan, recognizes that subjective "truth" is always poetic rather than essential. This suggests that the Winnicottian True Self, somewhat counterintuitively, ends up foregrounding the ultimate impossibility of stable subjective truth. This of course does not imply that the self cannot experience itself as real, unique, or fully present in the world. It merely means that the self is free to direct its attention to endeavors other than the pursuit of an ever-elusive truth; instead of expending its psychic energies in chasing an impossible goal, it is invited to focus them on undertakings that may—fleetingly at least—give it a sense of aliveness. This is one way to understand what it might entail to live one's fragmentation and decenteredness as empowering rather than debilitating.

WHO CAN AFFORD CREATIVE LIVING?

I have sought to demonstrate that despite the obvious differences between Winnicott and Lacan, the two thinkers share the insight that a falsely coherent psychic structure prevents the subject from living in the world in supple and creative ways. I would in fact suggest that the Winnicottian False Self is conceptually quite close to what Lacan means by the ego-bound self that is unable to overcome its narcissistic fallacies. Both display an artificially coherent psychic organization that is designed to conceal a less stable reality. Both suppress elements of the self that deviate from the painstakingly constructed (yet ultimately hollow) image that is designed to sustain the psyche's pretense of perfection. And both function as desperate defenses against the danger of psychic disintegration.

This implies that Winnicott's desire to uncover the True Self underneath its false manifestations—very much like Lacan's wish to unravel the self's narcissistic delusions—is an attempt to show us that it is only by learning to cope resiliently with its lack of integration that the subject can begin to confront the challenges of its existence in innovative ways. Inasmuch as Winnicott's True Self functions as an antidote to the psyche's false solidity, it, like Lacan's theory of foundational alienation, reveals that it is precisely to the extent that the self can tolerate states of incoherence that it is creative.

Both Lacan and Winnicott are deeply suspicious of excessive displays of coherence. Self-consistency taken to an extreme, both thinkers imply, can be an impediment to inner vitality and multidimensionality. This, I believe, gives us a productive way to approach the question of creativity (and even of psychic potentiality) in the constructivist context. I think that a constructivist model of creative living cannot be directed at making our lives more coherent but must instead convey something meaningful about coping with its intrinsic incoherence. Its aim cannot be to conjure away life's tensions, ambiguities, and points of bewilderment but rather to teach us how to live through these without breaking our spirit. By this I do not mean to argue that we should not respect our desire to feel grounded in the world but merely to suggest that one of the best things we can do for our well-being is to learn to accept the fact that life's unpredictability invariably exceeds our capacity to control it. As a matter of fact, the more we cling to the notion of predictability, the less dexterously we are able to deal with life as the erratic and capricious stream of unanticipated events, encounters, and developments that it often is. No matter how carefully we strive to organize our lives around certain centers of security—ideals, ambitions, or relationships, for instance—it is our lot as human beings to learn to survive less than secure circumstances. I think that psychoanalysis at its best—when it curtails its dogmatic and prescriptive tendencies—can empower us to meet the unforeseen with a measure of inner resilience.

Lacan and Winnicott help us to understand that living creatively in the postmodern era entails accepting existential insecurity as something that none of us, insofar as we are creatures of consciousness (and unconsciousness), can elude. This of course raises the question of who can afford to accept insecurity as a precondition of creative living. We have already established that the world is full of obstacles to creative living, that certain kinds of environments actively assault the individual's psychic life. This means that some individuals are confronted by forms and degrees of insecurity that far exceed what is "normal" in human life (even in a postmodern world). For example, oppressive sociocultural and economic conditions can erode the subject's psychic resources for the simple reason that they oblige it to focus on survival. In this manner, deprivileged subjects are compelled to experience the external world as inherently hostile and impinging. As a result, extreme anxiety—the sinking feeling that there is no respite from the world's intrusiveness—may be an unavoidable component of oppression.[6] And it would be a mistake to equate this kind of anxiety with the foundational anxieties of human existence.

In Lacanian terms, one could say that to the extent that oppression seeks to turn the deprivileged subject into an object of use for the oppressor—to the extent that the oppressed becomes a mere instrument of the oppressor's sadistic *jouissance*—the outcome of oppression is to force the subject into a nonpoetic (monotonous, repetitive, and predictable) relationship to the signifier. In practical terms, this means that oppression annihilates the subject's capacity to construct the parameters of its own being, robbing it of voice and narrative agency. By coercing the subject to internalize the very discourses that are designed to denigrate and humiliate it, oppression compels it to experience language—the agency of the letter—as wounding rather than as (at least potentially) enabling. The signifier, in other words, gets stuck or immobilized in debilitating circuits of meaning, marking the subject with—and making it the bearer of—the oppressor's sadistic desire. In this manner, oppression not only imposes a significatory rigidity that drains the subject's capacity for existential versatility but also reinforces the traumatic logic of the repetition compulsion whereby the very signifier that injures and carries harm is also the signifier that is the most powerfully prominent, dictating the destiny of the subject's psychic life. This is one of the mechanisms by which oppression destroys the deprivileged subject's

[6] There are many excellent analyses on the psychic effects of oppression. See, for instance, Layton (1998), Cheng (2000), and Oliver (2001, 2004).

self-regard. In Winnicott's terms, it causes the subject to feel that it has ceased to exist.

Here we come against one of the limitations of Lacanian theory, namely the fact that Lacan's adamant critique of the narcissistic tendencies of the ego makes it rather difficult to appreciate instances where the ego has been so profoundly wounded by abusive or oppressive interpersonal relationships that its capacity for narcissistic fantasies has been destroyed. While Lacan is correct in being suspicious of the ego's capacity to mislead the subject to think that it is more coherent or powerful than it actually is, his theory is less useful when it comes to cases where a damaged ego misleads the subject to believe in its own worthlessness or insignificance. This explains why Lacanian theory is not particularly effective when it comes to understanding the debilitating effects of contingent (circumstantial rather than constitutive) forms of trauma. The notion of learning to live with one's lack or insecurity takes on a wholly different valence when the lack or insecurity in question emerges from past neglect, abuse, or oppression.

In instances that involve the forceful robbing of the subject's sense of self-worth—as in the case with subjects who have been devastated by painful formative experiences or whose sense of inadequacy arises from inequalitarian social arrangements—it may be necessary to reconstitute the ego before embarking on a critique of its ontological status.[7] It is equally possible, however, that individuals who have experienced a high level of trauma possess a heightened awareness of the manner in which lack and insecurity constitute an inescapable component of human existence. The question may be too case specific to be resolved on a purely theoretical level. Yet there is no doubt that there are specific signifiers—signifiers that carry the unequal effects of power—that defile the subject, that cut and wound the subject in devastating ways. The subject who is under assault in this manner may find it difficult to relax its wakeful vigilance in relation to the world; it may find it difficult to allow for unintegrated states of being to emerge.

In this context, it is worthwhile to keep in mind Winnicott's assertion that the individual's capacity for creative living can never be entirely destroyed—that although the spontaneous gesture can be compromised, it cannot ever be definitively extinguished. Indeed, as we have already learned, one of the main tasks of the False Self is to protect the True Self from being found and exploited. In this sense, the False Self, rather than designating the annihilation of the True Self, can (in certain situations) function as a crucial defense against a debilitating world. In its most positive incarnation, it may

[7] Kirshner's (2004) sensitive analysis of forms of mirroring that offer a vulnerable self much-needed and legitimate recognition (rather than merely feeding its narcissistic fantasies) seems relevant here. More generally speaking, Kirshner's ability to address the problematic of trauma from a specifically Lacanian perspective forges valuable connections between Lacanian and non-Lacanian approaches.

even work to create the conditions under which the True Self might eventually be able to risk revealing itself. In this last scenario, the True Self is "acknowledged as a potential and is allowed a secret life" (1960, p. 143). In this paradoxical way, the False Self can carry the responsibility for sustaining and (in the long run) resuscitating the individual's capacity for creative living. As Phillips (1988) puts it, "The False Self is playing for time until a sufficiently nurturing environment can be found in which development can start up again" (p. 125).

Throughout my discussion, I have accentuated the idea that Winnicott's distinction between the True and False Selves in many ways grants us a psychoanalytic rendering of what phenomenology describes as the divide between authentic and inauthentic existential modes. What I find most interesting about Winnicott is that he recognizes that this is not a categorical either/or distinction, but that we tend to vacillate between these two ways of being in the world. Indeed, even when we fail to live creatively, we hold onto the idea that we have the potential to do so at some future point. As Winnicott (1971a) explains, "In a tantalizing way many individuals have experienced just enough of creative living to recognize that for most of their time they are living uncreatively, as if caught up in the creativity of someone else, or of a machine" (p. 65). Ironically, then, the fact that we feel disconnected from our capacity for creative living—that we are aware that something is missing in our lives—is a sign that, psychically speaking, we are still alive, that some untamed or unbroken part of us is still aspiring for recognition. From this perspective, even oppression need not, in the end, definitively obliterate the subject's will to (a creative) life.

This, however, does not erase the question of theoretical and political responsibility. How do we adequately and ethically distinguish between psychic insecurity as a universal existential predicament on one hand and insecurity as a state of affairs that arises from oppressive social or interpersonal arrangements on the other? If the False Self serves, as Winnicott proposes, as a protection against a potentially traumatizing external world, then under what conditions does it become possible to relinquish it? These are questions that I pose not only to psychoanalysis but also, more generally, to those of us who are invested in constructivist theories of subjectivity. How does the self know that in risking itself—in letting down its psychic defenses—it is not risking too much?

REFERENCES

Cheng, A. A. (2000). *The melancholy of race: Psychoanalysis, assimilation, and hidden grief.* Oxford: Oxford University Press.

Heidegger, M. (1971). *Poetry, language, thought* (A. Hofstadter, Trans.). New York: Harper & Row.

Kirshner, L. (2004). *Having a life: Self-pathology after Lacan.* Hillsdale, NJ: The Analytic Press.
Lacan, J. (1953). The function and field of speech and language in psychoanalysis. In *Écrits* (pp. 197–268). New York: W. W. Norton & Company, 1966.
Lacan, J. (1960). *The seminar of Jacques Lacan: Book VII. The ethics of psychoanalysis* (J.-A. Miller, Ed., D. Porter, Trans.). New York: W. W. Norton & Company, 1992.
Lacan, J. (1966). *Écrits: The first complete edition in English* (B. Fink, Trans.). New York: W. W. Norton & Company, 2006.
Lacan, J. (1975). *The seminar of Jacques Lacan: Book XX. On feminine sexuality, the limits of love and knowledge* (J.-A. Miller, Ed., B. Fink, Trans.). New York: W. W. Norton & Company, 1988.
Layton, L. (1998). *Who's that girl? Who's that boy? Clinical practice meets postmodern gender theory.* Northvale, NJ: Jason Aronson.
Oliver, K. (2001). *Witnessing: Beyond recognition.* Minneapolis: University of Minnesota Press.
Oliver, K. (2004). *The colonization of psychic space: A psychoanalytic social theory of oppression.* Minneapolis: University of Minnesota Press.
Phillips, A. (1988). *Winnicott.* Cambridge, MA: Harvard University Press.
Rudnytsky, P. L. (1991). *The psychoanalytic vocation: Rank, Winnicott, and the legacy of Freud.* New Haven, CT: Yale University Press.
Silverman, K. (2000). *World spectators.* Stanford, CA: Stanford University Press.
Winnicott, D. W. (1960). Ego distortion in terms of true and false self. In *The maturation process and the facilitating environment* (pp. 140–152). London: Karnac, 1990.
Winnicott, D. W. (1963). Communicating and not communicating leading to a study of certain opposites. In *The maturation process and the facilitating environment* (pp. 179–192). London: Karnac, 1990.
Winnicott, D. W. (1965). *The maturation process and the facilitating environment.* London: Karnac, 1990.
Winnicott, D. W. (1967). The concept of a healthy individual. In *Home is where we start from: Essays by a psychoanalyst* (pp. 21–38). New York: W. W. Norton & Company, 1990.
Winnicott, D. W. (1970). Living creatively. In *Home is where we start from: Essays by a psychoanalyst* (pp. 39–54). New York: W. W. Norton & Company, 1990.
Winnicott, D. W. (1971a). Creativity and its origins. In *Playing and reality* (pp. 65–85). London: Routledge, 2004.
Winnicott, D. W. (1971b). *Playing and reality.* London: Routledge, 2004.
Winnicott, D. W. (1971c). Playing: Creative activity and the search for the self. In *Playing and reality* (pp. 53–64). London: Routledge, 2004.
Winnicott, D. W. (1990). *Home is where we start from: Essays by a psychoanalyst.* New York: W. W. Norton & Company.

Chapter 9

Human nature

A paradoxical object

François Villa

In this chapter, I reflect on the surprises of reading Donald Winnicott's posthumous work, *Human Nature* (1988). This work could be termed a *bizarre object*: it is not, properly speaking, a book. Reading Clare Winnicott's preface and the editorial note, we learn that Winnicott occupied himself with it for more than 24 years. Its necessity emerged after 7 years of university lecturing, mostly to students wishing to become social workers. Its copies would have been handed out to students to free their attention from note taking during courses that Winnicott continued to teach until his death in 1971. We should then ask what status this text had for Winnicott, given that it had always remained a work in progress, never really being finished. Perhaps it offers us a kind of access to the workshop, the always busy construction site, from which Winnicott's published texts emerged.[1] This comment concerns methodological questions with which this type of work confronts us. Starting from clinical experiences, which he was able to manage only with the help of theoretical formulations, Winnicott attempted to transmit what he had learned from them. Mostly what was revealed to him, however, pertained to his ignorance.

Of course, the desire to master our ignorance is one of the bases of systematizing thought. But he then found himself in the dilemma that transmission requires putting experience into a particular shape or structure, a shaping that inevitably leads to reductionism and carries the risk that the result will be mistaken for a "real" that of necessity must *escape* our understanding and control. At the same time, a refusal to attempt a theoretical overview out of caution or an overestimation of purely empirical approaches presents a comparable danger to our capacity of thought. One key to reading *Human Nature* is to appreciate Winnicott's struggle to avoid falling into either of these traps.

To present my point of view as a Freudian psychoanalyst, I will focus on certain of Winnicott's arguments, the development of which allowed me to orient myself in this difficult work. The choice of the formulations that make

[1] To mention only the 1951 "Transitional Objects and Transitional Phenomena."

up the different parts of his text was determined by my effort to understand better the meaning that he gave to the notions of cure, health, emotional maturation, and the nature of the relationships between individuals, their inner world, and the world outside. My approach to reading Winnicott is eminently one of a French psychoanalyst. Having been trained at the Association Psychanalytique de France according to what the International Psychoanalytic Association has called the "French model of training," I inscribe myself in an "orthodox" Freudian tradition. Although I do not belong to the Lacanian school, in the course of training I was inevitably confronted with the effects that Jacques Lacan's project of a return to Sigmund Freud had on the French psychoanalytic community as a whole. Lacan's reading of Freud and the questions it raised are a part of the French psychoanalytic heritage, and no reader, whether he or she agrees with Lacanian theorizations, can ignore the fact that one now reads Freud *informed* by this history.

In my thinking about *Human Nature*, I will try neither to confront Winnicott directly with Freud or Lacan nor to establish quick equivalences between them. However, it seems clear to me that the question Winnicott tried to tackle through the enigmatic notion of human nature resonates with questions of the conditions of possibility and the limits of analysis that never stopped insisting through Freud's texts and Lacan's interrogations of them. The concept of human nature resonates with the themes of necessity (the Greek ανάγκη) and Freud's phylogenetic memory, and, although it appears contrary to Lacan's nonessentialist approach, it can benefit from being critically compared with his categories of the real and the symbolic. The clinical sources of the Winnicottian notion of the detail likewise deserve to be compared with those of the Freudian partial object and the Lacanian *object a*. However, to pursue this line of thinking, it is first necessary to try to "digest" what Winnicott offered us.

Paraphrasing Winnicott, I would say that reading *Human Nature* evokes a metaphoric process of digestion. During the theoretical meal being served to us, there are a certain number of courses, the complexity, composition, tastes, and smells that blur our perceptions and subject us to a kind of metabolic process. We feel that through this complexity Winnicott comes close to a reality that lies at the very core of what it means to be human, even though his reasoning is puzzling and not always easy to follow. If the construction produced may not be completely correct, it turns out to approach reality closely enough for us to be able to say "*se non e vero, e ben trovato*." Through his endeavor in writing *Human Nature*, Winnicott constituted human nature as an object, one that, having *survived* the work of destruction and construction proper to its making, is no longer reducible to a subjective object created by the author. This created object situates itself beyond the area of objects established by the subject's mental mechanisms of projection, and, therefore, outside of the subject's field of omnipotent control. The use of this object, which belongs, once it has been described, to the world of shared reality, now becomes possible. Its use leads to a return to the subjectivity of its user of something *other-than-me*, which makes the nature of the *me* all the more palpable. We witness in this work the personal creation of a theme, which, turning out to be without limits, brings out the limits not only of personal description but also, as the author points out, of personhood itself. In what follows, I extract a few samples from the richness of this work.

"A HUMAN BEING IS A TIME-SAMPLE OF HUMAN NATURE."

According to Winnicott, all human beings represent all of human nature; they are human nature, and at the same time they represent only a part. It is because they are only a part that they can misrecognize the unity on which they are staking a claim. A sample cannot fully comprehend what is only a temporarily determined representative, a moment of expression. Subjects are never fully capable of saying what they really represents. Being a time-sample of human nature brings us up against the paradox, which we must transcend, of the necessity to think together permanence and change. Winnicott forces us to recognize that human nature, which can be conceived of only as something permanent, something that does not change,[2] must also be thought of as becoming, at least in part.

Let us briefly note that Winnicott's thinking follows in the footsteps of Freud's *Project for a Scientific Psychology* (1895). In this text, Freud differentiated between two components of a wishful cathexis: one always remaining the same; the other variable. The constant part of perception, the "constant structure," was designated by Freud as "*das Ding*" (the "thing"), whereas the inconstant part of the perceptual complex of a fellow human being (*Nebenmensch*) is, on the contrary, to be understood through the work of recollection. Lacan's theorizations of *the thing*, *the big Other*, and *the small other* represent another attempt at pursuing and renewing the perspectives opened by Freud on the problem of what changes and what remains as a rigid, unchangeable core. To bring these intersections into view is not to suggest that the three authors have come to equivalent conclusions but rather to emphasize the points in which psychic life resists thought's grasp. These points are often the places where clinical psychoanalytic work confronts us with the very limits of our art and forces us to pursue a theoretic–clinical research. The point of departure for this thinking remains the same, however, encountering a point of clinical resistance. From here on, the authors follow singular and often divergent paths. The fate of "what does not change" is not

[2] More carefully, we should think of this change as only possibly intervening on the scale of geological temporality, therefore remaining unperceivable and thus meaningless on the level of human temporality.

the same in the Freudian perspective of mixed neuroses, in the Winnicottian concept of transitional phenomena, and in the Lacanian notion of structure, yet finding their common point of departure appears essential in preventing us from forgetting, on the beginning of each author's answer, that the clinical question remains open.

For Winnicott, ontology can originate only from an ontogenesis of a being in the process of becoming. This also explains how Winnicott's analysis of being and existence understands being in its relational aspects. His attention to the environmental provision (having to do with relationship) amplified what Freud had previously sketched out as the complex of the fellow human being. We find a similar preoccupation again in Lacan, when we read in his writing that the subject becomes meaningful only as being articulated through the discourse and the desire of the Other (who represents the treasure trove of signifiers). The relational aspects do not stand for the substantial element of being, yet the fact that they, too, constitute being can no longer be ignored. The substance of human nature is not an *all* closed up on itself; it is essentially a bundle of relations. Afflicted by the process of becoming, human nature in its determinations nevertheless becomes what does not change. Only the modalities of its expression vary, according to the times and to the progress of humankind's knowledge about this nature. While independent of history, human nature comprises in itself, as its constitutive dimension, the source of all possibility of historicization, in the process of which it materializes itself precisely as a unique time sample. This is, in essence, what Winnicott argued at the beginning of his lecture on *Morals and Education* (1963):

> The title of my lecture gives me scope to develop the theme not so much of society that changes as of human nature that does not change. Human nature does not change. This is an idea that could be challenged. Nevertheless, I shall assume its truth, and build on this foundation. It is true that human nature evolved, just as human bodies and beings evolved, in the course of hundreds of thousands of years. But there is very little evidence that human nature has altered in the short span of recorded history; and comparable with this is the fact that what is true about human nature in London today is also true in Tokyo, in Accra, in Amsterdam and Timbuktu. It is true for whites and blacks, for giants and pygmies, for the children of the Harwell or Cape Canaveral scientist and for the children of the Australian aboriginal. (p. 55)

"HUMAN NATURE IS ALMOST ALL WE HAVE."

This enigmatic formulation, which we find in Winnicott's preface, may seem to us ironic. Should we not understand it as putting greatest emphasis on the "*almost*"? We have almost all we need "to be" human nature; we would not need much more, but we have only enough for the "I" to be but a time-sample of human nature. "Mother Nature" settled for being lenient enough to enable us to exist in a world that wants nothing (Gribinski, 2006). This is for most humans intolerable; they experience this condition dramatically, while it is in fact only tragic. For example, the oedipal drama revolving around the parental imagos obscures the essentially impersonal operation of the drives, Freud's evocation of the demonic. The Oedipal organization permits a dramatization of existence by attributing happiness and unhappiness to parental images. Behind this organization, individuals can forget the demonic dimension of the drive and their fundamental inability to master it. "Being as being's becoming" forces us to create objects so we can have a certain supplement and allow the drive to be a process through which the "I" happens.

For Winnicott, when the loss of the subjective object occurs at a moment in which the developing human being has gained the capacity to get to know it as a separate object, the gap revealed by this loss gives access to human nature. This is of course another paradox, since one might well argue that a human being never turns out to be ready to meet with loss. Nonetheless, on the occasion of this particular loss we reveal ourselves, from the psychic point of view, as having been more or less ready for it.

"PROBABLY THE GREATEST SUFFERING IN THE HUMAN WORLD IS THE SUFFERING OF NORMAL, OR HEALTHY, OR MATURE PERSONS."

We must now tackle the problems of health and the limits of analytic work. Should we desire health? Had we previously considered it obvious that each one of us wishes to be healthy or to have good health, having read *Human Nature* we certainly might now come to doubt this assertion. Health probably cannot be as desirable as we once might have believed. Still, Winnicott's position does not really come as a surprise. Indeed, we find similar formulations by other psychoanalysts (Freud, Sándor Ferenczi, Lacan, Wilfred Bion). We must also recognize that this affirmation resonates completely with our experience as both analysands and psychoanalysts or simply with our experience of human life. This argument is nevertheless a kind of lever, allowing us better to understand what it is that Winnicott was trying to reach through the object of his study.

Let us first look at how Winnicott defended his statement. The previously quoted sentence belongs to a passage called "The Depressive Position: Recapitulation," in which he discussed this position as one that arrives only "as the child integrates finally to one responsible person and looks back" (1988, p. 108). This is a moment when children become conscious of the ruthless character of the primitive love impulse, of the aggressive, destructive, and possessive elements that this impulse also carries. The recognition of this dimension, which has until now been acting quite unrecognized, will bring about, on one hand, guilt, which constitutes a heavy burden children can tolerate only with difficulty, and, on the other hand, fear of reprisal. Both of these types of feeling become tolerable progressively, in a process children can accomplish only by putting in place a *benign circle* (with the mother, who, day after day, manages the situation), allowing for the development of the capacity for mending. Yet, "even so," writes Winnicott (1988), "the primitive love impulse continues to provide the basis for the difficulties inherent in life—that is, difficulties that belong to the healthy and more to the healthy than to those who have not been able to reach 'the depressive position,' which enables the full experience of concern" (1988, p. 108).

At this point a valuable detail emerges: the difficulties of psychosis are not inherent in life but belong to the struggle to reach a life. In fact, the difficulties of psychotics exonerate them from having to confront life's natural difficulties, which, inherent to human nature, specify[3] humankind rather than being an effect of life's contingencies. Emerging in the temporality of life, these last determine the type of sample that each of us will be. Following the author's logic, by defending the hypothesis that it is mainly the healthy who really encounter life's difficulties, we arrive at a definition of who such people are. To position oneself in this way can lead us to infer only that the problems that afflict the psyche first enable the subject to avoid an encounter with the inherent difficulties of human life. That is, the suffering they cause protects subjects from the greater sufferings that are the prerogative of the mature person. Further along these lines, it becomes clear what, according to Winnicott, psychoanalysis brings to the table—an increased awareness of human nature and a greater tolerance of that which within this nature escapes comprehension (1988, p. 50). Analysis would thus strive to complete the developmental task of achieving emotional maturity, which means recognizing that in reality it is life itself that is difficult.

From the point of view of the psychoanalytic cure, we cannot fail to see that humans resist taking this step to avoid the painful effects of the depressive position. They will rather impute their difficulties to contingent factors like heredity, constitution, hormonal imbalance, or faulty life management. Human subjects therefore seem ready to do all and anything, as long as it allows them not to see the real source of their difficulty. It is only the complex work of culture that leads us to admit that psychic conflict originates in the very nature of the primary impulse. Maturation requires us to absorb psychically the fact that the impulse strives toward its aim ruthlessly. This means that we must give up trying to rid ourselves

[3] Specific in the sense of being proper to human species.

of this reality by projecting its ruthless character onto the environment (1988, p. 10). The limits of the analytic cure, limits inherent not to the cure but to life itself, must be recognized as an extension of this discovery. Against our wishes, we must admit that the cure cannot give more power to individuals than what life can give to the human species, despite our tendency at times, perhaps too often, to believe that it might be possible for analysis to succeed where life itself can only fail.

"THE WORD 'HEALTH' HAS ITS OWN MEANING IN A POSITIVE WAY."

Let us come back to life's specific difficulties. The specific difficulties inherent to life can remain unrecognized inasmuch as they predominate in the state of illness. "Infants could not be studied in their development until the fear of physical disease and disorder had been cleared away. Now [thanks to pediatrics] we can see that healthy development is not a matter of weight-watching but a matter of emotional development" (1988, p. 113). For Winnicott, "the word 'health' has its own meaning in a positive way, so that absence of disease is no more than the starting point for healthy life ... and health in child care is not the end but the beginning" (p. 112). The advances made by medicine and more specifically by pediatrics over the last century have allowed us to have the time[4] to imagine health as such. We are now able to turn to other difficulties, which science seems unable to overcome and which attack healthy children simply because they are growing up in a society composed of human beings. To take these inherent problems of individual development and of the socialization process into consideration, clinicians must accept that all they really do is meet, in childhood psychology, "the struggles that we ourselves have been through, though for the most part we have forgotten these struggles or have never been conscious of them" (p. 10). Human nature refers to what lies beyond the mask of individual history. It is a rock to which individuals cling tenaciously for survival. It is therefore connected to life, but in an almost impersonal way. It is a time of egoism without an ego,[5] time ruled by the primary impulse, whose ruthless character is unrecognized since there is not yet a subject able to become aware of it.

However, we should think neither that Winnicott has an essentialist notion of health nor that he makes health into a supreme good that we would "naturally" all desire without ambivalence or conflict. The author has not failed to learn his lesson from both Aristotle and the psychoanalytic

[4] Only a century ago child mortality was extremely frequent.

[5] For more on this basis of impersonality see Maurice Blanchot (1969) in a passage dedicated to *L'espèce humain* in *L'entretien infini*, and also Zaltzman (1998).

clinic, which would like to make the supreme good the absolute and radical possession of the mother. This possession turns out to be as much prohibited by "human nature," the unremitting force of "what does not change" in "what is becoming," as it is restricted by social taboos. But let us take a closer look at what Winnicott means by health.

"EXCEPT AT THE START, THERE IS NEVER EXACTLY REPRODUCED THIS FUNDAMENTAL AND INHERENT ALONENESS."

Health is indeed posited as a first state, a basic, fundamental state, to which individuals who have lost it can try to return to start anew. But how do we conceive of this basic state, proper to human nature, where being emerges from nonbeing? For there to be health, it is necessary that in the beginning there exists fundamental, inherent aloneness, which will never again be accessible as such. This state of aloneness will be lost for good, yet the mode of its loss is seen as paradoxical. It is lost without ever really being lost, or, rather, it is lost only in the sense that it will never again be possible to find it as such. But only on the condition of its being lost can it be preserved as the base to which one can return to set off again. "Except at the start, there is never exactly reproduced this fundamental and inherent aloneness. Nevertheless throughout the life of an individual there continues a fundamental unalterable and inherent aloneness, along with which goes unawareness of the conditions that are essential to the state of aloneness" (1988, p. 132).

With Winnicott, things are never simply linear. In the beginning is a state of aloneness, but it is a false beginning because there was already a state before this first state—the state of un-aliveness. The introduction of this state before the beginning complicates the notion of aloneness, because we are asked to think that aloneness, before the encounter with dependence, is a fact that becomes a state in making itself dependent only on a maximum of conditions. And only in this way will it be possible to encounter dependence, the fact of which obviously precedes its conscious discovery and which does not make its recognition automatic (in the sense both of becoming conscious of this dependence and appreciating what is has made possible).

Aloneness, then, as a fact is only conceivable by imagining a time before the life impulse. We should specify that this *before* of the impulse does not mean the impulse is absent. It has simply not yet acquired a perceptible or meaningful character; it has not yet assumed a central position.[6] The latter

[6] "The essential principle is that by active adaptation to simple needs (instinct has not yet taken up its central position) the individual can BE and need not know of environment ... Primary narcissism, or the state *prior to* the acceptance of the fact of an environment, is the only state out of which environment can be created" (Winnicott, 1988, p. 130).

state is qualified in a number of ways: a peaceful state of un-aliveness, a state before aliveness, a relaxed state, a quiet state. It is only the experience of "the first awakening [which] gives the human individual the idea that there is a peaceful state of un-aliveness that can be peacefully reached by an extreme of regression" (1988, p. 132). Following this awakening, infants enter into an alternation between an excited state and a state of return to nonexcitement. The passage from a fact to a state of aloneness happens only through the coupling of the environment's active adaptation and infants' primary creativity. This passage leads to a ruthless state setting in where the instinct is defined as a powerful biological drive, which comes and goes in the infants' or children's life and which demands action. We should add that Winnicott makes a crucial connection between the state of un-aliveness and the primitive inorganic state, from which, according to Freud, each individual emerges. For Winnicott, what is primary in the arrival of being is not the inorganic but aloneness. Though it allows one to remain unaware of the environment, aloneness connects individuals, primarily and indestructibly, with the human community. By experiencing this dependence on others without having to acknowledge it, individuals gain access to the resources available in the community, enabling them to manage excitement and return to a calm, peaceful state. From the place of the other, they receive what Winnicott called "details," which can help them carve (like a sculptor) a psychosomatic whole by extricating the psychic from the somatic. This possibility arises, he suggested, from the creation of erogenous zones. The calm time of nonexcitement is a time of preparation for the consolidation of the impulse, which will sooner or later take central stage.

"IF THE CREATIVITY OF THE INFANT IS ABSENT, THE DETAILS PRESENTED BY THE MOTHER ARE MEANINGLESS."

This environment, on which the not yet individuals will find themselves depending, is not only not going to be recognized as such, but, quite to the contrary, also requires that it is encountered in a way that for the moment allows subjects not to have to recognize it, not to know anything about it. On this condition, little humans enter actively into dependence on an environment that, not anticipating this encounter, will not prematurely stamp out their creativity. Clearly, this human environment was already there well before the children's coming into the world. This is an indisputable fact, yet the encounter must happen in such a way that individuals do not have to take this reality into consideration too prematurely. This is necessary so that they can experience this encounter as a moment of personal creation.

We will not linger on the founding dimension that Winnicott attaches to the constitution of this area of illusion, where children can feel themselves capable of creating the world without anyone contesting it. It is however essential to pay attention to the way the author deals with the question of the existence or inexistence of primary creativity inherent to the human, independent of the environment, which is not a projection of what has previously been introjected or an excretion of what has been incorporated (1988, p. 110). This creative potential is a central element of the Winnicottian human nature. This cannot be stressed enough: *potential* defines a field of possibilities that, to be realized, will not spare life's contingences and accidents that inevitably and necessarily make others intervene in our lives. From this encounter spring the minute changes (Lucretius's *clinamen*) of the world, which would otherwise remain too ordered and too predictable and would have thus been sterile, even unlivable. Without others' interventions and without the investment in objects that give the drive to its vicissitudes, the death drive would rule in complete sovereignty.[7] Before becoming individuals, singularized by the particular history of their own development, little humans already belong to humankind, to the human species, as Freud would say. Before being a singular representative of the species, they are the species itself, a virtual vehicle of all of its potentialities. Their singular history will allow them to express some of them while sacrificing others. Some will be lost irreversibly because they were not actualized at a suitable moment. Others will stay in the background, ready to be actualized once a chance of life's fortunes smiles at them.

At this point, Winnicott comes up against the Freudian question of the presence, within humans, of a "memory" not linked solely to the experiences actually lived through by individuals but an ancestral memory concerning experiences of the species from before their coming into the world.[8] It is an impersonal memory, of which individuals find specific prototypes they will then draw on to give personal form to the tremendous forces at work within them and that eventually compel them to invent the psyche. If we think of this memory in terms of a precise, already formed content, the hypothesis appears improbable (which narcissistically is a relief), but it becomes defensible once we imagine it as a function, originally available to each individual and a source of primary creativity. In what Winnicott calls the "first awakening," a moment in which the unalive finds itself seized not just by the living but also by its excess, this function of memory causes a movement of creation to emerge, giving an

[7] On the same topic see Freud, *Beyond the Pleasure Principle*, and Lacan, "Le temps logique et l'assertion de certitude anticipée."

[8] Lacan's notion of the symbolic appears to me to signal the same necessity, that is to say, that in order for a being to happen, there must already previously exist a dimension whose overdetermination will have a conflictual effect on the process of individuation.

object to the drive. Humans as creators do not have the least idea of either the form or the content of what they will create. What they feel is that something must happen for the excited state to disappear. This is where the specific memory intervenes, carrying in itself a memory of other individuals of the species who have previously found a solution, our existence being the proof of their ability to survive.

In the moment of creation, creators will discover, for the first time, the content and the form of what they have created. We must admit, however, that no matter how original the creation, it will seem strangely to resemble the forms previously appearing in the history of the species. It is at first necessary that creators' illusion of the creation's first-time appearance be preserved. Yet, inevitably, creators will have to deal with the fact of their creation's debt to heredity, instincts, body particularities, and environmental factors. Based on this recognition, they will then elaborate their personal relations, their likes and dislikes, a personal conscience, and their hopes for the future (1988, p. 63).

In Winnicott's theory, human nature comes to take a place analogous to phylogenetic memory in Freud's work or to the symbolic in Lacan's. However, it would be inexact to put a sign of equation between these different notions. This is even more so because the notion of human nature probably entangles the registers of the real and the symbolic that Lacan firmly distinguished from each other in the first period of his work but that he later came to recognize were not as separable as he initially supposed. In the same way, if human nature refers to phylogenetic memory, it also touches on the Freudian bedrock of biology, which every psychical treatment eventually comes up against. This is why I conclude that each of these hypotheses attempts to confront the enigma of the emergence of being from nonbeing, the passage from an un-alive state to too much liveliness, which must be sufficiently reduced so that it does not become a threat to "staying alive."[9] We are faced here with a set of very complex problems: how to reconcile the fact of the existence of multiple hereditary dispositions and of an environment constituted prior to our coming into the world with the fact that, in spite of these overdeterminations, an essential personal contribution is still needed for life to take distinctive form? The solution toward which both Freud and Winnicott moved opposes both a theory of pure autopoesis, whereby subjects closed on themselves emerge from the world, and, simultaneously, a conception of subjects constructed solely on the basis of hereditary or environmental determinations.

"If the mother adapts well enough, the baby assumes that the nipple and the milk are the results of a gesture that arose out of need, the result of an idea that rode in on the crest of a wave of instinctual tension"

[9] On this point we refer the reader to the works of Fédida, especially *Des Bienfaits de la Depression: Eloge de la Psychothérapie* (2001).

(1988, p. 110). Not without malice, Winnicott writes that we know that the world was here before the child. I say not without malice, because we are obliged to admit that our functioning seems to want to neglect this reality once again. Regarding this world that was already there, we must add that the world was there not only around the child but, also, potentially inside of the child. Reading *Human Nature*, such a formulation is necessary; the Winnicottian environment is specific in being internal as well as external, an outside milieu as well as an interior one. Primary creativity is primitively independent of the environment, but, for it to be realized, it is essentially dependent on it. Winnicott explains, "What the infant creates is very largely dependent on what is presented to that infant at the moment of creativity, by the mother who makes active adaptation to the infant's needs, but if the creativity of the infant is absent the details presented by the mother are meaningless" (1988, p. 110). The origin of the creative movement is independent of the world. It is a movement inherent to the being that is yet to come. But its passage from a state of in potentiality to that of in action is contingent on an encounter with an environment that allows it to find, in the details present, its fate the possibility to fulfill itself in a trajectory of individuation.

"THE RESULTS OF AN IDEA THAT RODE IN ON THE CREST OF A WAVE OF INSTINCTUAL TENSION."

The contribution of the environment to the creating function would then consist only of presenting the details at the moment when the wave of the drive's tension reaches the crest carrying the possibility of representation as well as calling for it. The detail, presented to this crest of possibility that has not yet been realized, catalyzes the emergence of the first psychic representative of the impulse, the representation becoming the shore where the wave finds peace and to which each new wave returns. The importance attributed to these details that the environment presents seems all the more justified as they appear to be the medium of a return to the state of nonexcitement. However, in the human, there is an inevitable tendency to overestimate this importance and to idealize the impact of the details. Through the effect of deferred action, this process may then result in these details becoming the first cause of life's difficulties, of life's unhappiness. Underneath those details may lie the repressed knowledge that life itself is difficult. This is of course not to deny that some details may make it more difficult than it naturally would be and others easier; details are the spice of life that environment adds to human nature.

We now understand why Winnicott, taking human nature as the starting point of his study, argued that such study could be pursued only by those who have "read a certain amount of psychology of the dynamic kind and have had personal experiences, both in work and in life and living" (1988, p. 1). It is only after having paid acute attention to these details and after having listened to the place the human being tends to assign to them in his suffering that we can recognize the function they come to hold for us as that of a stimulus barrier. Only by looking at what details *do* for us we can break them down and bring to light the realities of human nature that lie behind these details. In fact, Winnicott suggested that a personal experience of this process is necessary for us to learn to "take care not to be expecting successes or afraid of failure" (p. 105). As noted earlier, what he understood by human nature is comparable to what Freud (1937) called the "biological bedrock of castration" and what Lacan named the real. What both men were trying to understand is what all analysis eventually encounters as its own unsurpassable limit. For psychoanalysis even to attain this limit is already a considerable accomplishment, as it means that the cure has succeeded in bringing neurotic suffering to the level of the ordinary misery of the human condition.

EMOTIONAL MATURITY

What does this statement have to do with the end of the cure? For Freud (1910, p. 39), the cure aims to attain a "necessary degree of independence and security against relapse." The analyst can consider his task accomplished not when he has definitely ruled out pathological reactions, but when he has given "the patient's ego *freedom* to decide one way or the other" (1923, p. 50), raising "the power of resistance of the inhibitions, so that they are equal to much greater demands than before the analysis or if no analysis had taken place." (1937, p. 228).

To conclude, we return to Winnicott's (2008) conclusion:

> Inheritance of personality traits and tendencies towards psychiatric types and disorders belongs to the physical, and limits are set to psycho-therapy by inheritance. These limits are relatively unimportant in the treatment of neurotic disorder, more important in the treatment of psychotic disorder, and most important of all in the psycho-analysis of the healthy, that is to say, of those who are (by definition) the nearest to being what they came into the world equipped to be. (p. 19)

Nothing is more difficult than to recognize and to deal with this reality to be able, eventually, to transform it. Yet this is the way toward what Winnicott called emotional maturity, a maturity that obliges individuals to give up trying to impute their misfortunes to the environment alone but, instead, to become fully responsible for it.

REFERENCES

Blanchot, M. (1969). *L'entretien infini*. Paris: Gallimard.

Cyssau, C., & Villa, F. (Eds.) (2006). *La nature humaine à l'épreuve de Winnicott*. Paris: Petite collection de psychanalyse.

Fédida, P. (2001). *Des bienfaits de la depression: Eloge de la psychothérapie*. Paris: O. Jacob.

Freud, S. (1895). Project for a scientific psychology. In J. Stracehy (Ed. & Trans.), *The standard edition of the complete psychological works of Sigmund Freud* (Vol. 1, pp. 295–387). London: Hogarth Press, 1949.

Freud, S. (1910). Letters from Sigmund Freud to Oskar Pfister. *The International Psycho-Analytical Library*, *59*, 38–40.

Freud, S. (1920). *Beyond the pleasure principle*. In J. Stracehy (Ed. & Trans.), *The standard edition of the complete psychological works of Sigmund Freud* (Vol. 18, pp. 1–64). London: Hogarth Press, 1949.

Freud, S. (1923). The ego and the id. In J. Stracehy (Ed. & Trans.), *The standard edition of the complete psychological works of Sigmund Freud* (Vol. 19, pp. 295–387). London: Hogarth Press, 1949.

Freud, S. (1937). Analysis terminable and interminable. In J. Stracehy (Ed. & Trans.), *The standard edition of the complete psychological works of sigmund Freud*. (pp. 211–253). London: Hogarth Press.

Lacan, J. (1945). Le temps logique et l'assertion de certitude anticipée. In *Ècrits* (pp. 197–213). Paris: Seuil, 1966.

Lacan, J. (1953). Le symbolique, l'imaginaire et le reel. *Bulletin de l'Association freudienne*, *1*, 1982.

Lacan, J. (1973). *Le seminaire, livre XI: Les quatre concepts fondamentaux de la psychanalyse*. Paris: Seuil.

Vanier, A. (2000). *Lacan*. New York: Other Press.

Villa, F. (2008). Retour sur la notion d'introjection chez Ferenczi. *Psychologie Clinique*, *2*, 88–103.

Winnicott, D. W. (1954). *Human nature*. London: Free Association Books, 1988.

Winnicott, D. W. (1963). Morals and education. In W. R. Niblett (Ed.), *Moral education in a changing society*. London: Faber.

Zaltzman, N. (1998). *La guérison psychanalytique*. Paris: Presses Universitaires de France.

Index

G

H

I

J

K

L